MISSING

THE UNSOLVED CASES OF IRELAND'S VANISHED WOMEN AND CHILDREN

Barry Cummins

Gill Books

Gill Books
Hume Avenue
Park West
Dublin 12
www.gillbooks.ie

Gill Books is an imprint of M.H. Gill and Co.

978 07171 8393 7

Design and print origination by O'K Graphic Design, Dublin
Copy-edited by Djinn von Noorden
Printed by CPI Group (UK) Ltd, Croydon CRO 4YY

This book is typeset in 11.5/16 pt Adobe Caslon.
The paper used in this book comes from the wood pulp of managed forests. For
every tree felled, at least one tree is planted, thereby renewing natural resources.

A CIP catalogue record for this book is available from the British Library.

5 4 3 2 1

For everyone who has been lost

Barry Cummins is a journalist with RTÉ and the author of four bestsellers: *Missing, Lifers, Unsolved* and *Without Trace*. His most recent book is *The Cold Case Files*. He is the recipient of three Justice Media Awards. In 2013 he helped to coordinate the inaugural National Missing Persons Day.

WOMEN WHO DISAPPEARED IN LEINSTER 1987–1998
(cases examined by Operation Trace)

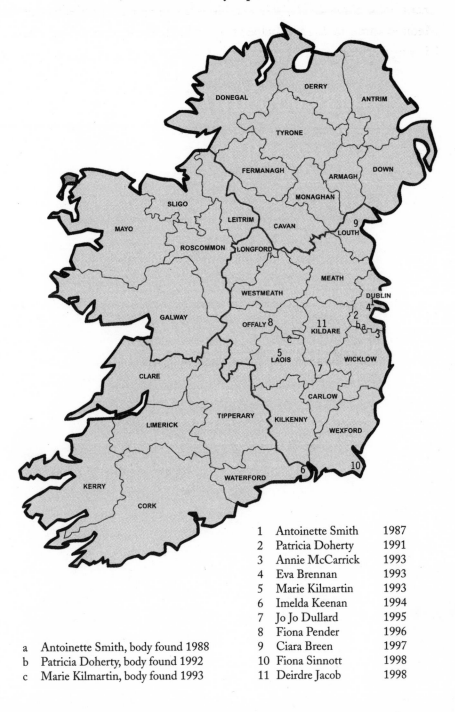

1	Antoinette Smith	1987
2	Patricia Doherty	1991
3	Annie McCarrick	1993
4	Eva Brennan	1993
5	Marie Kilmartin	1993
6	Imelda Keenan	1994
7	Jo Jo Dullard	1995
8	Fiona Pender	1996
9	Ciara Breen	1997
10	Fiona Sinnott	1998
11	Deirdre Jacob	1998

a	Antoinette Smith, body found 1988
b	Patricia Doherty, body found 1992
c	Marie Kilmartin, body found 1993

CONTENTS

INTRODUCTION

In the 1990s eight women vanished without trace in Ireland, all abducted, murdered and their bodies buried by killers who have not been brought to justice.

All the crimes took place in Leinster: two of the victims were found buried in bogland, the other six women have never been found. The disturbing reality is that the killers responsible have not been caught, having gone to extraordinary lengths to conceal their crimes. In some of the cases profiled in this book, it is believed the killer was known to the victim. Yet more than half the cases were random abductions and murders. Either a serial killer is responsible for many unsolved abductions and murders in Ireland, or a number of killers, who have so far evaded justice, could strike again.

Before the 1990s there had been a number of other horrific random attacks in the country, where killers who had struck in the 1970s and '80s had not been brought to justice. In July 1987 Antoinette Smith, a mother of two, vanished in Dublin after enjoying a concert in Slane. In April of the following year the body of the 27-year-old was discovered buried in a bog at Glendoo Mountain near Glencree in the Wicklow Mountains. Two plastic bags covered her head. Her daughters Lisa and Rachel were only seven and four when their mother was killed.

Eight years before Antoinette's killing, a young woman was abducted, raped and murdered in Newbridge, Co. Kildare. Twenty-three-year-old Phyllis Murphy was last seen alive at a bus stop at Ballymany on the outskirts of the town at 6.30 p.m. on Saturday, 22 December 1979. Phyllis had spent the day Christmas shopping in

Newbridge and was waiting to get a bus home to Kildare. By the time the bus arrived at her stop, Phyllis was gone.

For twenty-seven days her naked body lay at the edge of a pine forest in the Wicklow Gap, where Phyllis' killer had left it just 20 yards off the road, having driven her there in the boot of his car. She was found during a massive search throughout Kildare and Wicklow. Gardaí knew Phyllis was most likely dead, as they had gathered many of her belongings dumped at various spots in Kildare. Phyllis was discovered on 18 January 1980 and, remarkably, the freezing cold temperatures that year meant that semen stains on her body remained intact. But it would be another nineteen years before this forensic evidence would be linked to John Crerar, a former soldier living in Kildare town. He was arrested and charged in July 1999. A jury later unanimously accepted the forensic evidence that the DNA on Phyllis' body matched Crerar's to a certainty of one billion to one. Crerar, a father of five with no previous convictions, was found guilty and jailed for life for a murder he had committed two decades earlier.

But two other vicious killers had been incarcerated since 1976. John Shaw and Geoffrey Evans had fled England in the early 1970s where they were suspected of committing a number of rapes. The men settled in Ireland and made a pact to abduct, rape and murder one woman every week. They managed to murder two women before they were caught in Co. Galway; the first victim near Brittas Bay, Co. Wicklow, in August 1976. Elizabeth Plunkett, a 23-year-old Dublin woman, was abducted from the roadside, raped and strangled in a wooded area nearby. The men then tied a lawnmower to her body, rowed out to sea and threw her overboard. It would be weeks before her body was recovered.

Shaw and Evans went on to commit a spate of robberies over the next few weeks while gardaí in Co. Wicklow investigated the disappearance of Elizabeth Plunkett. In September 1976 the killers committed their second rape and murder when they abducted 23-year-old Mary Duffy from the roadside at Castlebar, Co. Mayo. She was tied up and driven to Ballynahinch, Co. Galway, where the horrific assault continued. She was then suffocated, and the two murderers took her body to Lough

Inagh, where they stole a boat, rowed out onto the lake and threw the body overboard, weighted down with large cement blocks.

Just days later Shaw and Evans were captured in Barna, Co. Galway, when a garda spotted the pair in a stolen car. By this time Elizabeth Plunkett's body had been recovered in Co. Wicklow and, while under arrest, John Shaw agreed to show detectives the location where Mary Duffy's body lay hidden at Lough Inagh. Shaw and Evans were later jailed for life, serving most of their sentence at Arbour Hill Prison in Dublin. Evans died in 2012, having been in a coma since 2008. John Shaw is now in his seventies and is one of Ireland's longest-serving prisoners, having spent more than forty years behind bars.

The first of many women to disappear in the 1990s was mother of two Patricia Doherty. Patricia was a 29-year-old prison officer who, on the day of her disappearance, had been to The Square shopping centre in Tallaght buying Santa hats for her son and daughter. Sometime after 9 p.m. on 23 December 1991 she reportedly left her home at Allenton Lawns in Tallaght and was not seen alive again. The following June a man cutting turf near Lemass Cross at Killakee in the Wicklow Mountains found Patricia Doherty's body in a bog drain around a kilometre from where Antoinette Smith's body had been hidden in July 1987. Nobody has ever been arrested in connection with the murder of Patricia Doherty or that of Antoinette Smith.

In March 1993, 26-year-old American woman Annie McCarrick was abducted and murdered, most likely near the Wicklow Mountains. Annie first arrived in Ireland when she was nineteen and studied in Dublin and Maynooth. She had fallen in love with Irish culture and Irish people and moved from New York to make her home in Dublin. On the day she disappeared in March 1993 she had told a friend she was planning to go for a walk in Enniskerry, Co. Wicklow. Her body has never been found, and her killer has never been caught.

Nine months after Annie McCarrick vanished, 35-year-old Marie Kilmartin disappeared in Port Laoise. All that was known was that Marie had left her home late in the afternoon of Thursday, 16 December 1993. Garda enquiries established that a call had been made to Marie's home from a public phone box at 4.25 p.m. The phone box was on the Dublin Road close to Port Laoise Prison, and the call lasted two and a half minutes. Whoever made that call may have enticed Marie to meet them. For almost six months Marie's body lay hidden in bog water in a large drain at Pim's Lane, north of Mountmellick, on the Laois–Offaly border. Her body was found by chance when the water receded in dry conditions. She had been strangled to death.

One case where it's clear that the killer didn't know his victim was the abduction and murder of 21-year-old Co. Kilkenny woman Jo Jo Dullard. Jo Jo was trying to hitch a lift in Moone, Co. Kildare, on the night of 9 November 1995 when her killer pulled over. Jo Jo had already hitched lifts from Naas to Kilcullen, and then from Kilcullen to Moone, but she was still more than 40 miles from her home in Callan, Co. Kilkenny. There are a number of suspects for this random abduction and murder, but without Jo Jo's body being found the killer remains at large.

Fiona Pender was twenty-five years old and seven months pregnant when, in August 1996, she was murdered and her body concealed in the midlands. The prime suspect for Fiona's murder was once arrested and questioned. It's believed he subjected Fiona to a ferocious attack some months before her disappearance, when he strangled her to the point of unconsciousness. Fiona's case differs from those of Annie McCarrick and Jo Jo Dullard in that gardaí ascertained that Fiona knew her attacker, and that the victim had previously suffered a history of violence.

The next to disappear was seventeen-year-old Ciara Breen, who sneaked out of her bedroom window in Dundalk in February 1997. Gardaí believe she was going to meet a man twice her age, and that this person was responsible for her abduction and murder.

A prime suspect was identified and arrested twice, in 1999 and 2015. However, on both occasions the man denied any knowledge of what happened to Ciara, although by the time of the 2015 arrest, he acknowledged he had met her secretly and had kissed her once. Many other witnesses claimed the relationship was much more serious.

The 2015 arrest led to a major excavation of bogland in Dundalk, but Ciara's remains were not located. The murder suspect died of a suspected heroin overdose in 2017.

A year after Ciara Breen's murder another teenager disappeared in sinister circumstances, this time at the other end of Leinster. Nineteen-year-old Fiona Sinnott was the proud mother of an eleven-month-old baby girl when she vanished from her home in Broadway, Co. Wexford, in February 1998. A number of people have been questioned about Fiona's suspected murder, but no charges have been brought. Several searches, including one where a lake was drained in south Co. Wexford, also failed to find the teenager. A suspect has been identified, but, as in the other cases, without a crime scene, witness, or body, a prosecution is unlikely.

Hundreds of buildings and thousands of acres of land have been painstakingly searched for these missing women. The recovery of the bodies is crucial for their distraught families, who long for some kind of closure, and vital for gardaí, who know that some of the most callous crimes to be committed in Ireland remain unexplained and unsolved.

The last woman to vanish in the Leinster area in the 1990s was eighteen-year-old Deirdre Jacob who disappeared in broad daylight from close to the front gate of her home at Roseberry, near Newbridge, Co. Kildare, in July 1998. Deirdre had been walking home from Newbridge town after visiting the bank and post office. Unlike the previous missing women cases, the garda response to Deirdre's disappearance was immediate. Detectives combed the area for clues within hours of her disappearance – in stark contrast to a number of the other cases when the alarm was not raised for hours or even days, and for more than a week in the case of Fiona Sinnott.

While it is generally accepted that Fiona Pender, Ciara Breen and Fiona Sinnott were murdered by people they knew, the cases of Annie McCarrick, Jo Jo Dullard and Deirdre Jacob were different. Theirs are considered random and opportunistic attacks. Speculation about whether any of the cases might be linked led to the establishment of a special garda initiative, Operation Trace, in September 1998.

Over time the six-member team of detectives analysed the movements of more than 7,000 convicted or suspected sex offenders who had lived or travelled in Ireland since the early 1980s. As subsequent crimes were committed in the 2000s, information relating to those attacks and the perpetrators were fed into the mix. Detectives compiled information on all known sex offenders, victims and violent incidents to have occurred in the previous two decades. It was a massive task, with every piece of information being logged in the hope that a new link might be established between any of the cases. From the Operation Trace headquarters at Naas, Co. Kildare, detectives would coordinate the arrests of nine men and women in connection with the investigations – but no charges were ever brought.

Despite the massive amount of information collected, no clear links could be established between any of the missing women. Although the objective of Operation Trace was to examine if two or more of the disappearances might be linked, detectives have long considered the possibility that none of the cases may be linked at all. If this is true it would mean that – including the murderer of Antoinette Smith in 1987 – nine separate killers operated in Ireland in an eleven-year period from 1987–98, all of whom got away with their crimes: nine separate killers, who abducted nine women, murdered them and buried their bodies.

Members of the Operation Trace team were conscious they were only analysing information relating to known sex offenders. It was always possible that some of the killers might be seemingly upstanding members of the community, men who had no previous convictions. Indeed, in the years after Operation Trace was set up, a number of violent men who had never before come to the attention of gardaí were caught for some of the most shocking crimes Ireland has known. These offenders were typically married men with children, who had somehow been able to keep their evil and violent tendencies hidden from even their closest family members.

There are so many questions. Are these killers family men who have never come to the attention of gardaí? Do their parents or wives or children or siblings suspect them? Are they local people who know the area around the site of each disappearance? Or are they living a vagrant life, travelling around Ireland or beyond, evading detection? Have some of them already taken their secret to their grave, or are they in prison serving sentences for other crimes?

One convicted rapist, now believed to have been a serial killer, was hiding in plain sight for decades. Robert Howard, originally from Wolfhill in Co. Laois, spent much of the 1990s travelling between Ireland, Scotland and England. He was already known to be an extremely dangerous individual. In 1973, aged twenty-nine, he raped a woman in Youghal, Co. Cork, after breaking into her home. Before he committed that attack Howard had already served time in prison in England for breaking into another house in 1965 and sexually assaulting a six-year-old girl. After serving a ten-year sentence for the rape in Youghal, Howard was free throughout much of the 1980s and '90s and travelled extensively between Ireland and Britain. Any time a neighbour would become aware of Howard's previous convictions or suspect he was a danger, he'd simply move on to somewhere new. Howard had a number of addresses in the Republic of Ireland: Lower Beechwood Avenue, Ranelagh, Dublin 6; Yellow Meadows Drive, Clondalkin, Dublin 22; Belgium Park, Monaghan; Primrose Grove, Coolock, Dublin 5; Barntown, Co. Wexford. He also had addresses in Newry, Co. Down and Castlederg, Co. Tyrone, and he lived in Glasgow and in London. The extent of the harm he caused during all that time has never been fully established. Howard died in prison in 2015 while serving a life sentence for the murder of Hannah Williams, a fourteen-year-old girl who vanished in London in 2001 and whose body was found a year later.

Right up to his death Howard was the prime suspect in the murder of fifteen-year-old Arlene Arkinson who vanished in 1994 after taking a lift from Howard in Co. Tyrone. Despite numerous searches in counties Donegal and Tyrone, Arlene's body has not been found. Howard did stand trial for Arlene's murder in 2005, but, controversially, the jury was not informed of Howard's other proven crimes and he was acquitted.

One violent man not known to gardaí until February 2000 was Larry Murphy, a 36-year-old father of two from Baltinglass, Co. Wicklow, who committed a shocking abduction, rape and attempted murder. Although he admitted the crimes, he maintained he had acted on the spur of the moment, and insisted he had only gone into Carlow town to buy a bag of chips when he decided to commit the abduction. The circumstances of Murphy's crime illustrate how one would-be killer used split-second violence to abduct his victim and transport her covertly in his car to two other counties as he continued his attack.

Shortly before midnight on 11 February 2000, Ken Jones and Trevor Moody were hunting in a secluded forest area of Kilranelagh in west Co. Wicklow when they heard a piercing scream, followed by the sound of a car revving up. As the car sped past, the men recognised the driver: he was Larry Murphy from Woodside, a small community a few miles away in Baltinglass. Just then a woman came stumbling towards them. Still trying to comprehend what was going on, the men approached the woman and asked her if she was all right. She recoiled in terror; in her terrified state she thought they were with her abductor, who over the previous three hours had severely beaten, repeatedly raped and then tried to kill her.

The two men managed to convince the woman they were not going to harm her. They draped a jacket over her, brought her to their car and set off for the garda station in Baltinglass, where they were met by three gardaí. An officer took off the binds that were still on the woman's wrists. Ken and Trevor told gardaí the identity of the man who fled the forest and as the woman outlined the harrowing details of what she had endured, the officers realised she had survived a murder attempt.

Fifteen months later, on 11 May 2001, Larry Murphy was jailed for fifteen years after admitting four charges of rape and one charge each of kidnapping and attempted murder. A packed courtroom heard the shocking details of how he had attacked the woman in a secluded car park in Carlow shortly after she left the nearby business premises that she owned. He punched her in the face, fracturing her nose, and forced her to remove her bra, which he used to tie her hands behind her back. He used a GAA team headband to gag her and then put her in the boot of his car. He drove nine miles to Beaconstown, near Athy, Co. Kildare, where he raped her. He then forced her back into the boot and drove 14 miles to Kilranelagh, Co. Wicklow, where he repeatedly raped her again. During the attacks he spoke with the victim, and truthfully told her he had children, but lied about his own identity, saying he was 'Michael' and that he worked in Dublin. At one point, as he spoke with the victim, he removed the bra that held the woman's hands behind her back, but he then became more agitated and tied her hands once again, this time with the GAA headband.

Murphy didn't tie the woman's hands as tightly as before, and it was in Kilranelagh that, while being forced back into the boot of the car, the woman managed to free her hands and tried to spray Murphy in the face with an aerosol she had found in the boot. But the spray didn't work and events took an even more sinister turn. Murphy produced a plastic bag and put it over the woman's head, pulling it tightly around her neck. The woman showed great strength in fighting back. It was at this point that Ken Jones and Trevor Moody arrived on the scene. They heard a woman scream and, when the car drove past them, they both recognised Larry Murphy as the driver. They then saw the woman stumbling towards them. As Jones and Moody brought the woman to the nearest garda station, Larry Murphy drove to his home a few miles away and, having downed a large quantity of whiskey, looked in on his two sleeping children and got into bed beside his wife. He was arrested the next day.

On the day on which he pleaded guilty to rape and attempted murder, Murphy fainted in the Central Criminal Court. As barristers stepped over the unconscious abductor and rapist, it was left to two prison officers to lift him off the carpeted floor of the Central Criminal Court.

It is a sobering fact that prior to abducting and attempting to murder his victim in February 2000, Larry Murphy had never come to the attention of the gardaí. By all accounts the self-employed carpenter was a dedicated family man and a loving husband. His main passion was hunting, through which he became familiar with the forested land of west Wicklow.

Had he succeeded in killing his victim, what had he planned to do with her body? He never gave any explanation or motive for his attack on the woman, whom he did not know. Murphy was a model prisoner and benefitted from remission whereby he only had to serve three-quarters of his 15-year prison sentence. He was released from prison in 2010 and left Ireland. Since then he has lived in Holland, Spain, and more recently London.

The depraved nature of Larry Murphy's crime gives us an insight into the mind of a potential killer who chose his victim at random. When he set out to abduct, rape and kill, he was confident and calculating. Had he succeeded in murdering his victim and her body was never discovered, or not discovered until years later, we might never have known of the horrific ordeal she had suffered or who was responsible.

One killer who knew his victim – and who planned his crime – was Graham Dwyer, convicted in 2015 of murdering Elaine O'Hara. Dwyer first contacted Elaine in the late 2000s via a fetish website for people with an interest in bondage and sadomasochism. Elaine was a vulnerable woman who met up with Dwyer not realising that his talk of wanting to stab someone to death was a very real desire. Dwyer, a family man with no previous convictions, was leading a double life. He orchestrated a situation whereby Elaine O'Hara was last seen alive walking through Shanganagh Park in Shankill, Co. Dublin. He told her to park her car at one end of the park and to meet him at the other side. He then drove her to a forest at Killakee where he murdered her. He left her body on open ground and her skeletal remains were found thirteen months later. Dwyer later dumped phones and other material at Vartry reservoir near Roundwood in Co. Wicklow.

A curious garda, James O'Donoghue, spent several days recovering items from the scene at Roundwood after some local men had handed in unusual objects, including handcuffs: these were recovered because an unusually dry summer had caused lower water levels, exposing the silt. Digital experts reactivated a number of SIM cards, which led to Dwyer. Good garda work, combined with luck, meant that one killer was eventually brought to justice.

Many killers go to great lengths to hide bodies, but concealing all evidence of a crime is difficult. In January 2004 Gary McCrea murdered his wife Dolores in Co. Donegal and burnt her body in a large outdoor fire. McCrea also threw several tyres on the fire and added an accelerant in an effort to completely destroy Dolores' body. However, forensic anthropologist Laureen Buckley was able to sift through material and find bones and teeth, which were identified as that of the mother of four. Dolores' family got some measure of justice when Gary McCrea was jailed for life the following year.

Other killers have also gone to extreme lengths to try and conceal their crime. Sisters Charlotte and Linda Mulhall killed their mother's boyfriend Farah Swaleh Noor in Dublin in March 2005 and dismembered his body at a house at Richmond Cottages in Ballybough. The two women then carried the body parts to the nearby Royal Canal and dumped them. But the pieces were soon discovered by passers-by, and after an extensive investigation the women were convicted and jailed for the killing. One distressing aspect of the case is that the victim's head was never recovered.

More recently, Paul Wells Snr was convicted in 2018 of murdering Kenneth O'Brien. The jury in the trial heard how the killer dismembered the body of his victim and put body parts in a suitcase, dumping it in a section of the Grand Canal in Co. Kildare. The suitcase, which did not sink, was soon found by a couple out walking.

Several other bodies that have been dumped in water have been located. Fourteen-year-old Melissa Mahon was killed in a house in Sligo town in 2006 by a neighbour, Ronald Dunbar, who then dumped the teenager's body 15 kilometres away. Melissa's body was located almost a year and a half later in February 2008 in Lough Gill. The jury at Dunbar's trial heard how he had strangled Melissa, put her body in a sleeping bag, weighed it down with stones, driven to Lough Gill and thrown Melissa's body into the water. Dunbar was convicted of manslaughter rather than murder but given the appalling nature of the crime the judge used his discretion to impose a life sentence.

Although rare, there are a number of cases where criminal charges have been brought without the body of a victim being located. In November 1977 IRA man Liam Townson was given a life sentence by the Special Criminal Court after being convicted of the murder of British soldier Robert Nairac, whose body has never been found. Soon after the soldier's disappearance in May 1977, gardaí discovered the scene where he had been shot dead, near Ravensdale, Co. Louth, and Townson was convicted largely on his own confession. Although the IRA has assisted in returning the bodies of some of the other people killed and secretly buried by its members, it has not provided any information on where Robert Nairac's body lies hidden in north Co. Louth.

Another cross-border investigation involved the murder of Gerald McGinley at his home in Enniskillen, Co. Fermanagh, in August 2000 by his wife, Julie McGinley, and her lover, Michael Monaghan. When Gerald McGinley was reported missing, a forensic examination of the family home showed that a bedroom had been redecorated to cover up evidence of the murder. Julie McGinley and Michael Monaghan were charged with murder before Gerald McGinley's body was found. It was not until June 2001, ten months after his violent death, that the body was discovered by a girl walking in a wood at Ballinamore, Co. Leitrim. Both Julie McGinley and Michael Monaghan were jailed for life.

In most cases, however, it is difficult to bring criminal charges in the absence of a body. Cases are difficult to prove. For instance, a man was charged with the manslaughter of Michelle McCormick, who vanished in Cork in July 1993. The trial at Cork Circuit Criminal Court heard how it was alleged the young woman had died following an assault at a caravan park in Owenahincha. It was further alleged that Michelle's body had then been dumped in a river in Kinsale: it was never found. A trial in May 2003 ended dramatically when the judge in the case directed the jury to acquit the accused.

Another trial to be halted, this time at the Central Criminal Court in Castlebar in May 2014, was that of a Co. Mayo man charged with the murder of Sandra Collins. Sandra was twenty-eight years old when she vanished in Killala, Co. Mayo in December 2000. Her fleece top was found four days later at the pier in Killala, and gardaí long believed the clothing was planted by her killer because it hadn't been spotted during extensive searches over the previous days. A garda investigation established that on the day she vanished, Sandra had found out she was pregnant and had contacted a man who detectives believed was the father of the child. A prosecution, based on circumstantial evidence, was brought against a 49-year-old man but at the end of the proceedings the presiding judge directed the jury to acquit the accused, and he walked free. Sandra's family continue to appeal to people in Co. Mayo and beyond to help them find their sister.

A similar appeal continues to be made by the family of teenager Arlene Arkinson, who went through the agony of seeing her suspected killer, Robert Howard, found not guilty in 2005. The verdict was a massive setback in the search for the body of the fifteen-year-old. In 2018 a body was exhumed in a graveyard in Co. Sligo amid suggestions it could be Arlene, but it was soon established that the body was that of a man. Detectives strongly believe Arlene's body lies buried somewhere close to the Donegal–Tyrone border.

Arlene is just one of a number of children who are long-term missing on the island of Ireland. The disappearance of six-year-old Mary Boyle in March 1977 and the abduction of thirteen-year-old Philip Cairns in October 1986 continue to baffle detectives, who have been investigating both cases for decades.

Mary Boyle was last seen walking near her grandparents' home near Ballyshannon, Co. Donegal, on a bright afternoon in March 1977. Her disappearance devastated her parents, Ann and Charlie Boyle, her twin sister, Ann, and her older brother, Patrick. There is still no firm evidence of abduction, yet numerous searches of lakes and surrounding bogland have failed to yield any results. Whether it was through an accident or through a violent act, what happened to Mary Boyle remains a mystery.

Philip Cairns was walking to school when he was snatched from the roadside in Rathfarnham, Co. Dublin, in October 1986. Philip was walking along a busy road at lunchtime when he vanished. An unsettling aspect of this case is that, a week after his disappearance, Philip's schoolbag was left in a laneway close to his home. The bag was left either by the abductor or by someone who found it after the crime and therefore has crucial information that could help the gardaí solve this tragic case.

Sometimes a body is only recovered with the assistance of the killer. In the early 1990s, before many of the missing women vanished in Leinster, Ireland was shocked by the chilling actions of Michael Bambrick, who killed his wife, Patricia McGauley, at their home in Dublin around September 1991; around July 1992 he then killed another woman, Mary Cummins, also at his home. Both women were classified as missing from the time of their disappearances until the truth caught up with Bambrick when his young daughter bravely began to tell gardaí how her daddy had killed her two pets. Detectives soon established a link between Bambrick and Mary Cummins, whom he had met for the first time on the day he killed her. Soon after his arrest he claimed he had killed both women during bondage sex sessions that had gone wrong. He dismembered their bodies and disposed of them in old drains close to Balgaddy dump in west Co. Dublin. It was not until June 1995, when he was finally caught and admitted killing the two women, that their remains were found.

It was only as a result of Bambrick assisting gardaí and giving details of what he had done with the two bodies that the remains of Patricia and Mary were found. The only substantial evidence in relation to the cause of death of the two women came from Bambrick himself. In 1996 Bambrick was jailed for eighteen years on two charges of manslaughter: he served his sentence in Arbour Hill Prison and, having been given a quarter off his prison sentence for good behaviour, was released in 2009.

Another body that was only recovered because of precise information was that of Marioara Rostas, who was eighteen years old when she was enticed into a car in Dublin city in 2008. For four years Marioara was a missing person, until a person brought gardaí to a forest in Co. Wicklow and pointed to the general location where she was buried. The person who showed detectives the burial site said he had not been involved in the murder but had helped to bury the body.

The abduction and murder of Marioara is an unfortunate and upsetting reminder that very dangerous people still live among us. The fact that the abduction occurred in broad daylight on a busy street in the capital, yet nobody saw anything suspicious, calls into question whether any lessons have been learnt from what happened across Leinster throughout the 1990s.

Conscious that most missing person cases are not crimes, this book highlights developments in honouring the memory of all missing people, and the sterling work of some families of missing people to keep their loved ones' cases on the media and political agenda. Cases where mistakes have been made during investigations are examined, while work being undertaken by gardaí to try and identify bodies recovered in previous decades is also outlined.

Close to 9,500 people are reported missing in Ireland every year. Most of those cases will be solved, with people returning home after days or weeks, or being located elsewhere. But at the end of every year some people will become part of the long-term missing person statistics. The reality is shocking: from 1950 to the present day, there are more than 870 people long-term missing in Ireland, the equivalent of a vibrant village – all gone, vanished without a trace. Many of those cases are not suspicious, but there are dozens upon dozens that are.

This is the story of some of Ireland's missing, the unsolved cases of vanished women and children.

CHAPTER 1

THREE BODIES FOUND: ANTOINETTE SMITH, PATRICIA DOHERTY AND MARIE KILMARTIN

The body of Antoinette Smith was found just before 4 p.m. on Easter Sunday, 3 April 1988 by a family walking in a remote part of the Wicklow Mountains. The warm, dry weather of the previous few weeks had caused a section of peat bog at Glendoo Mountain to subside, and Antoinette's leg had become exposed. In an era before mobile phones, the family who made the shocking discovery had to travel many miles away from the scene to get to a landline and raise the alarm. The family, from Ballinteer, rang their nearest garda station at Dundrum. Gardaí immediately went to the scene.

Detectives would eventually come to believe that two men murdered Antoinette. Her killers had chosen a burial place they thought would remain concealed forever. They had taken her body up the side of a mountain and buried her in a section of bog three-quarters of a mile away from Military Road, which traverses the Wicklow Mountains. A narrow disused bog road runs much closer to the scene, about 30 feet from where Antoinette's body was hidden. It's possible the killers had driven that road but they could have carried Antoinette's body from Military Road up to where they buried her beneath the soil. Antoinette's body lay undiscovered for almost nine months. The killers would have thought they had chosen a good spot to hide their victim's body. Only for dry weather causing the soil to shift, the mother of two might never have been found.

The real investigative work began on Easter Monday. The state pathologist, Professor John Harbison, arrived at the scene in the afternoon. His work at the burial site, and during the subsequent post-mortem examination at Dublin City Morgue, provided much of the information that led to the body being identified as Antoinette Smith. His work also unearthed a number of clues that remain very important lines of enquiry to this day, including the two plastic bags covering the victim's head.

Professor Harbison was brought by detectives to the spot at Glendoo Mountain where he saw the lower part of a body exposed eight feet from the mountain track. A few feet away from the body, a trickle of water flowed down the gully. During wet winter periods that trickle would have become a significant amount of bog water and risen to the level where the body lay hidden. However, after a long dry spell the water had become significantly lower than in winter and the soil had shifted.

Detective Brendan McArdle of the Technical Bureau brought Professor Harbison closer to the scene. As they approached the body they noticed five or six small pieces of denim cloth, similar to material from jeans or a jacket. Detective McArdle removed sods of earth that had been placed by the killers on top of the upper part of the victim's body. Professor Harbison could now clearly see the victim was wearing a denim jacket. A plastic bag covered the victim's head. When Professor Harbison opened the bag he found a second bag tied tightly around the head.

Professor Harbison searched around the body and found two items in the soil. One was part of a small heart-shaped earring, the other a Union brand key, which looked like a house key. The unidentified body was placed into a special coffin and carried by gardaí to the Military Road. Sergeant John Nolan escorted the body to Dublin City Morgue. The post-mortem examination would take place the next day, and the victim would soon be identified as a 27-year-old woman who had vanished nine months earlier.

Seven-year-old Lisa and four-year-old Rachel Smith last saw their mother on 11 July 1987. It was a Saturday afternoon and Antoinette and her friend Marie were heading off to the David Bowie concert in Slane. Antoinette lived with her two young daughters at Kilmahuddrick Court in Clondalkin. She was separated from her husband Karl: the couple were married in 1979 but the relationship had ended by 1987. Karl saw his daughters on Saturdays and sometimes they would stay overnight with him. It was an arrangement that was working well.

The previous Friday Antoinette had met Karl to ask him if the girls could stay with him on Saturday as she was going to the concert in Slane. Karl agreed and organised to meet Antoinette and the girls the following day. They met on the Naas Road, close to where Karl worked at a tyre factory. Karl took Lisa and Rachel and said he'd stay in Kilmahuddrick Court that night as Antoinette was going home with Marie after the concert. Antoinette said she'd be home by midday the next day. He gave her £30 to enjoy the day, which was on top of the maintenance he normally paid.

As she headed off to the concert Antoinette was wearing a denim jacket and jeans and carrying a red Texaco bag. Karl, Lisa and Rachel waved the two women off. Lisa described her memory of the last time she saw her mother.

I remember getting the bus with Mam and Rachel down to near the factory where my dad worked. I remember her saying we were to be good for our dad, and she said she would have a present for us when she saw us the next day. I remember us walking down the road then with our dad while Mam walked the other way.

Antoinette had worn a wig since she was a child, having developed alopecia and lost all her hair, but it was never obvious: she had different hairstyles at different times and on the day she went to the concert she wore a shoulder-length, dark-brown wig with a half-perm. The wig, made by Franca Ferretti, would later help to identify Antoinette when her body was recovered at Glendoo Mountain.

As Rachel was only four when her mother was murdered she does not have clear memories. She does have precious photographs of Antoinette with herself and her sister. Rachel says the full impact of her mother's loss is hard to describe.

Losing your mam is not natural, not natural when you are just four, and my sister Lisa was just seven. And losing her in the way we did is just horrific. The impact on us was horrendous, and the wider family too. Everybody was affected. The people who murdered our mam have to be caught, they have to be brought to justice.

It was a warm summer's day when Antoinette and Marie headed to Slane. Antoinette had dropped her daughters with Karl at 11 a.m. and met up with Marie in the city centre. The women bought matching T-shirts with the Bowie logo in pink on the front and an image of the singer. They bought two flagons of cider and got the bus from Dublin at 2.30 p.m, joining tens of thousands of other music fans at the venue, where they enjoyed a great atmosphere.

Antoinette and Marie arrived back in Dublin from the concert at around 11 p.m. The city was heaving with concert-goers, many heading off to pubs and clubs in the vicinity. The two women decided to go to La Mirage nightclub on Parnell Street. Marie would later tell gardaí that they had a pint of Harp each, by which stage they were both quite drunk, but they were in great form, dancing away. By chance they bumped into two men they both knew and at closing time Antoinette, Marie and the two men left the club together and walked down O'Connell Street. It was approximately 2 a.m.

Antoinette wanted to continue by herself – she rarely got a chance for a night out – but Marie decided to head home, gave a copy of her front door key to Antoinette and thumbed a lift home.

Antoinette walked on down O'Connell Street with the two men, but they decided to head home too and got a taxi to Ballymun. Both would later be questioned at length about their movements that night, but the taxi driver who brought them home knew one of the men and remembered the journey. The driver confirmed that nobody else was with them on the journey to Ballymun, which corroborated the two men's account that they had left Antoinette in the O'Connell Street area and had gone home at approximately 2.15 a.m.

When Antoinette failed to return home on the Sunday lunchtime as she said she would, Karl Smith checked at Antoinette's mother's house and with friends and family, but nobody had seen her. It was soon established Antoinette had never arrived back at her friend Marie's. Karl Smith promptly went to Clondalkin Garda Station and reported his wife missing, however it would seem that very little searching was conducted by gardaí for the missing woman, and very little publicity was given to the case until Antoinette's body was found nine months after her disappearance.

At the post-mortem examination Professor Harbison first removed Antoinette's clothing. He washed her T-shirt, which now revealed the wording 'David Bowie, Slane '87, Big Country, Groovy'. When the pathologist then began examining the body he realised that the unidentified woman was wearing a wig, and it became immediately clear to detectives that the body was that of Antoinette Smith, last seen in Dublin city the previous July.

When her body was found Antoinette was wearing her Sasparilla brand jeans and Primark denim jacket. Her shoes were never located, and it was established that her clothing had been disturbed before her death, indicating the attack had been sexually motivated.

As they began a murder investigation in April 1988 after the body was found, gardaí conducted a trawl of all taxi drivers known to have been working in Dublin in the early hours of 12 July 1987. They questioned if Antoinette had hailed a cab and tried to head home to Clondalkin. However, this line of enquiry would place Antoinette in an entirely different part of the county. Detectives eventually spoke with a taxi driver who remembered having driven two men and a woman from Westmoreland Street to Rathfarnham at about 3.30 a.m: he recalled the fare because the two men had made him feel uneasy during the journey.

He described both men as being in their early twenties. One was tall – the taxi driver remembered the passenger's knees sticking into the back of his seat. He was soft-spoken, with dark hair and a Dublin accent. The other man had dark hair parted in the middle and brushed back over his ears. The taxi driver said this passenger acted the tough guy although he was smaller than the other man. He also said the woman matched Antoinette's description. The three passengers had sat into the back of the taxi close to the Abrakebabra take-away on Westmoreland Street. He had brought them to a slip road near the Yellow House pub in Rathfarnham village where all three passengers got out. The witness said that, in his opinion, the woman seemed to know the two men.

Gardaí have long believed that the woman in the taxi was Antoinette Smith. What she was doing travelling to Rathfarnham, and just who the two men were, has never been established. While the taxi driver's description of the woman matched Antoinette's appearance, what was also of great interest to investigators was that Rathfarnham village is close to the Wicklow Mountains.

Two suspects would emerge during the murder investigation who were living in rented accommodation in Rathfarnham at the time Antoinette disappeared. These two men were staying in a property close to the Yellow House pub, although no firm evidence was established to link Antoinette to the property or to the men. At least one of the men had been to the David Bowie concert. By the time Antoinette's body was found the two men had moved out of the property. They are still considered as one line of enquiry in the case.

One issue that hampered the case was the lapse in time between when the murder occurred and when Antoinette's body was found. The killers had nine months in which to cover their tracks and in the interim some witnesses may have forgotten details of what they might have seen.

Some strong witnesses did emerge, however. A major appeal was made on the *Garda Patrol* programme on RTÉ a month after Antoinette's body was found, and this appeal brought forward information that is still relevant today. A man contacted detectives to say he had seen two men acting suspiciously. Even though it was ten months since the murder, the witness was able to say it was that very morning, 12 July 1987, that he had seen the men while walking his dogs at Cruagh Wood, close to Rathfarnham. This information was deemed potentially very relevant, given that Cruagh Wood was at one end of Military Road and just over a mile from where Antoinette's body was found.

At 5.50 a.m the witness was walking with his dogs from the car park towards the brow of a hill when he spotted a man coming towards him. The man hesitated when he saw the witness, but continued walking down the hill at quite a fast pace. As the two passed each other the witness said hello but the other man didn't answer. The witness described him as being in his late twenties, of medium build and with a heavy mop of dark hair over his forehead. He had a thin face and was in dark clothing.

The witness stopped walking, now worried about his van down below, and looked back towards the car park. In the distance below he saw the man meeting up with a second man with fair hair, in denims and who seemed smaller than the first man.

The witness later said that a photofit compiled by gardaí of the first man bore a very good likeness and was as good as a photograph.

Neither this man nor the second man has ever been identified. What they were doing in the Wicklow Mountains that morning has never been established. Could it be a coincidence that the two men were in the mountains on the same morning that Antoinette's body was likely buried at Glendoo?

Professor John Harbison was unable to determine the precise cause of Antoinette's death. As her body lay undiscovered for almost nine months, it was impossible to confirm if Antoinette had been strangled or suffocated, or perhaps beaten to death. The pathologist established that there was some bruising to Antoinette's jaw, which might have happened during an assault. He couldn't say if the plastic bags had been placed on Antoinette's head while she was alive or after she was murdered. The key found with Antoinette's body was the key Marie gave to her on O'Connell Street in the early hours of the morning of 12 July 1987.

The lives of Antoinette's two children have been shaped in so many ways by the horrific loss of their mother. To this day Lisa is very angry about the way she was told her mother was dead.

Two gardaí came to us in the school, two men, and one of them said we have good news and bad news, and asked which we wanted to hear first. The good news was that our mam had been found, the bad news was that she was dead. What a horrific way to tell a child something so traumatic. I can't understand what they were thinking.

Lisa can vaguely remember the funeral. Rachel was too young. Lisa didn't understand what was going on. She is very angry about the media intrusion at the time of her mother's funeral. Over the years, as the two girls started asking questions about the case, they have both become very vocal about the failure to catch their mother's killers.

Detectives from the Garda Serious Crime Review Team (also known as the Garda Cold Case Unit) brought Lisa and Rachel to the location where their mother's body was found. Lisa described visiting the spot.

You realise how inhumanely she was treated. It's gut-wrenching to think that someone would have so little regard for another human being. It's not just the fact that she was my mam, but the fact that someone is out there who could be so calculated towards another person. It's sickening to think that person is still out there somewhere. Where my mam was found, what hit me was how isolated it was. And the fact that it was thought out, that's what got me more, how many more people are buried up there? Whoever put my mam up there had no intention of her ever being found.

The investigation into the murder of Antoinette Smith was initially headquartered in Tallaght under the direction of Superintendent John Courtney who had significant experience of investigating serious crimes, having been a member of the murder squad, a team of detectives who had travelled throughout the country investigating crimes in the 1970s and early '80s. Courtney had worked on the case of John Shaw and Geoffrey Evans, who had abducted, raped and murdered women in counties Wicklow and Mayo before they were apprehended and brought to justice. He would have known that whoever murdered Antoinette Smith could likely strike again. However, despite intensive garda efforts in the months after Antoinette's body was found, her murder would remain unsolved.

In 2018 Lisa and Rachel Smith sought a meeting with detectives in Bray to ask that their mother's case undergo a complete review. As Antoinette's body was found in an area covered by the Wicklow garda division, it now falls to gardaí there to try and advance the investigation. The case was previously examined by the Garda Cold Case Unit, and several hundred recommendations for further action were made. Rachel says more needs to be done.

We need to keep our mam's case out there, keep her memory alive. We need the public to help us; it could be the smallest piece of information that leads to a breakthrough. And we need gardaí to properly look at the case, because at times down the years it hasn't been given the attention it should have received. It has been pushed down the line, and that's not good enough.

While there was no breakthrough in Antoinette's case, some other murders of women whose bodies were hidden in the Wicklow Mountains would be solved. Philip Colgan, who lived in Rathfarnham, is now serving a life sentence for murdering Layla Brennan. When Layla encountered 27-year-old Colgan in Dublin city in March 1999, she wouldn't have known that he was a convicted rapist. He had previously attacked an elderly woman and a Spanish student. Colgan murdered Layla and hid her body in a ravine in the Wicklow Mountains. He was finally brought to justice for the murder of Layla Brennan when he confessed to his wife what he had done.

In 2012 Graham Dwyer, a 42-year-old father of two, brought Elaine O'Hara to a forest in Killakee and murdered her, leaving her body exposed on open ground. Elaine's body lay in the forest for just over a year before it was found purely by chance. Dwyer would have driven the same roads used by Antoinette Smith's killers twenty-five years earlier.

Another murder with similarities to Antoinette Smith's was Patricia Doherty's, whose body lay buried in the Wicklow Mountains for almost six months. James Kelly from Tallaght found Patricia's body. He was stacking turf close to the county bog road dividing counties Dublin and Wicklow on 21 June 1992 when he made the shocking discovery. Just after 3.20 p.m. he spotted human remains at the Featherbed Mountain under a bog bank on the Dublin side of the road. James had previously worked on excavating bodies in a graveyard on behalf of the National Museum, so he knew at once he had found human remains. Looking closer, James spotted a pair of ladies' shoes. He immediately went to raise the alarm some miles away. Knowing the area well he was able to tell gardaí that the location where the body was found would have been filled with water the previous winter. James had dug a channel during springtime to release the water, and this, combined with the subsequent warm summer of 1992, meant that a section of bogland had shifted and Patricia's body had become visible.

Patricia's body had been hidden over a hundred feet in from the bog road. Detective Edwin Hancock of the Garda Technical Bureau noted that Patricia's remains had become visible in a hole at the base of a bank of turf, which had collapsed outwards. Detective Hancock and his colleagues Ollie Cloonan, Gerry Scanlon and Jim McLaughlin excavated the area around the body as State Pathologist Professor John Harbison looked on. It was clear the body was fully clothed, and that it was a woman who had been buried for some time. As the body was removed by ambulance, gardaí were already wondering if it was missing woman Patricia Doherty, last seen alive just a few miles away in Tallaght.

At 10 a.m. on Christmas morning 1991 Paddy Doherty walked into Tallaght Garda Station and reported his wife missing. He told Sergeant Patrick Madigan he had checked with his wife's workplace, Mountjoy Prison, but she hadn't reported for work the previous day. Paddy described how he had spoken with friends and family but nobody had seen Patricia. He said he had last seen his wife around 9 p.m. on 23 December when she left their home at Allenton Lawns in Tallaght.

Earlier on the day of her disappearance Patricia had been shopping in The Square shopping centre in Tallaght, where she had bought Santa hats for her son and daughter. Originally from Co. Kerry, Patricia had met her husband-to-be on the number 15 bus, where Paddy was a conductor. The couple had married and settled in Tallaght. Paddy was originally from Ballybofey in Co. Donegal but had lived in Dublin since the early 1970s. Patricia had previously worked as a school secretary in Tallaght, but in 1991 she changed career entirely, becoming a prison officer.

For six months Patricia Doherty was classified as a missing person. Her husband went on national radio appealing for help with the case. There were a number of reported sightings, but all came to nothing.

Paddy Doherty told gardaí he'd picked up a number of silent phone calls, which he thought were from Patricia; he believed she was still alive. He checked her AIB account in Tallaght but it hadn't been touched.

Patricia Doherty was identified by dental records and also by her jewellery and clothing. Paddy was shown a number of personal items by detectives, all of which had been recovered from the body found at Featherbed Mountain. Patricia's husband recognised a scarf; it was one she had bought in Dunnes Stores about two years before. Paddy also recognised Patricia's multicoloured jumper, and he identified her Mandarin watch, wedding band and an engagement ring. A key found with Patricia's body opened the door of her home at Allenton Lawns.

As in the case of Antoinette Smith, whose body had been found four years earlier in the mountains, Professor John Harbison was unable to give a precise cause for Patricia Doherty's death, describing the cause as 'unascertainable'. The pathologist did not find any type of head injury. It was possible Patricia had been strangled, but it could not be stated absolutely. It appeared Patricia was fully clothed when she was murdered and her body buried in the mountains. Although it was straying into the grounds of speculation, many detectives believed there was no sexual motive for her murder. Gardaí wondered if Patricia had known her killer. Was it someone living in Tallaght? Detectives examined her work at Mountjoy Prison, looking at prisoners she had been in contact with, but there was no prominent suspect. Nobody was ever arrested in connection with her murder. In recent years the case was re-examined by the Garda Serious Crime Review Team, and a number of recommendations were made to detectives in Tallaght to advance the investigation. Still her killer remains at large.

In March 1993, nine months after the discovery of Patricia Doherty's body, another woman vanished from Dublin. This time, despite a massive investigation, the body of Annie McCarrick would not be found. Four months after Annie disappeared, a third woman,

Eva Brennan, also disappeared in south Dublin. Just like Antoinette Smith's and Patricia Doherty's, neither Annie's nor Eva's cases would be solved. Then, in December 1993, another body of a murdered woman was found on bogland, this time in the midlands.

For 176 days Marie Kilmartin's body lay hidden in a watery grave. The large concrete block that lay on the left side of her chest ensured Marie's body stayed rigid beneath the bog water. She lay on her back, with her head turned towards her right shoulder. Like Patricia Doherty, Marie was still fully clothed, dressed in her matching jacket and skirt, double-breasted overcoat and boots. This time the pathologist was able to give a precise cause of death. Whoever killed Marie had used their bare hands to strangle her to death, before throwing her body into the bog drain and dumping debris on top of her.

This was no random abduction; it was a targeted killing by someone who knew the victim. Somebody rang Marie from a nearby phone box and tricked her into leaving her house in Port Laoise. Marie would rarely venture outdoors in the dark by herself but someone managed to entice her outside. It was around 4.30 p.m. on Thursday, 16 December 1993 when Marie set her house alarm and left her home. Marie Kilmartin would not be seen alive again. In the following hours she was murdered at an unknown location and her body taken 20 kilometres from Port Laoise to dark and isolated bogland.

An off-duty prison officer found Marie's body on the afternoon of Friday, 10 June 1994. Tom Deegan was on a break from a shift at Port Laoise Prison when he decided to bring some of his children to visit his other young son who was cutting turf in a bog at Pim's Lane, north of Mountmellick on the Laois–Offaly border. Tom's two-year-old daughter Rebecca began to wander off around the surrounding bogland, and Tom followed, holding her hand.

He spotted what looked like the wheel of a pram sticking up from a bog drain and on closer inspection noticed something else that resembled a boot and leg. Shocked, he brought his children home and told his wife what he had seen. They agreed he should go back and investigate further. It was still bright at around 9 p.m. when Tom ventured back down the winding laneway to the bogland. He again saw what looked like a leg and, moving closer, identified a second boot and leg. He immediately went to raise the alarm.

Marie Kilmartin was thirty-five years old when she was murdered, the third-youngest of four children born to Fred and Rose Kilmartin. Fred was a successful businessman in the Ballinasloe and Athlone area who had built up a multimillion-pound car dealership and garage business. Marie grew up in Ballinasloe with her sister Theresa and brothers Anthony and Noel.

Marie was diagnosed with a psychiatric condition at an early age. To this day, the initial cause of her mental illness has never been established. In late 1979, when Marie was twenty-one years old, she discovered she was pregnant. Marie was in such turmoil that she was placed under the care of a doctor at St Fintan's Psychiatric Hospital in Port Laoise. It was here that Marie met a nurse, Pat Doyle, who in time would become her best friend. Pat passed away in 2014. She once described how she and Marie became friends.

> My heart went out to her when I first saw her. She was such a frightened young woman, and on top of being in a psychiatric hospital, here she was pregnant. She was very lonely and very distressed. I spent a good deal of time with her right from the start. At first it was a nurse and patient relationship. Over time, as she became better, it was a friendship of equals, and we ended up sharing a house in Port Laoise for over a decade.

On the afternoon of 29 March 1980 Marie gave birth to a baby girl at Port Laoise General Hospital, having been transferred from nearby St Fintan's to give birth. She wanted to keep her baby but wasn't allowed to. A distraught Marie said that she wanted to call her baby Rosemarie and her wish was duly noted in hospital records. Within days the baby was taken from her and brought firstly to Dublin, then eventually back to Co. Galway to be adopted into the wider family. Two months later, as Marie remained in hospital, the infant was baptised in a church in

Dublin as Áine. She would be told at an early age that she was adopted but not that her real mother was a relative.

On the night of 10 June 1994 Garda Pat Lyne was on duty in Portarlington station when he received an emergency call about a body being found in a bog. He drove immediately to Pim's Lane where Tom Deegan was waiting. Tom pointed out the bog drain over towards the left. Garda Lyne looked closely at the darkened water and saw the two feet, then the rest of a body beneath the water covered with an old pram and parts of a gas heater. There was a fresh growth of furze and ferns on the water. It was clear the body had been there for some time.

The last definite sighting of Marie was by two friends on the afternoon of Thursday, 16 December 1993. Marie had spent the earlier part of the afternoon working at a care centre for the elderly in Port Laoise. She was a volunteer worker and was loved by the men and women she kept company. She served out meals, played cards with them and chatted for hours. Marie was comfortable in this environment. It was a form of sheltered employment for her, a social outlet that gave her a strong feeling of self-worth. Marie had a strong group of friends around her in Port Laoise. She normally worked part-time in the care centre, starting at around 11 a.m. and finishing up about 3 p.m. She didn't drive, and during the summer would sometimes walk the two or so kilometres to her home at Beladd on the Stradbally Road. Marie didn't like the dark and during the winter months she would always take a lift home.

That day Marie took a lift home with Frances Bleach and Frances Conroy. It was 4.10 p.m. when the car pulled up outside her home, one of a row of spacious bungalows set in off the Stradbally Road. The three women were in great spirits; they'd had a Christmas party that lunchtime for staff and those who attended the day centre. Marie invited her friends in for a cup of coffee, but the two women declined. She grabbed a bag of shopping she'd picked up earlier in the day, said goodbye, and went in her front door.

Perhaps the killer was watching Marie at this time. Perhaps he had followed the car all or part of the distance from the day centre back in the town. Or he may have been parked near Beladd waiting until he saw Marie go into the house. It was only a short time later, at 4.25 p.m., that a phone call was made to the house from a coin box near the town centre.

Áine was thirteen years old when Marie was murdered. Growing up in a town in Co. Galway, she had been told from an early age that she was adopted, but never knew the full truth. She had met Marie a few times, always believing she was a distant relative. It was long after Marie's murder that Áine learnt who her birth mother was.

I would have seen Marie once every few years, and I didn't really think twice about her, I didn't have a clue. I have one particular memory of her, which is quite endearing in retrospect. My adopted mum was driving me one day in Galway, it was during the summer and we saw Marie and a friend walking along. For some unknown reason I made Mum stop the car and I gave Marie a Wispa bar that I had, and I gave her a big hug. At the time I didn't know why I was doing that. I am so happy now that I gave her that Wispa bar. Such a simple thing, but it must have meant the world to her at the time.

At midday on Saturday, 11 June 1994, Professor John Harbison travelled with Inspector Philip Lyons to the bog at the end of Pim's Lane. The pathologist studied the body as it lay in the water. One of the first things he did was to remove the large concrete block lying on the victim's chest. The block was around twelve inches wide, six inches long and four inches deep. In order to remove the body, a pram and parts of a gas canister had to be taken from the water first. It was a very distressing scene.

Professor Harbison began the post-mortem at five o'clock on Saturday, 11 June 1994. It was already clear from the clothing that the body was that of a woman, and gardaí strongly suspected it was Marie Kilmartin. Professor Harbison first looked at the victim's hands. Two rings were removed from her right middle finger, including a Claddagh ring. He then removed a nine-carat gold cameo ring and from her left hand he removed a sovereign ring. The pathologist looked at Marie's left wrist and removed a Guess watch with a beige leather strap. He removed a gold chain with a heart-shaped locket from around her neck. Marie Kilmartin was known to wear scapulars around her neck and Professor Harbison was asked to check if he could find them. He found one shoelace-type cord.

An examination of dental records would later confirm Marie's identity, but it was through her jewellery that she was initially identified. Detective Pat Egan took possession of Marie's jewellery, watch and necklace. When Marie's best friend Pat was shown the items she immediately recognised everything. She had bought the Claddagh ring for Marie herself, and had also given her the sovereign one as a present. Marie had bought the cameo ring in Dublin. Pat recognised the heart-shaped locket as one she had bought for Marie in Newbridge in the late 1980s. The large Guess watch, with mother-of-pearl surround and roman numerals was the one Marie's father, Fred, had bought her as a present from China some years before. The green scapular looked similar to one Marie had got in the Poor Clare Convent in Carlow the previous summer.

Marie and Pat had shared a house in Port Laoise for more than a decade. Pat knew within hours of Marie going missing that something awful had happened. She described the last time she saw her friend.

I remember we had a cup of tea that morning, I was heading to work early and Marie was going to work at around eleven. Marie was talking about who might give her a lift home after work. And she mentioned that some of the girls might go out for a Christmas drink after work, and she was wondering if she might go. I arrived home from work just after six that evening, and when I saw Marie wasn't home I wasn't too surprised initially because I thought she might have been with the girls somewhere. But as the evening wore on and there was no word I just got very concerned. It wasn't like Marie not to phone to say where she was.

When Marie left St Fintan's Hospital in the early '80s she and Pat had first lived in a flat on the Dublin Road in Port Laoise. The call that led Marie her to her death was made from a phone box just across the road on the left-hand side as one drove out of town in the direction of the nearby prison. It was made at 4.25 p.m. on 16 December 1993 and lasted around two and a half minutes. Phone records from Telecom Éireann showed no other phone call was made from the call box between 4.11 p.m. and 4.42 p.m. A woman who was hitchhiking on the road that day later came forward to tell gardaí she had seen a man in the phone box at around half past four. She described him as being five feet eight inches tall and around thirty years old.

When the state pathologist finished his post-mortem examination in Tullamore Hospital on 11 June 1994 he came to the conclusion that Marie had been manually strangled to death. There was no sign of any other injuries to her body. Although Marie had been fully clothed, Professor Harbison examined whether she had been sexually assaulted. There was no evidence to suggest that she had.

Marie may have been strangled to death in a car or van, or at some location in the Port Laoise area. Gardaí have been frustrated by the fact they never found a murder scene.

Whoever killed Marie had been meticulous, planning not only how to get her out of her house under false pretences, but they also had an isolated spot earmarked 20 kilometres away to dispose of her body. While a clear motive was difficult to establish, the evidence suggested the killer knew Marie very well.

When Marie left the house she left her bag of shopping hanging on the back of a chair in the kitchen. She didn't leave a note for Pat so she probably expected to be back in the house within a short time. She did set the house alarm as she normally would, indicating she was not just walking out to meet someone at the roadside, but was going some distance to either meet the person or was being picked up to go somewhere. Whatever the reason for Marie leaving the house shortly after being dropped home from work, she did not sense danger.

Áine was thirteen when Marie went missing, and fourteen by the time her body was found. She clearly remembers attending Marie's funeral. She can remember Marie's mother Rose holding her hand tightly the day after Marie was laid to rest. Áine can remember feeling so upset on the day of the funeral, feeling something she couldn't explain.

The funeral was so sad; it was the saddest day of my life ever. I remember Marie's best friend Pat put her hand out to the coffin at the funeral and said 'don't go'. It was just so sad. I remember at the funeral I cried and I cried. I've never cried as much in my life, and I couldn't understand why, because I didn't know her very well and didn't know she was my real mam.

In 2000 Áine found out Marie was her mother. A cousin confirmed it when they were out socialising. Even after she found out the truth, it would take much more investigative work by Áine until she would discover she had a birth cert, and she had been born as Rosemarie Kilmartin in Port Laoise in March 1980. Almost everything Áine has learnt has been through her own initiative and persistence.

Marie used to worry what Áine would think of her. She spoke about Áine a lot with Pat and with her friends at the day centre in Port Laoise. She worried Áine would think badly of her if she ever found out she was her mother. She asked Pat that if ever Áine came looking for answers, that she'd help to tell Áine that Marie loved her dearly, and that she had wanted to keep her but knew in her heart that she couldn't.

Marie's murder was investigated as part of Operation Trace that examined the disappearances of a number of women in the Leinster area in the 1990s. Marie's murder was included, to see if the case might be linked to any of the disappearances in Leinster; similarly the murders of Antoinette Smith and Patricia Doherty were also examined by the specialist garda team.

On 25 June 1994, two weeks after Marie Kilmartin's body was found, two men were arrested in Port Laoise and questioned in relation to her murder. The pair were arrested at around eight o'clock that morning: one was taken to Port Laoise Garda Station and the other was held in Abbeyleix. Both men were released without charge after being questioned for twelve hours, and no file was sent to the Director of Public Prosecutions. One of the men knew Marie, and his vehicle was thoroughly searched, but no incriminating evidence was found.

Gardaí have long considered whether more than one person was involved in Marie's murder. There's nothing to firmly indicate this and it's entirely possible that one person murdered Marie, dragged her body to the bog drain and then threw in the concrete block, pram and gas heater. However, detectives still wonder if there was a second person keeping a lookout, or who may have helped carry Marie's body and dump it in the drain. From early evening it would have been pitch black in the laneway leading to the bog: there are no houses in the area and no street lights. Two people would have been much quicker disposing of Marie's body and, more importantly, ensuring that there were no witnesses.

In October 2006 it was decided that a full reinvestigation of the murder should be undertaken with every person originally interviewed about the case being re-interviewed. A team of eight detectives were initially assigned to work full-time on the unsolved killing, with an incident room being set up in Abbeyleix Garda Station. This culminated with the arrest of three people in 2008 – two men and a woman. Similar to the 1994 arrests, each person who was detained was released without charge.

The failure by gardaí to solve the murder of Marie Kilmartin has frustrated many detectives. Those officers who saw her body as it lay in the bog drain will never forget the scene. But there is an added frustration, as one detective explains.

In cases of missing people believed murdered, we are always talking about how if we could only find the person's body, we would not only bring some peace for a grieving family, but we would have a much better chance of catching the killer. But here we have a case where a body was found and we have a certain number of pieces of the puzzle, but still the case is unsolved.

Áine is angry at the way the State has handled her mother's murder. She points to one simple example.

The information on Marie's death certificate is incorrect. The official cert states Marie was thirty-six and that she died on 17 December 1994. In fact Marie was thirty-five years old when she died and she disappeared on 16 December 1993. So, how can you trust that the bigger picture is being looked at properly when small but hurtful mistakes like those are being made? And nobody else seemed to notice those mistakes or didn't seem to care until I came along asking questions.

In December 2006 Áine began a public campaign to get justice for her mother. She spent days handing out thousands of leaflets in Port Laoise and neighbouring towns, appealing for the public's help in catching her mother's killer. Since then she has fought a lonely but persistent battle to get answers. Most recently in 2018 she approached newly appointed Garda Commissioner Drew Harris, handing him a dossier relating to the case with the many questions she has about its lack of progress.

When Áine launched her campaign in 2006, she visited the spot where her mother's body lay hidden for six months, and she vowed she would never give up her fight for justice.

The person who murdered Marie and left her here with a brick on her chest and a pram covering her must have a very hard heart. I've been through a lot in my life, but there is nothing I could go through that could give me such a hard heart. This is such a sad place. It just makes me feel so cold inside. It's the laneway leading up to this spot that disturbs me the most. A long narrow lane, it's the darkest, gloomiest, saddest place I've ever been.

More than a quarter of a century after her mother was murdered, Áine says she is fighting not only on behalf of her murdered mother, but for all murder victims.

As dreamy as it sounds, my wish is for every unsolved murder to be solved. I want to see a reinvestigation of every murder that has not been solved. There are far too many cases that have not been solved. I want to see every unsolved murder being given adequate resources to catch those responsible. And if necessary, private detectives should be used, or retired gardaí should be brought back if they are available. If you were in my position you would feel the exact same.

Áine has been affected in many ways by the murder of her mother. She has become particularly alert to things going on around her.

It's not so much paranoia, but if I'm walking down the road, there's never a number plate of a car that passes by that I don't look at. I'm looking to see if it has LS on it, or WH or G or whatever, and that is always there. Before I knew who my mother was I used to look at women wondering if they might be my mam. And after I found out who my mam is, I've ended up looking at men in Port Laoise and in Galway and other places and wondering if any of them is the person responsible for my mam's murder.

There is nothing to suggest that the murders of Marie Kilmartin, Antoinette Smith and Patricia Doherty are linked. It's quite possible that three individual killers committed the crimes and used a similar modus operandi to hide the body of their victim. It is a chilling fact that, before six other women would disappear in Leinster between 1993 and 1998, there were up to three separate killers capable of hiding bodies in bogland in Leinster. And any one of those killers could have struck again.

Antoinette Smith's youngest daughter Rachel attended the National Missing Persons Day event in 2018. For the first time she met other families in the same position – people whose loved ones were once missing but were later found. As Rachel was only four when her mother was murdered she doesn't have memories of her. Her family have told her lots about Antoinette, and the photographs of them together provide a link to the past. More than three decades since Antoinette Smith was murdered, Rachel says the person or people responsible for the crime must be brought to justice.

It makes me sick to think there are people that can actually plan that, burying a body. There was planning put into the disposing of another human being. You wouldn't do it to an animal. The person responsible knew what they were doing. Where my mam was found, it's just by chance that she was found. We are one of the lucky families.

CHAPTER 2

ANNIE McCARRICK

I n March 1993 Annie McCarrick was abducted and murdered somewhere in either south Dublin or in Co. Wicklow. The 26-year-old native of Long Island, New York, left her home in Sandymount, Dublin, late on the afternoon of Friday, 26 March. She travelled to nearby Ranelagh, where it's believed she got on a bus for Enniskerry, a picturesque village in north Co. Wicklow. Hours later a woman matching Annie's description was seen by members of the staff in Johnnie Fox's pub, close to Enniskerry, in the company of a man in his twenties. Annie McCarrick was known to have visited this pub before, where she loved to listen to bands playing traditional Irish music.

If the woman in Johnnie Fox's wasn't Annie, she has never been identified. Likewise the man spotted with that unidentified woman has never come forward. Was it Annie and the man who would murder her? Although Annie's case officially remains a missing persons investigation, many gardaí say it was privately considered as a murder investigation almost immediately. The fact that she was probably murdered by a man who has attacked or murdered other women has caused immense frustration for gardaí, who admit they never got a break in the case. Indeed, whether Annie was ever in Johnnie Fox's pub that particular night, or if she ever got as far as Enniskerry at all, continues to be a source of much discussion among detectives.

Annie McCarrick's disappearance was totally out of character. She was no stranger to Ireland, having lived in Dublin for three years while studying in Dublin and Maynooth. Her murder, and the fact that her body has not been found, deeply affected her parents, John and Nancy McCarrick, who lost their only child. The couple later divorced and John passed away in 2009, aged sixty-six. Nancy still lives in Bayport, Long Island.

In January 1993 Annie McCarrick left New York for the last time to travel to Dublin. She wanted to see, once and for all, whether she would settle down and make her home in Ireland. Three months later she would be abducted and murdered.

Just after three o'clock on the afternoon of Friday, 26 March 1993, Annie McCarrick pulled the door shut on her apartment in Sandymount. Although the weather would later turn wet, Annie was planning a walk in Enniskerry. Earlier that day she had phoned her friend Anne O'Dwyer in Rathgar, asking her if she would like to join her for a stroll in the foothills of the Wicklow Mountains. In an era before mobile phones, Annie had made the call from a public phone box in Sandymount village. There was a phone in the apartment Annie shared with two flatmates, but it was for incoming calls only. Anne told Annie she had hurt her foot and wouldn't be able for the trip. Annie wished her friend a speedy recovery and it appears she decided to head for Enniskerry by herself. It was her day off and she wasn't due back at work in Café Java on Leeson Street until the next day. Annie had arranged for two friends to call over the following evening for dinner, and she might meet another old college friend for a drink on Sunday. That day she was at a loose end, and it was just the weather for a walk in a part of Ireland she had grown to know and love. She put on her favourite tweed coat, grabbed her handbag, and headed out the door.

Annie had left laundry in the communal laundry room. She had only recently moved into the apartment complex and it wasn't like her to leave her laundry unattended when other tenants might want to use the machines. Also, she left food she had bought that afternoon hanging on a chair, as if she was only heading out for a short time. Annie didn't leave her apartment for the intended walk until after three o'clock – more than four hours after she had spoken with Anne about heading for Enniskerry. Mid-afternoon was quite late to be heading to Co. Wicklow for a walk. She had told a flatmate earlier that day that her watch had stopped, so she may have simply lost track of time. The ironing board was also left out – perhaps she had been doing some housework before heading off. Annie would have known that if she left by three o'clock she could be in Enniskerry by 4.30 p.m. There would still be a bit of daylight left.

As Annie McCarrick left her apartment at St Cathryn's Court in Sandymount, a plumber, Bernard Sheeran, was working at a nearby apartment. He spotted her leaving her home and heading down the road. She was also seen by Bruno Borza, who ran the local chip shop: he saw her heading down Newgrove Avenue towards the terminus of the number 18 bus. This would bring her over to Ranelagh, where she would get a number 44 to Enniskerry. She saw a number 18 at the terminus but was still about a hundred yards away when the bus began to leave. She ran towards it, trying to catch the driver's attention. He spotted her, and slowed down to let her on. She paid the fare to bring her to Ranelagh.

Annie McCarrick loved Ireland. By March 1993 she had spent several years flying back and forth between Dublin and New York. It was 1987 when she first arrived in Ireland, coming for a week's holiday at Christmas when she was twenty and visiting Ireland as part of a group led by her cousin, Danny Casey, who taught Irish studies at the State University of New York. She instantly fell in love with the country and the people. Her great-grandfather and grandmother on her mother's side had left Ireland many decades earlier and there were also strong links with Ireland on her father's side. Her Long Island childhood was a very Irish-American one.

Annie McCarrick lived in Ireland for three years while she studied at St Patrick's Training College in Drumcondra, Dublin, and later at St Patrick's College, Maynooth. In between her studies in Ireland she returned to New York in 1990 to continue her studies there for a year. But she missed Ireland, where she had made so many friends. In a home video recorded in Dublin by Annie's aunt Maureen in 1989, it's obvious that Annie's American accent has developed a slight Irish lilt, to such an extent that she says other Americans in college think she is Irish.

By Christmas 1992 and back on Long Island having completed her studies in Ireland, Annie had decided that she wanted to return to Dublin. She discussed the matter with her parents, telling them she wanted to see once and for all if she wanted to make her life there. Ideally she wanted to get a job as a teacher. John and Nancy didn't want to their only child to leave America again, but they knew Annie was restless and had her heart set on returning to Ireland. On 6 January 1993 they kissed their daughter goodbye for the last time. Annie stepped on board a plane at JFK airport and left for Dublin. They would never see their daughter again.

Annie McCarrick spent the first eighteen years of her life in the leafy suburbs of Bayport on the south shore of Long Island, New York. Bayport is an hour's drive from JFK and an hour and a half south-east of Manhattan. It is a prosperous town in Suffolk County, with wide streets and large detached houses with open lawns out front. Just south of Bayport is the Atlantic Ocean, where Annie spent many happy hours standing on the shore looking across at the lights of Fire Island, south of Bayport.

Annie McCarrick's parents are both New Yorkers. From the mid-1960s until the mid-nineties they lived together in Bayport, raising one daughter, but divorced in the wake of Annie's abduction and murder. John suffered considerable ill health in later years. Nancy told me that Annie had a very happy childhood.

Annie was born in March 1967 at Bay Shore, just a few miles from here. When she was about fourteen months we moved into our first house at Dolores Court, which is just a few hundred yards from here. When she was twelve the three of us moved to Bayview Avenue. Annie was living there right up until she went to Ireland. For her primary, middle and high school Annie went to the local school for the towns of Bayport and Bluepoint. I worked as a secretary in the school, and her father was a teacher. This is the area where Annie spent the first eighteen years of her life. She had so many friends. It was wonderful.

It was from their home at Bayview Avenue that, on an evening in late March 1993, Nancy McCarrick rushed to JFK to board a flight to Dublin. A phone call from Hilary Brady, a friend of Annie's in Dublin, had set alarm bells ringing. Nobody had seen Annie in Dublin in more than three days. She hadn't turned up for work, and wasn't to be found in her apartment. Nancy has vivid memories of that time.

Annie's friend Hilary had phoned on the previous Saturday to say he was trying to reach Annie in Dublin and had forgotten her phone number. He said there was no answer from her apartment and they were meant to meet for dinner. We thought nothing of it, but it was a couple of days later that Hilary phoned again. He still hadn't spoken to Annie. But now alarm bells started to ring. Hilary had gone to where Annie worked on Leeson Street and discovered she hadn't turned up for work. Her flatmates who had returned to Dublin after the weekend hadn't seen her either. When he phoned that second time, Hilary said to me, 'No one has seen Annie.' I just knew something was wrong. Within four hours I was at JFK and on a flight to Dublin.

Nancy McCarrick arrived in Dublin the next morning. Hilary Brady met her at the airport. They travelled to the garda station in Irishtown, where Nancy McCarrick formally reported her daughter missing. John McCarrick arrived in Dublin shortly afterwards. The McCarricks still hoped that there might be some news of Annie at any moment.

They didn't know it then, but they would be staying in Ireland for the next two months. By the time they left Ireland broken-hearted in May 1993, they would be faced with the terrible realisation that their daughter would not be coming home.

When Annie McCarrick was formally reported missing, the gardaí in Irishtown had a difficult job in trying to piece together her last known movements. The fact that she was going about her normal routine made the job even more difficult. The gardaí had no crime scene. In tracing Annie's friends, detectives were quickly able to establish that she had intended travelling to Enniskerry; but had she made it there? One detective noted that the last sighting of Annie by someone who knew her is very helpful in this regard.

> We knew that Annie got on the number 18 bus in Sandymount. We knew that she would have intended getting off in Ranelagh to connect with the 44 to Enniskerry. But we had to consider every possibility, like whether she fell asleep on the 18 and ended up across Dublin city, miles from her intended destination, or whether she felt unwell and got off the bus before Ranelagh. These were all things we had to consider; but then we got a positive sighting from a former workmate of Annie's that put her on a number 44 in Ranelagh. All the indications are that she was going to Enniskerry.

Just before four o'clock on the afternoon of Friday, 26 March 1993, Annie McCarrick joined the queue at the bus stop in Ranelagh, opposite the Ulster Bank. She had walked from Chelmsford Road after getting off the number 18. She was wearing her dark tweed jacket, a pair of jeans, and oxblood-coloured boots. She carried a tan-coloured shoulder bag. Also waiting for a bus was Éimear O'Grady, who was ahead of Annie in the queue. She recognised Annie from their time working together in the Courtyard Restaurant in Donnybrook the previous month.

The number 44 arrived, and Éimear got on. She sat downstairs, because she was only going a short distance to her home at nearby

Milltown Court. She saw Annie get on the bus after her and go upstairs. Little did she know it, but Éimear's sighting of Annie going upstairs on the bus was to be of immense importance and led to the gardaí concentrating the bulk of their subsequent investigation on the Wicklow Mountains. Éimear O'Grady got off the bus a short time later, unaware that she was now the last person to positively identify Annie McCarrick. Within hours, Annie would be murdered.

The positive sighting of Annie on the number 44 bus gave the gardaí encouragement that they might be able to trace her movements thereafter. However, all their enquiries to establish where she went after that led nowhere. The driver, Paddy Donnelly, couldn't remember Annie being on the bus. None of the passengers who came forward could remember her getting off the bus at the terminus in the centre of Enniskerry, or at any stop before that. One detective remembered the garda team's frustration.

> Annie was a striking-looking young woman, and she stood out because of her accent. She was tall, and she was wearing a distinctive jacket and cowboy-type boots. And yet nobody saw anything. We knew from Éimear O'Grady that Annie had got on the number 44 bus, and this would correspond with her telling her friend Anne that she was planning to go to Enniskerry. But after that we don't have any positive sighting of her. We know she had to get off the bus somewhere between where Éimear got off, at Milltown, and the last stop at Enniskerry. My instinct says Enniskerry. But there is no one to positively identify her there.

Less than a mile south of Enniskerry is the Powerscourt Estate and Gardens – a popular venue for visitors. If Annie McCarrick did get the bus to Enniskerry, she would have got off in the centre of the village, which is shaped like a triangle, with three converging roads and a monument in the centre. If she did get the number 44 to Enniskerry she would have arrived there well before five o'clock. As day began to turn to dusk there would still have been at least a good hour of daylight left on that March evening. Did she decide to wander south towards Powerscourt waterfall? This would have been a logical journey for a young woman out enjoying the Co. Wicklow countryside. It would bring her along a fairly busy road, which heads on towards the Great Sugar Loaf. But this is speculation. Nobody has ever reported seeing Annie McCarrick heading out of Enniskerry towards Powerscourt. Even more frustrating, not one person has ever reported a positive sighting of Annie in Enniskerry. One woman who worked in the village's post office did say she served someone matching Annie's description that Friday evening, selling her three stamps for postcards. But the woman couldn't be sure it was Annie, and no postcards ever arrived to anyone from Annie. Frustratingly, there was no CCTV footage available. Quite possibly the customer in the post office wasn't Annie.

As the search entered its second week, a conference was held among detectives attached to Irishtown, Enniskerry and Bray garda stations. It was decided that a further appeal would be made for information. A photograph of Annie was circulated to television and newspapers. And then a man came forward with information that would bring a new focus to Annie's disappearance.

Sam Doran was working as a doorman at Johnnie Fox's pub on the night of Friday, 26 March. He phoned the gardaí to say he recognised the woman featured on the missing person posters: she had been to Johnnie Fox's that night. Another doorman, Paul O'Reilly, also told the gardaí that a woman matching her description had been in the back lounge of the pub at about 9.30 p.m. that evening. It was a busy night, and the Jolly Ploughmen band was playing into the early hours. Sam Doran was able to recall that the woman was in the company of a young man. He remembered telling the couple that there was a £2 cover charge for the lounge; the young man had paid for both of them, saying something like 'I'll take care of that.'

If Annie McCarrick did get to Enniskerry by five o'clock that evening, and if she was the woman seen in the pub four hours later, where had she been in the meantime? How did she get to Johnnie Fox's pub, if indeed it was her there that night? She was known to be a keen walker and could definitely have walked the four miles in that time, but the weather had turned bad. If Annie did walk to Johnnie Fox's, did she just meet someone outside the pub by chance, or had she arranged to meet them? Did she hitch a lift, or did she bump into someone she knew, someone who has never come forward? The gardaí had, and continue to have, many such questions.

Assuming that the woman identified in the pub by Sam Doran and Paul O'Reilly was Annie McCarrick, detectives now had a description of a man they would like to question. He was described as being in his mid-twenties, clean-shaven, of average build, with dark-brown hair. But despite repeated appeals for information, neither the woman nor the man has ever come forward. One detective believes this is significant.

> For one person to remain silent is not uncommon, but for two people not to come forward is highly unusual. If they were entirely innocent, surely one, if not both, would have come forward, even years later. It made us think that perhaps the woman was actually Annie, and the man in question was the man who would later attack her. It's still a valid theory; but it doesn't really get us any further. If it was Annie, nobody could identify the man she was with. Nobody saw them leave the pub.

There was another American woman in Johnnie Fox's pub that night who looked somewhat like Annie; but this woman was with her mother, not a young man. Gardaí later tracked down a group of French tourists who had taken photographs in the pub that night but there was no sign of Annie in the photos, nor of the unidentified man. Detectives who would later work as part of Operation Trace would often revisit the description of the man seen in Johnnie Fox's. One detective believes this unidentified man could hold the answer.

> If you consider the description of this fellow – clean-shaven, in his mid-twenties and with dark-brown hair – it actually matches a man who only came to our attention years later for a horrific attack

on a young woman in Co. Wicklow. He abducted this woman, raped her and then tried to kill her. He had never come to our attention before. We suspect he has attacked other women. It would make you wonder if he was the man in Johnnie Fox's. But in other ways, the description of a clean-shaven man in his twenties with brown hair is one which matches thousands of men. But we haven't ruled this man out. He was always clean-shaven; he was always charming. And underneath it, he's one of the most violent men I've ever encountered.

Within days of Nancy McCarrick arriving in Dublin in March 1993, her husband followed. Her brother, Tim Dungate, also travelled from New York, as did her brother-in-law John Covell, who was married to Nancy's sister Maureen. The four of them met gardaí to see how the investigation was going. Nancy remembers the detectives seemed at a loss to explain what might have happened.

It was just beyond their comprehension. Annie wasn't the first woman to go missing in Ireland, but she was the first of a number of women to disappear over a short number of years. But back then the gardaí just couldn't explain it. It was new to them. I remember suggesting that Annie might have responded to a particular ad for someone to work with horses. The ad was in relation to a place on the way from Dublin to Enniskerry. I remember asking if they had questioned this man, and a garda said, 'Oh, Mrs McCarrick, you don't think Annie responded to the ad, and the man thought to himself that he'd keep her; no such thing could happen.' It was just beyond their experience. Now it's different, they know that there are people capable of these terrible deeds. Gardaí worked extremely hard on Annie's case, but it was just so new to them.

Though the disappearance of Annie McCarrick is still officially classified as a missing person case, every detective who worked on it in the initial stages knew it was a murder enquiry from very early on.

As detectives began to consider where Annie's body might have been buried, some were conscious of the unsolved murders of Antoinette Smith and Patricia Doherty, whose bodies had been hidden in the Wicklow Mountains in 1987 and 1991. Both bodies had been found after dry weather caused turf banks to subside. Nobody had ever been charged in relation to these horrific murders. If the cases were not linked it was clear that, uncannily, two different killers used similar remote parts of the Wicklow Mountains to hide the bodies of their victims in the very same fashion. One detective says gardaí soon feared Annie McCarrick had suffered a similar fate.

> The bodies of Antoinette Smith and Patricia Doherty were buried in relative close proximity in the Dublin Mountains. The persons responsible for those murders are still out there – killers who know the Dublin Mountains; killers who knew where they could work undetected as they sought to hide their crimes by burying the bodies. In searching for Annie we were conscious of those murders; but it was only years later, when Operation Trace came on stream, that all these cases were really looked at for links. Whoever murdered Antoinette Smith is still out there, and whoever murdered Patricia Doherty is still out there. It's often speculated whether the person who killed Annie McCarrick killed other women later on. Annie was the first of a number of women to vanish in the 1990s and not be found. But what's not spoken about as much, and which we must always consider, is – had Annie's killer actually killed before?

Annie McCarrick had been sharing an apartment at St Cathryn's Court at Newgrove Avenue in Sandymount for a few weeks before she disappeared. Her two flatmates were Jill Twomey and Eda Walsh. They had first met Annie in January when she responded to an ad looking for a flatmate. They instantly took a liking to her and offered her a room. The three young women quickly became good friends. Jill and Eda last saw Annie on the morning of the day she disappeared. Eda remembers Annie had been sitting up in bed knitting that morning.

On that morning I had clothes to dry in the basement and I needed change for the machine. I knocked on Annie's bedroom door and she was sitting up in bed knitting. She asked what time it was and I said 7 a.m. Annie thought it was earlier and didn't realise that her watch had stopped. She gave me change for the dryer and we had breakfast together. She didn't have any real plans for the weekend so I gave her my sister's number in Newbridge, just in case she was at a loose end and wanted to come down to visit. This would have been the first weekend since Annie moved into the apartment in January that she would be alone as neither Jill nor I would be in Dublin. Annie had taken the single room when she moved in and I had a bigger double room. I promised Annie that whenever her mum was coming over we could swap rooms for the visit, so her mum would have space with her. I headed off to work and was going on from there to Newbridge. Jill left the apartment after me. She was heading to Cork that weekend.

Annie had brought Eda and Jill to Johnnie Fox's a couple of times in early 1993. She had been telling them about the pub and how much she liked it. The fact that she had been there just a few weeks before she vanished made it even more curious that more people, either staff or customers who might recognise her as a familiar face, hadn't seen her there on 26 March.

With Eda and Jill now gone for the weekend, Annie later left the apartment to walk the short distance to Quinnsworth in Sandymount. She bought ingredients to make some desserts for Café Java, where she was due back at work the next day. The receipt for the ingredients shows that she paid for the goods at 11.02 a.m. She then went to the AIB branch in Sandymount; she wanted to change her account from the Clondalkin branch to Sandymount. When she had arrived back in Dublin in January 1993 Annie had stayed for a while with her friend Hilary Brady at his home in Clondalkin.

The closed-circuit television tape of Annie in the AIB branch in Sandymount shows her going about her normal life. There is nothing out of the ordinary. After leaving the bank she walked back towards her apartment. From the phone box outside, she phoned Anne O'Dwyer to see if she wanted to join her for a walk in Enniskerry. She also phoned Hilary Brady to arrange that himself and his fiancée, Rita, come over for dinner the following evening. She didn't leave the apartment again until around 3.15 p.m., when she headed out to jump on the number 18 bus for Ranelagh.

Annie had been friendly with the Brady family for many years. Soon after she arrived in Ireland in 1988 to begin her studies at St Patrick's Training College in Drumcondra she started going out with Hilary's brother Philip. This was one of two serious relationships she had while she studied in Ireland. She later met Dermot Ryan, a fellow sociology student at St Patrick's College, Maynooth, and they dated for about two years. After Annie and Philip Brady broke up they remained on friendly terms, and Annie kept in regular contact with the Brady family, including Hilary and his fiancée. On the day she disappeared she was looking forward to preparing dinner the following evening for Hilary and Rita.

Hilary Brady was immediately concerned about Annie. It was around eight o'clock on the evening of Saturday, 27 March 1993, and he and Rita were standing outside Annie's apartment. He had been ringing the doorbell, but got no response. This was not like Annie: if she had to cancel the dinner engagement, surely she would have phoned. The apartment was in darkness. Hilary couldn't remember the number for the phone in the apartment. Hilary still had the McCarrick home number in New York from many years before. It would be the afternoon in New York, and John or Nancy would definitely have Annie's phone number.

Nancy answered the phone and Hilary explained that he and Rita were outside Annie's apartment but he didn't have her phone number and couldn't reach her. Nancy gave him the number and they had a brief chat. Hilary tried the number. It rang and rang, but there was no answer. It was now dark. Hilary had a mobile phone but Annie didn't. The only way to reach her was the apartment door bell or phone line.

Hilary and Rita decided they would try again in a while, and they went for a drink in a nearby pub. But when they tried again, there was still no answer. The couple decided there wasn't much else they could do at that hour of the night, so they headed home.

The next day Hilary called into Café Java in Leeson Street. What he was told only increased his concern. Annie had not turned up for work. She had been due in the day before, and had not phoned to say she wouldn't be in. It was quickly established that the last time anyone had seen her in work was about three o'clock on the Thursday afternoon.

Eda Walsh remembers that very soon after arriving home to Sandymount that Sunday evening she realised something was very wrong.

> When I came back on Sunday evening, the first thing I remember was hearing the phone ringing inside the apartment. There were two locks and it took a little while to open the door. When I got in, I answered the phone and it was Hilary Brady asking if I had seen Annie. I remember there were two or three bags of shopping from Quinnsworth just inside the door on the floor. The bags contained ingredients for making tarts for Café Java in Leeson Street. I remember the ironing board was out and a telephone directory was out too as if Annie had been looking through it. Hilary came to the apartment later that night. He said he had phoned all the hospitals to check if Annie had been admitted over the weekend. We waited until Jill arrived back from Cork to see if Annie had made contact with her over the weekend. Jill hadn't been in contact with Annie since Friday morning.

That night Hilary Brady made another phone call to John and Nancy McCarrick in New York. He told them nobody had seen Annie, no one knew where she was. She had missed a shift in work. She wasn't at home.

Annie McCarrick was a confident woman, chatty and friendly. She made many friends in Ireland from the time she first arrived in 1987.

For her to decide to go for a walk alone in the foothills of the Wicklow Mountains was the act of a confident and resourceful woman. When she arrived in Ireland in January 1993 her work papers weren't in order, but she just couldn't wait to get back to Ireland, to her friends. When one job fell through because of problems with her work visa, she wasn't too bothered: she just began looking for another job.

On 17 March 1993 – nine days before she was murdered – Annie joined thousands of people in O'Connell Street, Dublin, where she celebrated St Patrick's Day. She went with a local family from Sandymount. Naturally she missed her family back in New York, but she was where she wanted to be.

No one has ever been arrested for the abduction and murder of Annie McCarrick. There is no prime suspect. A number of men have been interviewed at length, but nobody has ever been detained for questioning.

By the time Operation Trace came to analyse Annie McCarrick's case, together with those of five other missing women in the Leinster area, one extremely violent man had not yet come to the attention of gardaí. The crimes committed by Larry Murphy in three counties on the night of 11 February 2000 shocked the most hardened detectives. Murphy abducted a woman from Carlow and raped her in his car at locations in counties Kildare and Wicklow. The crimes gave an insight into the modus operandi of one man who, by his own admission, had intended to kill the woman he abducted. He had a plastic bag over his victim's head and was trying to suffocate her when two hunters stumbled on the scene by chance.

The fact that Larry Murphy had no previous convictions, and was married with two young children, was also of interest to detectives. Here was an attacker who had not been on the garda radar.

Larry Murphy wasn't the only abductor to be exposed many years after Annie McCarrick disappeared. Annie was missing seven years when John Crerar was finally arrested for murdering Phyllis Murphy in Co. Kildare in 1979. Just like Murphy, Crerar had no previous convictions. Likewise, architect Graham Dwyer seemed like the perfect family man until he was arrested in 2013 and charged with the murder of a woman whose body lay in the Wicklow Mountains for thirteen months.

While there are many convicted sex offenders who have been considered as suspects in the murder of Annie McCarrick, the other possibility is that the killer was someone who, just like Graham Dwyer, John Crerar and Larry Murphy, had never come onto the garda radar before.

What if the answer to Annie's disappearance is closer to Sandymount? What if she did go for a walk in Enniskerry, and then returned home? Nobody realised she was missing until the following day, so what if she got back to Sandymount that Friday and something happened closer to home? However, there is nothing to indicate any of this happened. The last positive sighting of Annie is the Friday afternoon on a bus in Ranelagh that was heading for Enniskerry. But in the absence of any positive lead, every possibility has to be considered.

Two days before Annie vanished, a suspected serial killer from Spain was believed to have jumped into the waters of Dublin Bay from an approaching ship. Twenty-six-year-old Antonio Anglés Martins was wanted for the murders of three teenage girls who had been abducted while walking to a disco in Alcàsser, Valencia in November 1992. Crew members on board a ship that had sailed from Lisbon believed a stowaway they discovered was the wanted man, but he jumped overboard as the ship approached Dublin Port.

Following contact with Spanish and Portuguese police, gardaí believed Martins was very likely the stowaway who had jumped ship. Gardaí obtained an extradition warrant in case they located him, but no trace was ever found of Martins. It's most likely the stowaway drowned in the cold waters of the Irish Sea. To this day, in the absence of a body being located, Martins is one of Interpol's most wanted fugitives. Even if he had made it to shore, it's most unlikely he would have had the opportunity to cross Annie's path. However, the suspected arrival of such a dangerous man into Irish waters just two days before Annie's disappearance is uncanny.

The big question in Annie's case is this: was she in Johnnie Fox's pub on the night she disappeared? Gardaí believe the two doormen were absolutely genuine in their recollection of a woman bearing a strong resemblance to Annie in the company of a clean-shaven man. But what if that wasn't Annie? What if the whole focus on Johnnie Fox's was wrong?

If Annie was in Johnnie Fox's pub that night, one lead that still needs to be pursued is information received by detectives in the late 2000s that a member of the IRA may have murdered Annie. The account given to detectives from a credible source relayed information suggesting that an IRA member from Belfast was hiding out in south Dublin and had gone to Johnnie Fox's pub that night and struck up a conversation with Annie. According to the story, at some point during the night the IRA member believed he had spoken too much about his background, and decided to murder Annie.

While some believe the story may seem far-fetched, detectives would still like to question this man, whose identity is known to them. But they haven't been able to locate him for more than twenty-five years. When he was nominated as a suspect, gardaí were also told this IRA member was suspected of abusing a child and was then moved out of Ireland by the IRA leadership in 1993. It's believed he travelled to the United States, but after that he effectively went off the grid. Gardaí continue to liaise with a number of other police forces in an effort to track down this man.

The McCarrick family were greatly frustrated at the lack of any solid lead in the case. Within weeks of Annie's disappearance, John McCarrick decided to hire a private investigator to help find his daughter. The investigator, Brian McCarthy, had been recommended by an official at the US embassy in Dublin. However, he also failed to turn up any solid leads. Detective Inspector Martin Donnellan, who would later become an assistant commissioner, led the original search for Annie. Donnellan says they spent thousands of man hours on the case.

We carried out massive searches on foot, inch-by-inch physical searches. We chased up leads and possible sightings right around the country. Any person we knew to have a history of sexual assaults was looked at. There were numerous searches throughout north Co. Wicklow. Right from the start, Annie's case was treated like a murder investigation. A retired superintendent from Scotland Yard came over at John McCarrick's request and reviewed the file. He was satisfied with the scope of our investigation. But, at the end of the day, Annie is still out there somewhere.

In June 1997 new information was given to detectives about suspicious activity seen near Enniskerry on the day Annie McCarrick had vanished. A decision was taken that a pet cemetery near Enniskerry should be searched. The search, involving twenty gardaí, began on the morning of Monday, 16 June. Gardaí from the forensic science and ballistics sections were on hand to provide guidance on searching through the graves. The information given to the gardaí consisted of a report of a large box being buried at the pet cemetery shortly after Annie McCarrick had disappeared. As word spread of the search, two men contacted the gardaí. They told detectives they had buried a greyhound in the cemetery in late March 1993. The men's story was borne out when the remains of the dog were unearthed a short time later. By one o'clock the following afternoon, the search of the pet cemetery was completed. There were no new leads.

Annie McCarrick wanted to be a teacher. When she started her studies in 1988 she went to St Patrick's Teacher Training College in Drumcondra. She later studied at St Patrick's College, Maynooth, entering in the second year of a course in which she studied sociology and English. It was here she met fellow student Geraldine Delaney, who became a good friend.

Annie was an only child, and so was I, so we had a particular bond. Annie was what you'd call a real Celtic woman. She wore lovely cloaks and knitwear. And she was such a reliable person – even to the extent that when we studied in the reading room in the Arts Block in Maynooth, if Annie took a break she'd write on a note the time she had left. She'd leave the note on top of her books. She was that reliable, that predictable. I also visited her in New York after she finished her studies here. We would have great chats about everything. On the night before Annie disappeared, the Thursday, we had a chat on the phone. She was really looking forward to her mother, Nancy, coming over to visit her the following week, and she had made plans for what they would do together. We said we might meet up for a drink on the Sunday night. Annie was to call me. She never did.

Nancy McCarrick was also looking forward to visiting Annie in Dublin. During a subsequent search of Annie's apartment in Sandymount, gardaí found theatre tickets she had bought in anticipation of her mother's visit. When Annie was living in Ireland Nancy would visit her every Easter, staying for about a week or ten days. Nancy told me a simple story that shows how resilient and confident her daughter was.

It was the summer of 1989, and Annie was in Germany. She was there with her college friends from Maynooth. They all went to work there for the summer, and they had jobs already arranged in a pickle factory near Hamburg. But when Annie went to start work there she was told that she couldn't work with her friends in the factory because she didn't have a European passport. She didn't have the right permit to let her work there. Undeterred, Annie went down to the local fruit market, and within minutes she had found a job with a stall-holder. I remember she phoned me and she was joking, saying, 'I'm lifting all these wooden crates; wait till you see the muscles I've developed.'

Annie loved the way of life in Ireland, the culture, the music, the people. Late on 26 March 1993 some violent person shattered that view of Ireland. Nancy McCarrick bears no ill will towards the country where Annie chose to live.

> When I left Ireland in May 1993 without any news of Annie, I was just devastated. I managed to return to Ireland in August of that year for about a week. I didn't go back there for a long time after that. John and I later divorced. I feel as close to Annie here in New York as when I would visit Ireland. It was another eight years after Annie disappeared that I went back to Ireland. I went over in 2001, and I met a number of gardaí, including the Assistant Commissioner, Tony Hickey, who briefed me on their investigations into whether a serial killer might be involved in Annie's case. Despite the reason for my return there, I was very happy to visit Ireland. I don't blame Ireland at all. Even now, Dublin is a much safer place than parts of New York. There is just no comparison.

I asked Nancy about her feelings towards the person who murdered Annie. She paused, thought carefully, and after a few moments replied:

> I feel that if in any way Annie's death was not what the person intended to happen, or if it was accidental, and if that person responsible was not to harm anyone else, I would have no interest in seeing any person punished. I just want Annie back. I want her home.

John McCarrick was also devastated by the loss of Annie. He did everything he could possibly do to find his daughter: he made numerous appeals on radio and television; he hired both a private investigator and a retired English police officer to review the garda investigation; he offered a $150,000 reward for information leading to the recovery of Annie's remains. The loss of his only child shattered him. Before his health deteriorated he brought an Irish film crew to Bayport to show them where Annie grew up. He brought them along Bayview Avenue, down Dolores Court, and down to the beach from where Fire Island is visible across the bay. During the summers when Annie was a teenager, she and her father used to stand on the beach and look at the glistening lights across the bay, where groups of young people would party into the early hours. Visibly upset, he told the film crew that if he could have one wish, he would like nothing else than to be standing on the same beach with Annie by his side just like the old times, with them both listening to the sound of the water and looking across the bay.

Hundreds of acres of woodland and bogland have been searched in an attempt to find Annie McCarrick's remains. The search of the pet cemetery in Enniskerry, four years after her disappearance, is only one example of many searches that have been made for her some years after her disappearance. Another tip-off, that Annie would be found in a well in Co. Wicklow, was also investigated but led nowhere. Other information led to a search of Crone Wood, three miles south-west of Enniskerry, which also yielded nothing.

Barry Walsh was a detective based in Irishtown station for eight years until he was promoted in 2016. He read the full original file on Annie's disappearance. As he investigated Annie's case, he got to know Nancy, and was her liaison officer for a number of years. He says the case was hampered by a number of factors.

The challenge has always been to try and place particular evidence into perspective, from the point of view of what's more valuable versus what's not. Very few of the investigative methods available today were widely available in 1993. There was no CCTV available from Ranelagh, none from Dublin Bus of that number 44 bus, there was no CCTV available from Johnnie Fox's of that night. The lack of CCTV means that strong reliance had to be placed on the accounts of witnesses without any corroborative evidence. This placed a very significant burden on the initial investigative response, as those gardaí had to follow up numerous time-consuming reported sightings of Annie. All these reports were no doubt well intentioned, yet none yielded anything significant and virtually all served only to use up valuable time at the early stages of the investigation. Nowadays everyone has a mobile phone – that wasn't the case back then. The fact that no scene could be identified is also an obvious difficulty. I was first in contact with Nancy in New York by email and phone, updating her on the work we were doing in the detective unit in Irishtown, assisted by the Garda Serious Crime Review Team. I met Nancy in person when she came to Dublin in 2014 to make an appeal on *Crimecall*. I would be hopeful that someday Annie will be found.

Considering the time that elapsed before Annie McCarrick was reported missing, the killer had at least forty-eight hours to cover his tracks. While it is a remote possibility that he may have driven Annie back towards Dublin, this is thought to be unlikely, for the simple reason that there would not be as many places to conceal a body. The feeling of most detectives who have investigated the case is that Annie is buried in the Wicklow Mountains. Gardaí are conscious that there are miles and miles of bogland in which her remains may lie. This seems the most likely explanation; but without a witness, or a confession, or a chance discovery, she may never be found.

In May 2018 a young woman was abducted while walking on Kilcroney Road in Enniskerry. Several children in a passing car witnessed the woman being forced into a jeep. The woman's body was found in an isolated spot in south Dublin two days later. She had been asphyxiated. The day before her body was found, the woman's killer was shot dead by a garda during a confrontation at Cherrywood Business Park in south Dublin. On a note in his car the killer had written the words 'Pucks Castle', which led gardaí to where the killer had left his victim's body. Naturally there was speculation that this man might have murdered before, but although it seemed coincidental that the man had abducted a woman in the very village that Annie McCarrick had intended travelling to a quarter of a century before, detectives felt this man could not have been her killer. He would have only been fifteen years old in 1993.

In the 2018 investigation, gardaí were greatly assisted by having CCTV footage available from Dublin buses that had been in Enniskerry village, and also from CCTV cameras in the Enniskerry area. That footage led within hours to a suspect being identified. In March 1993 no such video footage was available to track Annie's last movements before her path was crossed by a killer.

Annie McCarrick touched the lives of many people in her twenty-six years. Apart from her devastated parents, she is survived by many aunts, uncles and cousins on both the McCarrick and the Dungate side. And she left behind many friends in Ireland, people who knew her in college and in work. Annie would talk of settling down and of one day having a family. Dermot Ryan, who went out with Annie for over two years, later met an Italian woman at Maynooth, whom he since married. He was nineteen when he started going out with Annie, who was a year older than him. Dermot remembers Annie as a gentle, sweet young woman who was often more romantic than practical.

I last saw Annie over two years before she disappeared. We broke up towards the end of 1990. I remember I visited her over in Long Island that summer, after she returned there for a while to study there. I stayed with her for about four months, and we had a really nice time. But eventually I had to come home, and Annie was staying there for the moment. She drove me to JFK airport from her home, and she wanted me to make a commitment to our relationship, but I didn't: I wanted to come home and think clearly. I remember she had $5 on her, and she bought me one of those toys, a little snow-shaker, as a memory of New York – you know, you shake it and snow falls over Manhattan. I never saw Annie again. I was living in Italy with my fiancée when I got the news over two years later that Annie was missing. I'm married now and have my own family. When I was going out with Annie and we were both studying at Maynooth, she was renting a cottage in Ballyboden in south Dublin. She was sharing this cottage with another woman, and it was out in the wilds. It took about two hours to get from there to Maynooth, but Annie wouldn't live anywhere else: she just loved that cottage. Annie had a romantic view of Ireland that most Irish people would find corny, but she just loved this country. She had the most beautiful warm voice, and she would never snub anyone. It's just so sad.

Before he retired in 2002, Detective Garda Val Smith looked once more over the file that consumed so much of his time over the previous nine and a half years: file C31/24/93, missing woman: Annie McCarrick. Val says this is the only case that he ever got personal about.

What is frustrating is that we never got a run for our money on it. The last sighting of Annie on the bus in Ranelagh heading towards Enniskerry opens up so many possibilities, so many avenues of enquiry. We never made an arrest in this case. We questioned a number of men at length about their movements around the time of Annie's disappearance, but we just never got that break. This case affected all the gardaí who worked on it. It was exhaustive. If it affects gardaí, God only knows how it affected Annie's parents and family and friends. If Annie's body was found, that would at least be one thing: that would be something. I served here in Irishtown for thirty years, and this is the biggest unsolved case we've had. I would dearly love to be called out of retirement one day to give evidence in this case.

Nancy McCarrick has many happy and funny memories of her only child, and she has many emotional ones. In the present circumstances one paints a particularly poignant picture.

Annie was such a romantic, she was such an emotional person. I remember she was in Manhattan one time and she phoned me. 'Mom,' she said, 'I'm at the opera. I'm at *La Bohème*; there's standing room only. I'm having the most wonderful time, it is so beautiful, and I am crying my eyes out.'

For Nancy there is no closure, no ending. Some years ago the New York State Police called to her and took a DNA sample, which was then forwarded to gardaí. The potential of DNA evidence was largely unknown when Annie vanished, but now advances in forensic science mean that if ever Annie's body is found, she could be identified.

More than a quarter of a century since her only child was cruelly taken, Nancy says she is not certain how she has coped.

> You always hope that she will be found. You do that forever. As you have heard many times, faith, family and friends play a tremendous part in helping you to keep going. And time is a great healer. Two of my brothers live very close by and two other siblings live only twenty minutes away. And we have many cousins who live on Long Island. I am truly blessed to have a large, caring family, and we all miss Annie very much. We will just have to wait and see if we are meant to know what happened to her. The gardaí have worked so very hard on her case, and we will see what God has in mind.

CHAPTER 3

JO JO DULLARD

ate on the night of Thursday, 9 November 1995, 21-year-old Josephine (Jo Jo) Dullard was abducted in Co. Kildare and murdered. She was halfway home when her killer struck. It was a cold winter's night in the village of Moone when, just after half past eleven, Jo Jo accepted her third lift that night. After spending the day in Dublin, she had then missed the bus that would bring her directly home to Callan, Co. Kilkenny. Instead she had got a bus from Dublin to Naas, Co. Kildare, and started hitching. She got lifts from Naas to Kilcullen, and from there to Moone. By the time she got to Moone she still had more than 40 miles to go.

Just after half past eleven Jo Jo entered the public phone box in Moone, just yards from the busy road. She phoned her friend Mary Cullinane, telling her where she was. She was now thinking of trying to hitch a lift 10 miles to Carlow, where she could stay with a friend. During the short, stilted conversation she was looking out of the phone box, trying to flag down passing motorists. Suddenly she dropped the phone and ran out to the side of the road: a car had stopped. Jo Jo ran back to the box, told Mary she'd got a lift, and hung up. This was the last anyone ever heard from Jo Jo.

At some point during the next few hours, Jo Jo Dullard was murdered. There are a number of different suspects whom the gardaí believe may be responsible for the killing. These include a Co. Kildare man who gave the gardaí false information about his movements that night and a man from Co. Wicklow who was later convicted of abducting a woman in Carlow and trying to murder her. Two members of a criminal gang of Travellers, who it's believed travelled the same road that night, are also earmarked as suspects.

Jo Jo's disappearance caused immense pain for her sisters Mary, Nora and Kathleen, her brother, Tom, and her nieces and nephews. The failure to find Jo Jo's remains led Mary to launch a national campaign for the establishment of a specialist garda missing persons unit and also the establishment of a National Missing Persons Remembrance Day. The Dullard family were instrumental in erecting the National Monument to Missing People in the grounds of Kilkenny Castle, which was unveiled by then President Mary McAleese in 2002. Whoever murdered Jo Jo will never be allowed forget their evil deed.

Early on Thursday, 9 November 1995, Jo Jo Dullard collected her last dole payment in Harold's Cross, Dublin, and spent the afternoon looking around the shops and having a few drinks with friends at the Bruxelles pub off Grafton Street. It was the end of an era in her life. Having spent more than two years living and working in Dublin, she had recently moved home to Callan, where she had got a flat in the centre of town and now had full-time work at a pub and restaurant there. The collection of her final dole payment was the last of her tasks in Dublin.

At some stage on the journey from Dublin Jo Jo fell asleep. She woke just as the bus was coming into Naas. She was still almost 60 miles from home. She began to hitch, hoping she might be lucky enough to find someone driving as far as Kilkenny or even Callan; a more realistic prospect might be finding a motorist heading towards Carlow. Jo Jo had a friend there who would put her up if she could only make it that far. It was already dark as she began thumbing, standing on the busy road. It was a cold night, and she was wearing a black cotton jacket, a shirt, blue jeans, and boots. One motorist stopped; he was heading for Kilcullen, five miles down the road. Again it was a step in the right direction, so Jo Jo got in. She had hitched lifts many times before in Co. Kilkenny and was aware of the dangers of taking lifts from strangers.

It was now after eleven o'clock and Jo Jo was standing in Kilcullen, 20 miles from Carlow and 45 miles from Callan. She had only put out her hand to start hitching a lift again when another car stopped. This driver was also heading in the direction of Jo Jo's ultimate destination but not going the whole way. He said he could bring her as far as Moone. Jo Jo got in, knowing that this lift would get her to within 10 miles of Carlow and closer to a bed for the night.

It was 11.35 p.m. when this motorist dropped Jo Jo off at Moone, Co. Kildare. The village was quiet but for the distant sound of people having their last drinks in a nearby pub. Jo Jo decided to phone her friend Mary Cullinane to let her know where she was. The motorist who left Jo Jo in Moone had dropped her close to a public phone box. At 11.37 p.m. she stepped into the phone box and made the call. 'Hi, Mary. I'm in Moone. I missed the bus,' she said. They had a general chat for three minutes, while Jo Jo kept an eye out for any cars heading south. Suddenly she said, 'Hold on.' She dropped the phone, left the phone box, and returned a few seconds later. 'I have a lift. See you, Mary.' She left the phone box and walked towards a nearby car. She would not be seen or heard from again.

Jo Jo Dullard was the youngest of five children. She never knew her father, John Dullard – he died when his wife, Nora, was pregnant with Jo Jo in 1973. Nora died in 1983, when Jo Jo was nine, leaving just Jo Jo and her sister Kathleen still living at home in Newtown, near Callan. The responsibility for raising Jo Jo fell on Kathleen, who was only ten years older. Soon afterwards Kathleen married her fiancé, Séamus Bergin, and they brought Jo Jo to live with them at Ahenure, just outside Callan. It was here that Jo Jo lived with Kathleen and Séamus until her mid-teens. When I met Kathleen the constant pain caused by her sister's disappearance was all too evident. Even with happy memories, tears welled up in her eyes.

I was only nineteen when Mam died, and it was just Jo Jo and me in the cottage in Newtown. I was quite nervous with just the two of us in the cottage, but we always felt safe in Mammy's room. I was going out with Séamus, and we got married in 1985 and had our first child, Aisling, in 1986. We decided to move up here to Ahenure, and Jo Jo came with us. She was about fourteen at the time. Myself and Séamus were just starting out, and we later had three more children. Our children were very close to Jo Jo: she was more like a sister to them than an auntie. She lived with us until she was about sixteen. I would do it all again in a second if I could. None of us can believe that Jo Jo is gone now; there's emptiness in our hearts that we just can't fill.

Kathleen Bergin reported her sister was missing less than twenty-four hours after Jo Jo had vanished. Yet despite the fact that she had disappeared from the side of a road on a dark night, Kathleen remembers an initial lack of urgency from the gardaí that she found distressing.

Jo Jo was meant to be at work at Dawson's pub in Callan on the Friday evening. I remember I got a call from the manager, Tom. He said Mary Cullinane – Jo Jo's friend – was with him, and Jo Jo hadn't arrived for work. Mary then told me about the phone call from Moone. Immediately I knew this was serious. I called a friend of Jo Jo's in Carlow, but she hadn't seen her. I contacted the gardaí in Callan, and the officer told me Jo Jo was twenty-one and might have decided to go back to Dublin. I called the gardaí three times, but I got the same type of response. Eventually I called in to the garda station. I went up to a garda and said, 'If there was a bank robbed you'd be out there with checkpoints.' In the years since, many gardaí have worked very hard on Jo Jo's case, but that initial response was so wrong.

It was the following Monday, more than three days after Jo Jo Dullard's abduction and murder, that the search and appeal for information began in earnest. One senior garda in the Kilkenny division later revealed that he wasn't even aware of Jo Jo's disappearance until the Monday. Vital days were lost during which suspicious activity, such as unusual digging, went undetected. The search, when it did begin, was extensive, but one detective says the delay may have given the killer time to cover his tracks.

There is a feeling among some detectives that the person or persons responsible for killing Jo Jo may have actually been questioned at some stage during the investigation. I mean the investigation was massive, and it stands to reason that we may well have spoken to the killer during our search. Over 800 statements were later taken, and 2,000 questionnaires were completed. A number of men who drove through Moone that night were detected. Some of them gave misleading or evasive answers. We even tracked people down in France and the USA who had driven through Moone that night, but we ruled them out. But the fact that the case lay dormant for the first few days gave the person responsible time to compose themselves, to concoct a story, to practise it, maybe even to start believing their own lies. Also, the killer had a clear seventy-two hours to conceal Jo Jo's body. There are a number of theories about where Jo Jo's body may lie. Given the time the killer had, even a particular theory put forward that she is buried at a certain location in Co. Kerry is a possibility.

Jo Jo's sister Mary Phelan and her husband, Martin Phelan, believed from day one that the answer to what happened to Jo Jo lies close to where she disappeared in Moone. Sadly, Mary died in 2018. She had often told me she knew the identity of a particular person who was in Moone the night Jo Jo disappeared, and who had made contradictory statements to gardaí when first questioned about his movements the night Jo Jo vanished. Mary always believed this man was the prime suspect, and that his private land should be searched for Jo Jo's body. Even in the months before Mary passed away she continued to call for a search to be carried out on a derelict three-acre farm in Co. Wicklow, close to the Kildare border.

Before Jo Jo vanished, Mary and Martin Phelan were farmers, tending to cows and sheep on their ninety-acre farm at Grange in Co. Kilkenny. They were also parents, rearing their two children. Imelda was eight and Melvin was five when their aunt Jo Jo was taken from them. From November 1995 Mary and Martin Phelan spent most of every day planning, pressuring, fundraising, phoning, faxing and pleading with the power-holders in society for help in finding Jo Jo. Mary once told me of the shock she felt when a garda told her they knew more than they were saying.

> This senior garda told me that they thought they knew where Jo Jo might be buried. It's a section of private land. The garda told me that a man had made contradictory statements. We later hired a private detective, who approached this man on the pretext of seeking directions to a golf course. All the detective could tell us was that he got a very uneasy feeling about the man. He also said the man had a deep scratch on his face. It could be something, or it could be nothing, but all we want is for this private land to be searched. Surely if someone makes two different statements there are at least grounds for serious suspicion.

The Phelans have long campaigned for all land within a twenty-mile radius of Moone to be combed thoroughly for clues to Jo Jo's whereabouts. This search would extend over both public and private land in counties Kildare and Wicklow, and would cover the land belonging to the person the Phelans always considered a suspect. Mary and Martin Phelan met successive Ministers for Justice and the Garda Commissioner to argue their point. The lands remain unsearched. One senior officer who reviewed the case strenuously denies that the gardaí were in any way reluctant to follow this line of enquiry.

Yes, this man did make two different statements about what he did and where he was on the night Jo Jo disappeared. We know he was in Moone at around the time Jo Jo was. He had earlier been over in Co. Offaly and was heading home. There were certain discrepancies in his statements. He told us he had been genuinely mistaken in his first statement and was sorry, that it wasn't malicious. You need more than that to get a search warrant. That's the law we work under.

Jo Jo lived at the Phelans' home in Grange from the age of sixteen, having moved from Kathleen and Séamus Bergin's house in Callan. For months after her disappearance Mary couldn't face going into Jo Jo's old bedroom, or looking at her old schoolbooks, or clothes, or posters. Eventually the precious keepsakes were gathered up and put away for safekeeping.

When the gardaí began their investigation into the disappearance of Jo Jo Dullard, a number of people came forward with information that suggests she may have accepted not three but four lifts that November night. Detectives quickly traced the two motorists who had given her lifts from Naas to Kilcullen and from Kilcullen to Moone. But witnesses were now reporting seeing a woman hitching a lift in Castledermot, Co. Kildare, five miles south of Moone, at about 11.55 p.m. This time would correspond with Jo Jo getting a lift in Moone at about 11.40 p.m. Four people reported seeing a woman matching Jo Jo's description in Castledermot that night; two of those witnesses saw the unidentified young woman thumbing a lift on the Carlow side of the town, near the Schoolhouse restaurant.

This new information threw a different light on the investigation, one that remains to this day. If the woman in Castledermot was Jo Jo Dullard, whoever gave her a lift from Moone to Castledermot has never come forward. Why is this? Did the same person circle back to Castledermot and offer her a further lift and then attack her? If the person is entirely innocent, why do they remain silent? Do they know the identity of the person who gave Jo Jo a fourth lift, or did they spot anything that might be of use to the gardaí? Was it Jo Jo at all who was seen in Castledermot, or was the sighting of someone else?

In February 1997, fifteen months after the disappearance of Jo Jo Dullard, gardaí released new information that raised the distinct possibility Jo Jo might have been taken against her will a further 50 miles south, as far as Co. Waterford. The news came after a taxi driver contacted gardaí with a deeply disturbing story that raised the possibility Jo Jo might have been attacked by not one but two men. The witness recounted something he had kept to himself for over a year. At about 1.20 a.m. on the morning of 10 November 1995, he was driving along the main road at Kilmacow, three miles north of Waterford, when he saw a red car with British number plates parked at the side of the road. A man was urinating beside the car. Suddenly he saw a woman running from the left-hand rear door of the car towards the front. She had bare feet, and seemed distressed. A second man suddenly appeared, also from the back of the car. He followed the woman, grabbed her by the hair, and got her in a bear hug; he then dragged her back to the car. It then took off in the direction of Waterford city. The taxi driver had seen all this happen in a matter of seconds as he drove past the car; yet it would be more than a year before he reported it. A garda who worked on Jo Jo's case from the beginning believes this reported sighting may yet yield results.

The report by the taxi driver opens up a number of lines of enquiry. I think the witness delayed coming forward after being advised by someone close to him that it was none of his concern and he should keep out of it. But thankfully he eventually came forward and better late than never. We have our suspicions as to who the two men were. The car was described as a red-coloured Ford Sierra Sapphire or Ford Grenada, with English registration plates. Despite the foreign registration, we believe the two men in the car were Irish. It just makes you think. If it was Jo Jo who was spotted by the taxi driver, she was taken over 50 miles from where she made the phone call in Moone.

Gardaí investigating the Waterford sighting focused their attention on a criminal gang who came from the Travelling community. One man in his twenties would come to feature as a suspect after he was convicted of raping a thirteen-year-old girl in Co. Louth in 1997. This man would in time be exposed as one of the most violent men to have lived in Ireland in recent times, and had committed crimes against both settled people and Travellers. Investigations would lead detectives to believe this man drove the road through Moone on the night Jo Jo disappeared. What particularly interested detectives was the discovery that the man was also living in Dundalk when teenager Ciara Breen vanished in 1997, although no evidence was found to firmly link him to either Jo Jo's case or Ciara's. The man is currently serving a 21-year sentence after being convicted of raping a woman in her eighties.

Over four years after Jo Jo disappeared, a 35-year-old father of two, Larry Murphy, abducted a woman in Carlow, repeatedly raped and then tried to murder her in a prolonged attack that occurred in three counties. Detectives from Operation Trace were conscious that the route Murphy travelled that night, with his victim in the boot of his car, was very close to both Moone and Castledermot. He had crossed over the N9 road close to where Jo Jo Dullard had been hitching a lift in November 1995. Murphy hadn't come to the attention of the gardaí before he repeatedly raped and attempted to murder the woman in February 2000. After he was sentenced to fourteen years' imprisonment, two senior gardaí went to meet him in prison. He politely told them he had no information about any missing women.

A total of nine people, including a number of women, were arrested for questioning by detectives from Operation Trace investigating murders including Jo Jo Dullard's. Some of those arrested were held on suspicion of withholding information. Others were arrested as suspected killers. Two members of a criminal gang from Waterford were among those interviewed. They are believed to have been socialising in Dublin on the Thursday afternoon and evening. One garda says it's believed the criminals drove through Moone later that night.

Many of the answers they gave us are evasive, but that could be because they don't want to reveal a totally separate crime they may have been involved in. But we received certain information that outlined in very clear detail an allegation that these two men had abducted Jo Jo and had killed her. The two men deny any knowledge of Jo Jo. We need a witness, or we need a confession, or we need a body. These men remain suspects.

In the days and weeks immediately after Jo Jo vanished, her family made many appeals for information. Jo Jo's disappearance was reported extensively in both the national and local media. Over time, as Mary and Martin Phelan would continue their campaign, constantly urging gardaí to do more to search for Jo Jo, they found many other families also suffering the loss of a missing loved one. Through their public campaign for more affirmative action, Mary and Martin were also providing a voice and a support network for other families. They recognised that the circumstances of every person's disappearance were different, but what united all families was the need to know what had happened to their loved ones.

Mary Phelan showed me a collage of photos recording Jo Jo as a young girl, as a teenager and as a young woman. At the top of the collage she is pictured as a baby in the arms of her mother, Nora. Another image records Jo Jo on the day of her First Holy Communion. Another photo is of Jo Jo in her school uniform, and the bottom of the collage features images of Jo Jo as an adult. In each of the photographs, she is smiling. The standard garda missing person's report, which was filled in for Jo Jo, recorded her height and weight, hair and eye colour and facial features. Such forms are important in terms of garda investigations, but it is only through studying photographs that a person's various expressions, including their smile, become apparent. In the months after Jo Jo vanished in Co. Kildare her image would become known throughout the country, with treasured family photos becoming a means to highlight the family's ongoing appeal for information.

Kathleen Bergin told me that Jo Jo had been thinking of not going to Dublin at all that fateful Thursday.

> Jo Jo had to get to Harold's Cross at some stage to get her last dole payment. She had just got a new job in Callan and so had to get to Dublin to tie up loose ends whenever she got a chance. She was actually meant to go earlier in the week, but she had to cover in work for a girl who was sick. The day before she went I told her that if she didn't go to Dublin the next day we could meet for a coffee in Callan. But Jo Jo went to Dublin, and I never saw her before she went.

Jo Jo Dullard lived in Dublin for two years. She and her friend Mary Cullinane both arrived in Dublin from Co. Kilkenny with dreams of becoming beauticians. Both young women signed up for a beauty course in Crumlin but found that the cost of books and materials was just too great; so they dropped out and got jobs working in pubs. If they made enough money they could always go back to the course. Jo Jo got a job in The Red Parrot in Dorset Street, where members of the staff remember her as a courteous young woman who was a hard worker. She and Mary Cullinane first lived in Dolphin's Barn for about a year then later moved to Phibsborough and then to Rialto.

It was during her time in Dublin that Jo Jo met her only long-term boyfriend, Mike, an American who was travelling around the world. He loved Dublin so much he decided to stay longer than intended. Kathleen Bergin remembers that Jo Jo was very excited when she first brought Mike down to Co. Kilkenny.

> She phoned me one time and said she was coming down to see us that weekend. Then she said, 'Do you mind if I bring a friend?' They both came down, and we met Mike. He really was a nice chap. We all went out for a pint. I know that Jo Jo was very keen on Mike. When they broke up I know Jo Jo was really upset. When we saw her with Mike we couldn't believe how grown up she was,

we all felt so proud of her. Jo Jo had a hard life, with Mam dying when she was so young and Dad dying just before she was born. Going up to live in Dublin is never an easy thing for a young girl to do, but Jo Jo was so brave, so grown up.

By the time Jo Jo disappeared, Mike had left Ireland to continue his travels on the Continent. The gardaí would later track him down in Spain, after a farmer made a discovery that detectives hoped might be a development in the case. In the summer of 1996 a farmer found a watch in a dyke on the Carlow side of Castledermot, seven miles from the phone box in Moone. The farmer thought nothing of his find until he saw a fresh appeal, later that year, for information on Jo Jo Dullard's disappearance. He contacted the gardaí, who immediately set about trying to establish whether the watch was Jo Jo's. Detectives learnt that her former boyfriend, Mike, had given her a watch. When they tracked him down in Spain and asked him to identify the watch, he couldn't. He later wrote to Kathleen and Séamus Bergin to say how sorry he was to hear of Jo Jo's disappearance.

In June 1997 a body was recovered from the river Shannon at Bush Island, near Ennis. The body had been in the water for some time, and it was not immediately clear if it was male or female. While forensic tests were carried out, there was huge media speculation that the body might be Jo Jo's. However, within days it was confirmed that the body was that of a missing Limerick man, who had disappeared early in 1997.

In the weeks immediately after Jo Jo Dullard's disappearance the gardaí had to sift through thousands of questionnaires and investigate hundreds of reported sightings. One senior garda says the search for the missing woman was extensive.

A garda sub-aqua team searched 36 miles of the river Barrow, just a few miles west of Castledermot and Moone. All the roads from Moone to Carlow were searched inch by inch for clues. Woodland and forests were searched. For twelve months, forest, woods and bogs were searched every weekend. Over 2,000 witness statements were taken, and detectives made enquiries as far as America and Australia.

Shortly after Jo Jo's disappearance, gardaí thought they had a concrete lead. Gardaí in Kilkenny remembered that the night following her disappearance, but before the alarm was raised, two Englishmen had been arrested for breaking open a phone box in the town, apparently looking for money. The two men were released and left the country. But detectives would later be alerted to the incident at Kilmacow, outside Waterford, where two men in a car with British number plates were seen in the company of a woman who was barefoot and in obvious distress. Gardaí tracked one of the men to Portsmouth; the other was found in Australia. At first neither man could account for his movements. One detective told me investigators thought they had two serious suspects.

These two men used to travel over by ferry from Fishguard to Rosslare and then travel around the country breaking into coin boxes in small villages. Although it was fairly minor-scale crime, they could make up to seven or eight thousand pounds over a week, and then head home on the ferry. We finally caught up with these fellows, and they couldn't tell us where they had been on the night of Jo Jo's disappearance. We took their car and we pulled it apart, checking it for any evidence of Jo Jo having been in it, or any crime having been committed. For three months we thought we might have our men, but then we found that they were effectively in the clear. We established that on the night Jo Jo disappeared they had checked into a bed and breakfast in Cork under the alias of Cunningham. An extensive check of phone records showed that they had actually called home to England at 12.20 a.m. on 10 November 1995. So these two could not have been in Moone or Castledermot only half an hour before, and were not the two men seen bundling an unidentified woman into a car outside Waterford city later that night. This pair weren't able to clear themselves; it was actually gardaí who eventually established their alibi for them.

In 1995 the main road linking Dublin and Waterford travelled through Moone. The closely knit community in Moone has suffered in the knowledge that some person who drove through their village that night was a murderer, a person out looking for a woman to kill. It is a distressing thought for local people, who know that the killer could very well have picked on any woman out on the road by the phone box that night.

Jo Jo disappeared before mobile phones were commonly used. On the night she vanished, her only way of making contact was to use the public phone box in Moone. That call box is now long gone. A lasting memory to Jo Jo, in the form of a memorial stone, now lies where the phone box once stood. It was at this spot that Mary told her friend she'd 'just got a lift'. However, putting the stone in place was not an easy task. There were objections from some local people, who thought the village was being unfairly defined by Jo Jo's disappearance. Jo Jo's family and friends decided to take matters into their own hands. One of those involved was John McGuinness TD, who has long campaigned for more action to be taken to find missing people. He described to me the covert operation that saw the memorial stone erected in Moone.

Mary and Martin Phelan came to me one day in 1998 and told me they wanted to put up some kind of memorial to Jo Jo in Moone. I had known them for about two years before, since they first came and basically demanded that I do something to help find Jo Jo. One thing that we could at least do was put up a memorial in Moone. The vast majority of people in Moone were supportive of the idea, but one or two people were not so keen. There was a real fear that there might be an objection if planning permission was sought. A memorial stone had been carved in Co. Kerry and was brought up to my office in Kilkenny, and we decided we would erect it ourselves. At around five o'clock one morning, myself, my brother Declan, Martin Phelan and his brother Gerard loaded the stone up into a jeep and we headed off for Moone with the cement mixed in the back. Before it was bright we had cemented the stone against the wall beside the phone box. To this day, that memorial stone has not been touched. It is a fitting tribute to Jo Jo, which has been accepted by the people of Moone. The memorial stone reads: 'Jo Jo Dullard, missing since 9 November 1995. What happened to her? Where is Jo Jo now?' Local people, and motorists passing through the village, often stop, lay flowers, and reflect on the enormity of the unexplained death of Jo Jo Dullard.

On 22 November 1998 Moone became the scene of the first mass for missing people. The families of many missing people attended the service at the Church of the Blessed Trinity. It was an emotional evening, with many families who thought they suffered alone meeting other families who suffer the same loss. The mass was organised by the Jo Jo Dullard Memorial Trust, which was set up by Mary Phelan. In May 2002, in another landmark in Mary Phelan's campaign for missing people, President Mary McAleese unveiled the National Monument to Missing People in the grounds of Kilkenny Castle.

Martin Phelan watched his wife campaign on behalf of her sister from the day Jo Jo was reported missing. He supported her every step of the way. Sometimes he took matters into his own hands. It was through his impassioned initiative that John McGuinness became a close associate of the Jo Jo Dullard Memorial Trust. It happened one day, about a year after Jo Jo's disappearance, when John McGuinness was Mayor of Kilkenny and Martin Phelan thought to himself, 'Enough is enough.' He marched into the mayor's office and got McGuinness's undivided attention by standing up on a glass table. For fifteen precarious minutes he spoke frantically at McGuinness from the top of the table and told him why the people of Kilkenny and the representatives of Kilkenny should be outraged that one of their own could go missing, be murdered and not be found. John McGuinness committed himself to fighting for the Phelans.

One lead from a member of the public led to a search of woodland near Clonmel, Co. Tipperary, in April 1999. A couple out collecting holly in November 1995 said they had seen two men and a woman in the forest. The woman appeared to be unwell or under duress. The couple had not reported the sighting at the time and forgotten about it, but subsequent publicity about missing women brought it back to them. When detectives received the information they believed they might be on to something. The woodland was about 15 miles from the reported sighting of two men and a distressed woman at Kilmacow on the night of Jo Jo Dullard's abduction. The witnesses were able to point out a specific area where they saw the two men and the distressed woman, but an extensive search revealed nothing.

The gardaí conducted an extensive trawl through Jo Jo Dullard's life in an effort to establish whether the person who gave her a lift had, by fluke, actually known her. One line of enquiry that was eventually ruled out as a coincidence was that Jo Jo was known to socialise in a particular pub where a now convicted murderer also drank. In December 1995, just over a month after Jo Jo's disappearance, David Lawler raped and murdered Marilyn Rynn as she walked along an isolated pathway in Blanchardstown, Co. Dublin. Lawler worked for Telecom Éireann as a van driver and would have had the opportunity to travel around the country alone. Detectives established that Lawlor and Jo Jo Dullard had frequented the same pub. One detective told me further investigations revealed it was just a coincidence.

We established David Lawler had never met with or spoken to Jo Jo in the pub. They had been there at different times. I suppose if Jo Jo disappeared in Dublin, close to or near her home, we would have been even more suspicious initially. But a receipt from an ATM machine put David Lawler in Dublin that night, and he didn't have access to a vehicle at that time. Certainly he was looked at purely because of his murderous activity only a month after Jo Jo's disappearance, and the fact they had been in the same pub fuelled our initial speculation. But Jo Jo was standing on a lonely road in Moone, many miles from Dublin. Whoever the killer is, it was a chance encounter.

On Christmas Day 1995 Mary and Martin Phelan rose early. Despite the trauma of Jo Jo's disappearance six weeks before, Santa had to arrive for Imelda and Melvin, then eight and five years old. The Phelans sat at the kitchen table and ate tea and toast. The four of them put on their coats and went to meet Martin's brother Gerard. They travelled towards Moone, where they spent all day searching for Jo Jo in hedges, drains and roadsides until evening. They found nothing. Mary never forgot that Christmas Day.

> We set off early for Moone; we couldn't just sit at home while Jo Jo was still out there. We started from the phone box once again and searched wherever we could. I remember thinking as we searched the roadside that the man who is responsible for murdering my sister would be sitting down having his Christmas turkey, sitting with his family, maybe sitting by a cosy fire. And here we were continuing to search for Jo Jo. It's just not right.

Shortly after Jo Jo Dullard went missing, Mary and Kathleen searched her flat at Green Street, Callan. They found a list that Jo Jo had made of Christmas presents she intended to buy for loved ones. There was her only brother, Tom, and his family in Kildare, and closer to home in Co. Kilkenny her sister Nora, her sister Kathleen and her family, and Mary and her family. Then there were her many friends in Callan. Kathleen Bergin told me of many fond memories she has of her little sister.

> Jo Jo was sometimes a little tomboy when she was growing up. She'd play in the fields and swim in the river; she'd climb trees, and play soccer. Then she became a teenager, and she was into music. She loved George Michael, Michael Jackson and A-ha and had posters of them all in her bedroom. Jo Jo loved animals, and she

had a cocker spaniel; she called him Freeway, after the dog in the TV show *Hart to Hart*. She got the dog just six months after Mam died, and she really loved him. When she grew up Jo Jo was still deciding what to do with her life. She was only twenty-one when she disappeared. She was working in a restaurant and a pub. She said some day she might go back to the beautician's course, but she was also talking about being an air stewardess. She had so much ahead of her.

Kathleen's husband, Séamus Bergin, believes more needs to be done to find missing women in Leinster.

There are five or six who have gone missing in very suspicious circumstances. Surely to God something should be found by now. It's hard to believe that nothing has been found. It would make you wonder if there is some kind of planning or organisation involved. It is so scary. There are some gardaí who have worked very hard on these cases, but their hands seem to be tied. I think that if gardaí believe certain people have information but are not giving that information to detectives, then gardaí should have the power to prosecute them. Something more needs to be done. There are people who know, or at least strongly suspect, what happened to Jo Jo. Life isn't the same without Jo Jo; she should be here with us now. It feels like a nightmare that never ends.

A detective who worked on Jo Jo Dullard's disappearance agrees that the circumstances of her abduction and murder fit the profile of a serial killer.

Jo Jo disappeared two and a half years after the disappearance of Annie McCarrick over the far side of Co. Wicklow. And then there was the disappearance of Eva Brennan, who may have been abducted as she was walking along a quiet road in south Dublin in July 1993. We definitely think that Annie McCarrick might have accepted a lift from a seemingly charming man. We know for a fact that Jo Jo was seeking a lift in Moone the night she disappeared. Whoever stopped for her in Moone was able to trick her or lull her into a false sense of security. Whatever happened, it wasn't a crime of passion. Jo Jo didn't know her killer, or killers. Whoever's responsible may very well have struck before, or have struck again afterwards. If they are not dead or in prison for something else, they may strike again.

Detectives have spent many hours teasing out different theories as to why Jo Jo may not have been immediately suspicious of the occupant or occupants of the car that she stepped into in Moone. One report made to the gardaí early in the investigation was by a woman who said she saw a woman matching Jo Jo Dullard's description about to get into a car in Moone. She had not come forward earlier because she had been on holiday and was unaware of the significance of what she had seen. She said she saw this woman walking towards a dark-coloured car, possibly a Toyota Carina, which had stopped about 50 yards from the phone box. One of the rear doors was open. The gardaí studied this reported sighting carefully. The make of car was vigorously pursued by detectives. It did not lead anywhere but continues to be a line of enquiry.

This sighting raised the possibility that Jo Jo might have got into the back seat of a car. This would suggest in turn that the front passenger seat was occupied. Was it possible that the front-seat passenger was a woman? This might have lulled Jo Jo into thinking she was safe in the car. Or was it occupied by a man who, like the driver, appeared to be normal? Or was Jo Jo immediately suspicious of the occupant, or occupants, but pulled into the car before she could get away? Might this be the car that was later spotted 50 miles south near Waterford, where a barefoot woman was seen trying to escape from two men? All these theories are credible, some more so than others. But it's all just speculation.

Within months of Jo Jo's disappearance her sister Mary, having failed to get satisfactory answers from certain gardaí in relation to her sister's case, was calling for the reintroduction of the murder squad. This specialist team of detectives had operated in the 1970s and '80s, travelling around the country, offering assistance to local gardaí dealing with particularly complex murder investigations. As more women continued to disappear after Jo Jo, Mary began calling for the establishment of a specialist missing persons unit. Such a unit would be able to get to the scene of a disappearance quickly, without any needless delay in deciding which garda division had jurisdiction over the investigation. Valuable scientific evidence might also be salvaged, and psychological profiling of suspects might also prove fruitful. However, despite all the disappearances, no such unit would be established.

For many years, the Jo Jo Dullard Memorial Trust was central to keeping the issue of missing people on the political and media agenda. The beliefs of members of the Trust often clashed with the opinions of certain gardaí. An internal garda document from the late 1990s described the group as 'tending towards a radical interpretation of the situation ... listing 84 people as missing since 1990 ... this would include fishermen lost at sea, and "presumed drowned" cases ... the general perception of their literature is distorted ... However in their particular circumstances they should be given as much leeway as possible.'

This clash of opinions relates to the fact that many missing people have chosen to go missing. The Jo Jo Dullard Memorial Trust did not differentiate between the families of missing people who have been murdered and the families of those missing people who have not been the victims of violence. Mary Phelan would often make the point that every missing person leaves behind a heartbroken family, every case is tragic.

When Jo Jo Dullard disappeared she was wearing a black zip-up cotton jacket, light-blue jeans and black boots with two-inch square heels. She had two weeks' dole money in her possession. No items of the clothing she was wearing have ever been found. There was no sign of a struggle along the roadside in Moone. Jo Jo Dullard's lonely death is in total contrast to the warmth, comfort and love of her family.

Mary Phelan holds a special memory of the night Jo Jo went to her debs' dance.

> I will never forget that night. Jo Jo had bought a lovely dress, and she was getting ready here. She had her hair all up in curls. I gave her a ring and a bracelet that had been given to me. I remember walking away from her for a moment and I looked back, and do you know, I'll never forget how she looked. It was amazing: she looked just like Mum. I was looking at Mum. When Jo Jo was ready to head out she came and gave me a big hug, and she said to me, 'I'll never forget you for this.'

On 26 May 2002 a National Monument for Missing People was unveiled in the grounds of Kilkenny Castle. The steel monument, featuring the handprints of members of the families of missing people, is in a quiet part of the castle grounds, surrounded on three sides by flowers and bushes. A significant number of families of missing people attended the event, including those of Jo Jo Dullard, Fiona Pender, Ciara Breen and Fiona Sinnott. President Mary McAleese unveiled the monument and was escorted around to meet all the families by Mary Phelan. As Jo Jo's sister made a speech thanking everyone who had made the day special, she broke down. Mary Phelan had been at the forefront of the tireless campaign for the monument. Her efforts had brought families of missing people together. But she, and all Jo Jo's loved ones, yearned for one thing: to have Jo Jo's remains returned to them.

Mary Phelan died in April 2018. She spent the last twenty-two years of her life campaigning for justice for her missing sister. She often said the person responsible for murdering Jo Jo needed to be brought to justice to protect others.

The person who killed Jo Jo will definitely strike again. Give him time and he will. This person has got to be caught and brought in. This person has to be caught to save the life of whoever the next victim is. And we have to find Jo Jo to put her with Mum and Dad. They're buried together in Kilkenny city, and that's where Jo Jo should be resting. We have to give her a Christian burial.

CHAPTER 4

FIONA PENDER

Fiona Pender, a 25-year-old model and hairdresser, was seven months pregnant when she was murdered in August 1996. The Pender family, from Connolly Park, Tullamore, suffered huge pain. Before Fiona's murder they had already lost a loved one. Fiona's younger brother Mark was killed in June 1995 when his motorbike hit a lorry near Killeigh, just south of Tullamore. And the loss of Fiona was not the last tragedy to hit the family: having murdered Fiona, her killer set in train a series of events that, four years later, would lead to Fiona's father Seán taking his own life.

The loss of Mark, Fiona and Seán devastated the two remaining members of the close-knit family – Fiona's mother Josephine and younger brother John. Josephine campaigned for more than twenty years on behalf of her missing and murdered daughter. She long believed she knew the identity of the person who had murdered Fiona. A prime suspect in the case now lives in Canada. A major search of woodland in north Co. Laois in late 2014 came as a result of very credible information relating to the suspect, but after two weeks' work the excavation ended without any trace of Fiona being found. This was just the latest blow to Josephine and John in their search for Fiona. Sadly, in 2017 Josephine passed away following an illness. The torch has now been passed to John Pender to continue the fight for justice.

John Pender says Fiona was previously attacked by the prime suspect when, in early 1996, he strangled her to the point of unconsciousness. Blood vessels in her eyes were burst during the attack, which occurred when she was in the early stages of pregnancy. Fiona later confided in her young brother what had happened, but swore him to secrecy. John was only thirteen and honoured his sister's request. It was following Fiona's disappearance that John told his parents, and then the gardaí, what Fiona had previously told him. He said Fiona had described how her attacker had 'cried like a child' after the assault and promised it would never happen again.

The Pender family never believed Fiona was the victim of a serial killer, a view shared by gardaí who worked on the case. Detectives believed there was a local answer to Fiona's disappearance. In April 1997 three women and two men were arrested and questioned. All five were released without charge twelve hours later.

The last person known to have seen Fiona Pender was her boyfriend, John Thompson. He described how he said goodbye to her at about six o'clock on the morning of Friday, 23 August 1996. He said Fiona, who was suffering from a bout of heartburn, was still in bed as he left their ground-floor flat in Church Street, Tullamore. He had a busy day's work ahead at his family's farm in Grange, Co. Laois, about eight miles away.

The next evening John Thompson received a phone call at the farm from Fiona's mother. 'Where's Fiona?' Josephine asked. 'I've been around to the flat. She's not there.' 'I thought she was with you,' he replied. 'I'll be in to you shortly.' Later that night John Thompson and Fiona's mother and father and her thirteen-year-old brother walked into Tullamore Garda Station. Fiona had not been seen for more than thirty-six hours. It is most probable that she was already dead.

The last time Josephine Pender saw her only daughter was at 7 p.m. on the evening of Thursday, 22 August 1996. The two had spent much of the day together, making two trips to the Bridge Shopping Centre in Tullamore. Fiona was in good form. Her baby was due in just over two months' time. John was working long hours at his father's farm.

Fiona was searching for a new home for themselves and the baby. The flat in Church Street was too small, a bedsit with a kitchen in one part of the room. Fiona had decided that once the baby was born she was going to take the infant home to her mother's house, where they could both rest for a few weeks, hoping that within a short time she and John and the baby would have a nice place of their own.

The last day that Josephine and Fiona would spend together they met at Dunnes Stores at the Bridge Centre, a few minutes' walk from Church Street. They did a bit of shopping and then decided to head back to the Pender family home at Connolly Park, about ten minutes' walk away. It was raining, so they got a taxi. Fiona's father was in the house, getting himself ready for a fishing trip. Tired after the walk around the shops, Fiona sat down and cradled her tummy. She picked up a copy of *Hello* magazine and began flicking through it. She found a photograph of the singer Eric Clapton on a fishing trip catching a salmon; she showed it to her father, getting his own fishing gear together, and they laughed. The expectant mother was just hours away from being abducted and murdered.

Fiona Pender was the eldest of the three children of Seán and Josephine Pender. The second was Mark, two years younger than his sister; John is the youngest. He was thirteen when his only sister vanished and sixteen when his father took his own life. But the first tragedy to hit the Pender family occurred when John was only twelve, when his older brother was killed in a motorcycle accident.

Mark Pender loved motorcycles. The one he was riding that day in June 1995 was a limited-edition Fireblade. It was a sunny day, and he and a friend had just stopped for ice cream and petrol in Killeigh, south of Tullamore. After finishing their ice cream they got back on the bike and headed for Tullamore. A few moments later the bike hit a grass verge and swerved into the path of an oncoming lorry. The passenger escaped with minor injuries, but Mark Pender died. He was twenty-one years old and the proud father of three-year-old Dean. Mark and Dean's mother, Gillian, were due to be married the following May. A week after Mark's death an insurance agent, unaware of Mark's death, called to say that the couple had been given approval for a mortgage.

Fiona Pender took the death of her younger brother very badly. With only two years between them, Fiona and Mark were close. Fiona shared his interest in motorbikes; she even bought her own, but she got rid of it after Mark's death. It was through her interest in motorbikes that she had met John Thompson, a farmer from Grange in north Co. Laois. It was Mark who introduced her to John, who he knew from working with motorbikes, fixing them up. Fiona and John hit it off immediately. Their relationship began in October 1993, when they went on a date to Birr, and the relationship continued up to the time Fiona vanished almost three years later. After Mark's death there were nights when Fiona could be found at his grave in Durrow, just outside Tullamore. It was at the church in Durrow that Mark and Gillian were to be married. As Fiona spoke to her brother at his graveside she promised she would be a great aunt and would always look out for Dean, now that Mark was gone.

The sitting room in the Pender home in Tullamore has always been cosy and welcoming. Down the years I met Josephine Pender a number of times at her home to discuss her daughter's case. The room was dominated by photographs and paintings. Most of the photographs were of Fiona, who modelled for magazines. The four paintings were by Seán Pender, a talented artist. There were two landscapes and a painting of boats tied up by a snowy pier; the fourth was an adaptation of the Mona Lisa. They were mostly painted in 1998 – two years after Fiona's disappearance, and two years before Seán would end his own life.

It was in this room that Fiona Pender sat with her mother and father on the afternoon of Thursday, 22 August 1996. While they were still suffering the loss of Mark, there was a lot to look forward to. Mark's son, Dean, was three years old. He and Gillian were living close by, and the Penders could visit Dean whenever they wanted. With Fiona's baby due shortly, Dean would have a new cousin, and Seán and Josephine would have a second grandchild.

Fiona's baby was due on 22 October 1996. There was great excitement. If it was a girl, Fiona said she was going to call her Emma, or perhaps Laura. If she had a boy she said she'd know immediately whether or not to call him Mark. While it was a time of happy expectation, there were also pressures. It would be a strain to find a new house or flat for herself and John and the baby, and that really needed to be done soon. However, the baby appeared to be perfectly healthy, and that was the main thing. Fiona had been through a scare in the first three months: she was told she was in danger of having a miscarriage.

Once, as Josephine and myself sat in the room that had held such excitement in August 1996, she recounted, with clarity, what was to be the last day she would spend with her only daughter.

Well, we sat here after coming back from the Bridge Centre earlier that day. It had been raining, but it eased off a bit. We had a chat and a laugh here, and we had a bit of lunch. Seán was getting ready to go off fishing. I said to Fiona that I needed to get a new pair of trousers for John; school was starting back in a couple of weeks. Fiona said she could get a few more things for the baby as well, so we decided to head back up to the Bridge Centre. I remember clearly I bought the baby a little grey tracksuit, and we got Fiona a pair of shoes that she'd be able to wear after the baby was born. And Fiona got some things for the baby: she got nappy wipes and gripe water and Sudocrem. Those things were still in the bag, unpacked, when gardaí later searched her flat. My son John joined us, and the three of us walked Fiona back to her flat at Church Street. We walked into the flat with her. It was around seven o'clock. I gave her a kiss. I remember clearly, as myself and John walked across the road I waved back at her. And that's the last memory I have of Fiona; her little face at the door.

The flat in Church Street where Fiona Pender was last seen is in the centre of Tullamore. In 2013 I visited the flat with Josephine and John.

It was a very emotional occasion for both of them. As we sat in the small room John told me hadn't been to the flat since 1996.

> There's something familiar about it, it's seventeen years since I visited this place, the last time I was in this room Fiona was here, she was on the bed, she waved me off. There's something familiar about this room, but Fiona is not here.

There was a twelve-year age gap between Fiona and her youngest brother. John remembers how his sister doted on him.

> Fi was bright and bubbly. Because of the age difference I got special treatment from her, she was very good to me. She brought me to the cinema, she spiked my hair for me.

A three-minute walk from the garda station, with the Bridge Centre even closer, the tiny flat is situated on the ground floor of a large converted building that houses twelve self-contained bedsitters. Standing at the front door you can see that there are only two routes that Fiona and her killer could have taken. Coming out of the flat, turning left brings you towards the town centre, while turning right brings you to a roundabout that leads on to the roads towards Port Laoise and Portarlington. Church Street is a busy street, with pubs, restaurants and flats. Despite this, nobody has ever come forward to say they saw Fiona leave her flat. There was no firm evidence of any violent attack in the flat; no evidence that an intruder broke in; no evidence of any type of disturbance. There was no evidence that she was placed in anything before being brought from the flat. It is still possible that Fiona was murdered in the flat, but it's also possible that she left the flat after someone coaxed her outside. Either willingly or unwillingly, she could have got into a vehicle with someone she knew. It most probably headed to the right, towards one of the roads leading to Co. Laois; this would be the quieter route. But this is just speculation, based on probabilities, not certainties.

John Thompson arrived at his family's farm in Killeigh early on the morning of Friday, 23 August. He had a lot of work to do; it was a busy time, with a baby on the way. John and Fiona had lived in London for four months in late 1995 and early 1996. They had tried to find a place so they could stay a bit longer in London, but it didn't work out. John was now working long hours at the farm owned by his father, Archie Thompson, who had played a large part in raising his family due to his wife's ill health. John was his only son, and during August 1996 they were at silage. He would need to take time off once the baby was born but right now he had to work. He told detectives he'd had no time to contact Fiona or to check on her that Friday. He thought she was with her mother.

In Tullamore, Josephine Pender went out to the shops on the Friday afternoon. She bought cabbage plants for Seán to sow in the garden. She walked down Church Street and knocked on Fiona's door, but there was no answer. The blinds were still closed. Josephine headed home. It was not unusual, at the weekend, for a day or so to go by with Fiona and her mother not meeting or talking on the phone. Josephine remembered that a few of Fiona's friends were home from America that weekend; perhaps Fiona was with them.

The next day, Saturday, Josephine and John went to evening mass. They walked down to Fiona's flat to say hello. Again it was in darkness. The blinds were closed, and there was no answer. This was now very unusual; something wasn't right. They walked the ten minutes home to Connolly Park, and Josephine rang John Thompson in Grange. 'Where's Fiona?' she asked. 'She's not at the flat.' 'I thought she was with you,' he replied. 'I'll be in to you shortly.' Josephine remembers that later that night they searched all around Tullamore for Fiona.

John Thompson came in, and I went with him to the flat at Church Street. I didn't see any kind of disturbance. The stuff Fiona bought for the baby on the previous Thursday was still there. But Fiona was nowhere to be seen. We went to the graveyard in Durrow: Fiona used to go and visit Mark's grave there late at night, but she hadn't been doing that for a good few months. She wasn't there. We then checked the hospital and her friends' houses, but she wasn't anywhere to be found. I said I wanted to go to the barracks, so myself and John Thompson and Seán and my son John went to the garda station. I told the garda there that Fiona was missing. I remember the garda didn't take us too seriously. He said something like she was twenty-five and an adult. But I knew something was wrong. She was seven months pregnant.

Though the gardaí were informed on the Saturday night that Fiona was missing, it was the following Monday before a public appeal was made. One detective involved in the subsequent investigation believes vital hours were lost, but this was perhaps unavoidable.

Hindsight is a great thing. But back then there was no similar disappearance. Jo Jo Dullard was abducted the previous November in Kildare, but the circumstances were different. It was obvious almost from the start that Jo Jo was the victim of a crime. But in Fiona's case there was no crime suspected at the start, and I mean the first few hours. There was no crime scene, no disturbance at her flat, no cry for help, no sound of a screeching vehicle. We had a missing pregnant woman who had been very upset when she lost her brother the year before. There was nothing immediately suspicious. And that's what I believe her killer wanted. He gained those first few valuable hours. Here we had a heavily pregnant woman, who was effectively on her own in her flat for a large part of each day. The last reported sighting was on a Friday morning, and the first report to gardaí was on the Saturday night. And it's the next day before a full missing person search is organised. Valuable hours were lost.

One image of Fiona that Josephine was particularly fond of was a black-and-white photograph of Fiona modelling a wedding outfit. It was taken for a women's magazine, but this photograph tells another story. Fiona Pender had a dream of making a happy life as a mother and wife. She wanted to get married, and she wanted herself and John Thompson to find a nice house and have a family. As she looked forward to the birth of their first child, Fiona's thoughts would often turn to getting engaged and getting married.

There are many photographs of Fiona that are posed shots. Fiona had been modelling since her late teens; she modelled dresses, hats, jackets, and casual wear. She did wedding fairs and other modelling events and had built up a large portfolio. It had started when a friend of hers, Emer Condron, set up her own agency in Tullamore. Emer did modelling work herself, and soon got Fiona involved. As well as her modelling work Fiona was also a talented hairdresser. She left Sacred Heart Secondary School in Tullamore after doing her Inter Cert and became an apprentice with Kassard's hairdressers in Tullamore.

By Monday, 26 August it was clear to the gardaí in Tullamore that Fiona Pender was not in any of the places that she might reasonably be expected to be. A heavily pregnant woman was missing. It was now more than seventy-two hours since the last reported sighting of Fiona by her boyfriend. At the time of Fiona's disappearance, Gerry Murray, who by then had thirty-six years' experience, was the local garda superintendent.

On the Monday I sent two gardaí up to Josephine Pender in Connolly Park and got her agreement for a nationwide public appeal for information on Fiona's whereabouts. The case was on the news that lunchtime. We immediately took possession of the flat Fiona shared with John Thompson. We combed that flat, looking for any indication of where Fiona might have gone. We began an extensive search of land in the greater Tullamore area. We searched all the local lakes. We went up to the Bord na Móna site and we searched silt ponds up there. And the Tullamore river, which runs at the back of the flat, where Fiona was last seen – we searched that inch by inch. We searched it from the back of the flat right down to where it flows to Rahan. When we found nothing I got the sub-aqua divers in a second time. We went over it, but again there was nothing. We searched the canal, and a local reservoir, all unsuccessfully. We checked out all Fiona's friends. One of her friends had left for Spain, and we tracked her down, but Fiona hadn't been in contact. We had no crime scene, no body. No expense was spared in this search. We spent more man hours searching for Fiona than we did on a couple of murder cases that we solved.

As gardaí in Tullamore began an extensive search of all surrounding public land for any trace of Fiona, her family travelled about 12 miles south on a hunch. After Mark Pender's death in June the previous year, the Penders had buried his biker gear and the bike at a spot in the Slieve Bloom Mountains close to Clonaslee, Co. Laois. Perhaps Fiona had travelled there. It was just a hunch, but at a time of desperation every possibility had to be investigated. However, there was no trace of Fiona.

The Slieve Bloom Mountains are made up of vast areas of dense forest as well as sections of mountain where steep inclines give way to deep gorges. The mountains extend for almost 20 miles from their eastern tip near Rosenallis, Co. Laois, past the Ridge of Capard and Wolftrap Mountain, down to the south-west tip of Co. Offaly. While the gardaí have also never ruled out the possibility that after killing Fiona Pender the murderer may have taken her to private farmland in an effort to hide her body, one detective who worked in the Laois– Offaly Division for more than thirty years believes the Slieve Bloom Mountains may hold the answer.

If the killer brought Fiona to private land, be it farmland or whatever, there would always be the chance that someone else would have spotted him digging the ground, or using machinery at an odd time, or whatever. There are two other possibilities that we always considered. Offaly is so flat, and there is so much bogland, the answer may lie there; or look south to the Slieve Blooms. I've always felt the Slieve Blooms could be the answer.

Retired Inspector John Dunleavy told me the search for Fiona extended across acres of land in a number of counties.

> The summer of 1996 had been very dry, which meant a vehicle might have travelled in farther over what might be normally wet, marshy terrain. So we searched deep into remote areas of woodland and bogland. We used metal detectors and spent weeks walking in the Slieve Blooms. We just put people in the mountains for days on end and gave them areas to search thoroughly. We found bodies of animals. We searched large private estates in Offaly, and we did thorough searches of scrubland south of Tullamore. We also carried out searches in three other counties, but there was no sign of Fiona.

During all of the searches for Fiona's body over more than two decades, gardaí have always used metal detectors. Such devices are important in any type of search, but particularly important in searching for Fiona Pender's body. Some time prior to her murder Fiona had been in a traffic accident and a metal pin had been inserted in her arm. Detecting that metal pin might be how Fiona's body will one day be found.

In the initial stages of the investigation, many detectives thought of another murder in the midlands, three years before, in which a woman was abducted and murdered. While it was soon believed there was no link between Fiona's case and the murder of 34-year-old Marie Kilmartin from Port Laoise, gardaí were aware that Marie's body lay hidden for six months before it was discovered in June 1994 in a bog drain at Pim's Lane, Borness, near Mountmellick. Detectives searching for Fiona were aware that one killer had previously used bogland around the Laois–Offaly border to conceal a body.

Marie Kilmartin's murderer had placed a concrete block on her upper body and head to weigh her down beneath bog water. However, the water had subsided somewhat during a warm summer and her body was spotted by chance. One detective says gardaí initially hoped they could find Fiona as quickly.

We checked out as much an area of land as we could. We would love to bring some closure for Fiona's family. We would dearly love to find Fiona. We've established to our satisfaction that Fiona's and Marie's cases are not related. So there are two evil people who killed women in the midlands in the mid-nineties and got away with it. If we could at least find Fiona for her family, that would be something.

Josephine Pender once told me how she knew Fiona had been murdered.

One date that stuck with us during that time was 22 October 1996. That was the date that Fiona's baby was due. We had spoken about that date many times. She was so much looking forward to the birth. After she disappeared, the gardaí contacted maternity hospitals all around the country, and they checked in England as well. That day – the twenty-second – was very difficult. It still is. It's a special day. But in the weeks and months after that, it began to hit us that Fiona wasn't coming home.

One thing the Penders always wondered about was whether Fiona's labour might have been brought on during the murderous attack she suffered. She was seven months pregnant when she vanished. Fiona's killer took two lives when he ended Fiona's life. A sobering thought in terms of the length of time this case remains unsolved is that if they were alive today, Fiona's baby boy or girl would be an adult.

The search for Fiona Pender was the largest garda investigation ever undertaken in the Tullamore area. Detectives even considered the possibility that Fiona might have been buried under the grave of her brother Mark at Durrow graveyard; but a preliminary search of the area ruled out that possibility.

Hundreds of people were interviewed and hundreds of questionnaires were completed – at the railway station, at bike rallies, at discos, in shops and pubs. As people wanted to do everything they could to help, gardaí were not short of reported sightings. Each of these was investigated, and ruled out. One woman was adamant that she had seen Fiona in Dunnes Stores that Friday afternoon, but when the supermarket receipt rolls were checked it was established that the witness had seen her not on the Friday but on the Thursday afternoon.

This was a case in which the gardaí were inundated but where that crucial piece of information was missing. Nobody could establish Fiona Pender coming out of her flat, either alone or with someone. Retired detective Mick Dalton, who worked in Tullamore for more than thirty years, remembers one occasion in late 1996 when the gardaí thought Fiona might have been found safe and well.

> We got a call from an Irishman who was over in London. He told us that he had been in a pub in London and had got talking to a woman who said she was from Tullamore. She said she was just after having a baby. He described her as a young woman with blond hair. Initially it sounded like Fiona. But we checked it out and it wasn't Fiona, it was actually another young Tullamore woman who had moved to England. The woman looked fairly like Fiona. It was certainly quite a coincidence. Sadly, it wasn't Fiona.

One lead gardaí investigated thoroughly was the possibility that Fiona might have travelled to London, to the area in which she and John Thompson had lived for four months in late 1995 and early 1996. They had decided to go to England in the wake of Mark Pender's death. It was a quiet time on the farm for John, and Fiona's aunt Bernie could put them up in London.

London was a totally new experience for Fiona. She had never been out of Ireland before. The couple got jobs in the Hilton Hotel in Croydon, and during their free time they visited all the tourist attractions. It was a carefree and exciting time. They even thought of settling in London, but they didn't have enough money and after four months they came home to Tullamore. They first moved into a small flat in Clonminch Road; a short time later they found the flat in

Church Street. Fiona sold all her bike gear and bought a young bull to be reared for her on the Thompson farm in Killeigh. Coming from the town, she didn't know much about farming, but she wanted to learn more from John.

In the early part of 1997 the gardaí continued a detailed study of the statements and questionnaires that had been completed by members of the public. They outlined the movements of hundreds of people and vehicles in the days during which Fiona Pender was believed to have been abducted and murdered. When the statements of a number of people were cross-checked an issue arose about the movements of a particular vehicle around the time of Fiona's disappearance. A conference was held, and a decision to question a number of people again was taken.

Early on the morning of Thursday, 24 April 1997 three women and two men were arrested at a number of places in counties Laois and Offaly. One of the men arrested was the person who was alleged to have previously strangled Fiona to the point she had lost consciousness. All five of those arrested were told they were being held under section 4 of the Criminal Justice Act, which allowed for their detention for a maximum of twelve hours. The five were taken to Tullamore Garda Station, where they were held in separate rooms, to be questioned by specialist detectives who had arrived from Dublin. The five people under arrest were asked probing questions about their knowledge of the movements of people and vehicles around the time of Fiona Pender's disappearance. Throughout the day there was information from the gardaí about whether anyone was going to be charged or not; then at seven o'clock that evening it was announced that all five people had been released without charge. Gardaí drove the five people, who were described as being shaken by the events of the previous twelve hours, back to their homes.

In Connolly Park the Penders received a phone call from a garda informing them that all five people had been released without charge. Years later, Josephine Pender's voice broke as she remembered that day.

When those people were arrested I answered the phone that morning and took the call from the gardaí. I remember telling Seán. He was sitting on the couch when I told him that they had arrested five people. Seán just aged in front of me. A friend of Fiona's, Emer Condron, came around and stayed with us the whole day. That day was so long. We were just waiting, hoping something positive was going to happen. And then we get the call to say they're all being released. I told Seán. He just went downhill from there.

Seán Pender took his own life on 31 March 2000. He was found by his son John. Seán had become unwell in the wake of his daughter's disappearance. Josephine told me Seán was hurting from the moment Fiona disappeared.

My husband cried for his children every night. He looked like a man with cancer: he was fading away, he looked so weak. We looked for help for him, but back then we didn't know the people that I know now. Seán just became so sick as a result of what happened to our family. He went so low he couldn't take any more. We had a wake here in the house, and Seán looked so much younger when he was laid out. He's at peace now. I've no doubt he's in heaven. He suffered too much hell on earth. Whoever murdered Fiona and her baby is also responsible for my husband's death. And they denied my grandson, Dean, a granddad, an aunt and a cousin.

Just a few months before Josephine passed away in 2017, John's partner had a baby girl, and in what was an emotional moment, Josephine held her newborn granddaughter. John says the birth of his daughter changed his life for the better in so many ways. Amid all the pain and loss, there was new life.

It was a proud moment to see my mother with her new granddaughter, it felt so right to see them together. I could see the joy she felt as she held my newborn child, we spoke of how good an aunt Fiona would have been, and couldn't help shed a tear for her own little baby. Over the coming months I brought her granddaughter to see Josephine as much as her failing health would allow. On those visits together she would forget for a short time about her ailments and become herself again, it was a beautiful thing to see. She used to always say to me I was her reason for living. And now I feel I have my own, a beautiful daughter and an incredible partner who has been there for me through my darkest of days.

In the aftermath of losing Seán in 2000, Josephine and John had a large extended family to help them. Josephine and Seán were married for thirty years. Their wedding took place in St Colmcille's Church in Durrow, where Mark was laid to rest in 1995, and where Seán was buried in 2000. Subsequently Josephine and John would often visit the graveyard and also think of Fiona and her baby. Josephine is now also laid to rest in Durrow.

The prime suspect for the murder of Fiona Pender is a man originally from the midlands who now lives in Saskatchewan, a vast province in the centre of Canada. This man moved from Ireland a number of years ago. He has two children in Canada and has worked as a delivery driver throughout his adopted country, driving thousands of miles of open road. At one point the suspect is believed to have become involved in a survivalist lifestyle in Canada. He had plans to build a large bunker at his rural house and wanted to stock it with enough supplies to last a year. He was said to be investing his money in gold and silver, believing banks were going to collapse and that various currencies were in danger of being devalued. It was also claimed that he had links to some dangerous elements in a Canadian biker gang.

Gardaí are aware that this is the man who is alleged to have attacked Fiona some months before her disappearance. This man was one of the five people arrested and questioned in Tullamore in 1997, before being released without charge. He's also the same man who, it's claimed, once visited the family of another missing woman, and said he might have been responsible for Fiona's disappearance, but had been on medication at the time and couldn't remember whether or not he had caused harm to Fiona.

In 2012 the man left Ireland for Canada after an expected inheritance failed to materialise. At the time he was also in significant mortgage arrears; he has not been back to Ireland in a number of years. One garda remembers speaking with the man in the initial stages of the investigation.

> We had this man in for questioning. He wasn't under arrest; he was there voluntarily. And we were talking, and we had our suspicions about him. I said something to him about it being terrible that there was no closure for the family, that Fiona was out there somewhere. This man put his face in his hands. He began to sob. I looked at the other garda with me. We were both thinking the same thing: we thought we were about to crack this thing. Then this man wiped his eyes with his arm and suddenly sat up straight and said, 'I can't tell you anything. You won't get me.'

In 2014 gardaí became aware of a potentially significant development in Canada. Police in Saskatchewan were investigating an allegation that the man had threatened and sexually assaulted his wife. The woman contacted officers with the allegation and during a search of the couple's home in a small town in Saskatchewan, police examined a number of laptops and videotapes. The videos were of the man and woman engaged in sex acts. The woman viewed the footage and said she had absolutely no recollection of the events. She told police that there were occasions when she woke up without any memory of going to bed, and she would find traces of make-up on her face that she had not applied herself. She said she had not consented to the sexual acts depicted in the videos. When police searched the man's car they found a bag of make-up in the boot.

Her husband was charged with two counts of sexual assault, one count of sexual assault with a weapon and two counts of uttering death threats. He stood trial before a judge-only court and the videos were played in court. The woman said she was unconscious in the footage. 'It's degrading and humiliating. It's a violation of me,' she told the judge. She explained she had been asleep during all of the occasions filmed by her husband. She also said the make-up was not hers and she had not applied it. Her husband must have applied the blue eyeshadow, red lipstick and fake nails and eyelashes that she was wearing in the footage.

The woman said she had found a tape of a similar incident when the couple were in Ireland some years before. She said the accused had got upset and left for a week before returning and apologising. She said her husband had wanted to get Canadian citizenship because there was no extradition arrangement with Ireland.

During this trial the man's wife told the court that her husband was linked to an unsolved missing person case in Ireland. She said her husband told her that gardaí were trying to set him up in relation to the disappearance of a missing woman.

She told the court that on one occasion her husband said, 'You know I've done it before. They'll never find you. You'll end up like her.' All of this was obviously of great interest to gardaí investigating Fiona's disappearance. Detective Inspector Martin Harrington, Detective Sergeant Jer Glavin and Garda Anne Marie Deegan flew to Canada to learn more about the claims. There was naturally an expectation that if the man was convicted of the charges in Canada, that there might be new leads in Fiona's case on the other side of the Atlantic Ocean.

However, in October 2015, following a four-day trial, Chief Justice Martel Popescul issued a 37-page judgement finding the defendant not guilty of all charges. The accused man had given evidence in his own defence and had denied making any threats, and had said his wife had consented to, or was aware of, him videoing various sex acts. In the absence of any other evidence, the judge found in the defendant's favour and he walked free from court. He later began proceedings to sue for wrongful arrest.

On the day the man was found not guilty at the court in Saskatchewan I visited Josephine Pender in Tullamore. She had been kept up to date on the case in Canada, and was hoping that developments there might help unlock information in Fiona's case. She knew the man on trial over 6,000 kilometres away was the same man she believed had murdered Fiona, and whom she had previously confronted. But when she heard the 'not guilty' verdict she was devastated. It was yet another setback in seeking answers about her daughter's murder.

Josephine had had her hopes dashed the previous December when a major excavation took place at Capard Wood in Co. Laois but ended without any trace of Fiona being found. Detectives had focused on a specific forested area, 18 kilometres from Tullamore, after receiving what they believed was credible information relating to the suspect now living in Canada. Gardaí sought the expertise of the Independent Commission for the Location of Victims' Remains who had successfully located the bodies of IRA victims buried in a number of counties. An expert from the commission was on-site at Capard where 2,500 square metres of woodland was to be searched. The site was photographed from the air, divided into grids, probes put into the ground and a sizeable number of trees felled. A specialist sniffer dog was also on-site, along with a large team of garda searchers.

The trees that were cut down were very tall but would have been only saplings when Fiona disappeared. For more than two weeks that December officers searched the woodland, hoping they were in the right area. However, on 18 December 2014 – day eighteen of the search – the operation was called off. There was no trace of Fiona in that part of woodland.

Josephine Pender and her son John visited the site on the last day of the search. All the gardaí and the machine operators stood by silently. The Penders shook hands with every person who had given so much of their time and effort to excavate the woodland.

Fiona's best friend, Emer Condron, ran a modelling agency in Tullamore for ten years. She first got to know Fiona when she approached her to see if she was interested in modelling work. Fiona was delighted to be asked.

I always thought that Fiona was beautiful, and she was very confident; and when I asked her to do some work for me she was thrilled. She entered the Miss Offaly competition to qualify for Miss Ireland, but she didn't reach the height requirement. Fiona had an openness to care for people, and she didn't want a big fancy lifestyle, just a secure home for herself and her baby. She stopped modelling after Mark died in June 1995. She and Mark were very close, and she just loved her little brother John to pieces. I sold my modelling business in the summer of 1996, when Fiona was pregnant and looking forward to a happier life. We were planning to set up a mobile wedding unit to cater for hair and beauty.

On the weekend in August 1996 when Fiona Pender disappeared, Emer Condron had called to the flat in Church Street a number of times, but didn't knock because the blinds were drawn. She assumed that Fiona was resting and didn't want to disturb her. It wasn't until just before ten o'clock on the evening of Saturday, 24 August that she realised something was terribly wrong.

Fiona's boyfriend, John Thompson, knocked on the door, and Fiona's mother, Josie, was with him in the jeep. They were looking for Fiona, and John asked me if I knew where she was. I was never so scared: it soon began to sink in that she was missing. It is just so horrific to think that someone did this to Fiona, when she was seven and a half months pregnant. It's so frightening to think of what she may have gone through. Not knowing what happened to Fiona, or where she is, it's just horrible. It is an empty death: nobody can grieve, there's no grave to visit.

To help her missing friend, and all missing people, Emer Condron coordinated a campaign in the late 1990s that sought to use the postal system to maintain awareness of the plight that many families suffer. She asked An Post to consider raising awareness of the issue of missing persons by issuing stamps bearing a photograph and details of missing people, but the authority declined. Emer was disappointed, but undeterred.

I get a little upset when I see what does appear on stamps – musicians and the like. All I wanted was a stamp to honour missing people, or to somehow keep the issue in the eye of the public. I still hope that An Post may take the initiative and be the first to do something like this. In the meantime I printed special appeal envelopes with a photo of Fiona, and a short description, and over 22,000 of those were circulated. Fiona was the soundest person I knew. It makes me so angry that in relation to all the missing people who are presumed to have been murdered, that for each of these people there is a person or persons responsible for these cowardly acts of murder, and they are walking around freely in our society. And they have a free hand to do it again to another family.

In 2018 John Pender narrated a documentary about his missing sister. In *My Sister Fi* John stood outside the flat on Church Street and remembered the last time he saw Fiona. He also outlined his clear memory of her confiding in him that a person, described as the chief suspect, had previously attacked Fiona, strangling her until she passed out. In the documentary (which is available online) John credits his partner and young daughter for giving him strength and focus, and he vows to continue the fight his mother had kept up from 1996 until her death in 2017.

John told me that public pressure is very important so that Fiona will never be forgotten.

It is vital in a missing person's case for families to take the lead in the investigation. When the person is not here to speak for themselves we must be a voice for them. It's always been clear in Fiona's case that there has been a lack of enough evidence and more information is needed. I feel what is known to gardaí at this stage should be enough to declare this a murder investigation. It was heartbreaking to bury my mother without finding Fiona, after all her campaigning and years of suffering. To leave Fiona and her baby in an unmarked grave somewhere is simply unacceptable. There is currently a cold-case team of investigators reviewing the case and that leaves hope for the future. I have witnessed myself that even after many years new leads can develop. It was my mother's dying wish to find Fiona and her baby's remains to give them a proper burial and I will not stop until the person responsible for their deaths is brought to justice for their crime. My father Seán used to say, and I have to trust that, 'the wheel always turns'.

A permanent reminder of Fiona is a sculpture designed by John and situated along the Grand Canal in Tullamore. The sculpture signifies the bond between mother and child, and remembers both Fiona and her unborn baby. A four-and-a-half kilometre stretch of scenic walkway along the canal is named Fiona's Way in her memory.

In May 2002 Josephine Pender and John attended the unveiling of the National Monument to Missing People by President Mary McAleese in the grounds of Kilkenny Castle. Later that day, in a private meeting, Josephine Pender and President McAleese held hands and spoke about Fiona. It was an emotional meeting for both. Josephine introduced John to the President, who remarked that he was a fine young man. 'He's had to grow up too fast,' replied Josephine, as tears streamed down her cheeks.

All the gardaí who initially investigated Fiona's disappearance are now retired. The current team of investigators are led by Chief Superintendent John Scanlon, and detectives are in close contact with John Pender. The original superintendent in the case, Gerry Murray, told me the one regret of his career was that Fiona's disappearance was not solved.

> The people of Tullamore were terrific in their assistance, but that is the one disappointment in my life. We thought we would crack this case; and I still believe that Fiona will be found some day and that the person responsible will be held responsible. Right now we have no scene, no body. But I believe this will be solved.

In 2002 I spoke with John Thompson but he declined to be interviewed. He told me he believed the gardaí made many mistakes early on in the investigation. He said certain leads were not followed up, or were not followed up quickly enough.

Josephine Pender's death in 2017 affected many other families of missing people. Josephine was a great listener: she had manned a helpline for people in distress in Tullamore and she extended that listening ear to people across the country in the same situation as her own. Her strength and fortitude gave so many other families strength to continue their campaign for answers.

Josephine Pender once told me she always wanted a large family. She had two miscarriages before John was born, and two afterwards. On one occasion as she looked at photographs of her dead children, Fiona and Mark, she gave a long sigh.

> I should have seven children, now I only have one. Whoever took Fiona damaged so many people. John and myself go out to Seán's and Mark's graves in Durrow to think of Mark, Seán, Fiona and the baby. On the twenty-second of October of every year, the date that Fiona was due to give birth, we go to the graves and we light a candle. I bring a little toy for the baby.

CHAPTER 5

CIARA BREEN

Ciara Breen is commonly referred to as one of Ireland's missing women, but she was a child when she was murdered in the early hours of 13 February 1997. She was most likely killed by a man she had arranged to meet close to her home in Dundalk, Co. Louth.

Ciara had gone to bed that night but had waited until her mother was asleep and then sneaked out of a downstairs window to meet someone. Ciara's mother Bernadette, gardaí and many local people focused their attention on a man who lived on the same street at Bachelors Walk, and who had previously shown an unhealthy interest in the teenager. That man, who was in his thirties at the time, emerged as the prime suspect, and was arrested twice in connection with Ciara's disappearance – in 1999 and 2015. He admitted having previously kissed the teenager but, despite many witnesses claiming he had been in a long-term relationship with Ciara, denied this and refused to answer several questions while under arrest.

In 2015 a massive search for Ciara's remains was undertaken in bog and marshland in Dundalk, close to the garda station and railway line. Eighteen years after Ciara was murdered, a significant number of new witnesses emerged after a fresh garda appeal. New information now linked Ciara and the suspect on the night of her disappearance, including a reported sighting of the teenager close to Balmers Bog soon after she had sneaked out of her house. Over a three-week period in August and September 2015, four acres of land were excavated. It was difficult terrain to search, with gardaí wading through bog water and cutting eight-foot-high reeds to allow access to the ground, but no trace of Ciara was found. A forensic archaeologist at the scene said the work had been hampered by hundreds of tonnes of rubble and rocks, which had been dumped at the site in 2003. It was possible Ciara's body had been buried at the site, but the dumping of hard fill had reduced the possibility of finding her.

During the excavation at Balmers Bog in August and September 2015, the prime suspect was spotted walking by the area a number of times, observing what was going on. Despite the fact that the man had made self-incriminating comments following Ciara's disappearance and denied a relationship with the teenager, the Director of Public Prosecutions decided not to prosecute him for Ciara's murder.

Bernadette Breen lost her only child when Ciara was murdered. She died in 2018, following a long illness. Bernadette often told me there were so many reminders for her of what she has lost.

> Ciara was my life. She was my identity: I wasn't Bernadette, I was 'Ciara's Mam'. And I know I always will be. But my baby is lying out there somewhere.

Bernadette always knew the identity of the prime suspect. Many months before Ciara vanished she had chased the man away from their door as he was trying to strike up a conversation with Ciara, enquiring if she had a boyfriend.

Ciara Breen was abducted and murdered a month before her eighteenth birthday. She would never know her mother had organised a surprise trip to Disneyland in Florida for her birthday. Ciara and Bernadette had been to Florida the previous October, and Ciara had often said she would love to go back.

Twelve hours after her only child vanished in February 1997, a doctor in the Blackrock Clinic in Co. Dublin told Bernadette Breen she had cancer. She had kept her appointment, hoping that Ciara would be back before her. Bernadette knew there was £100 still in Ciara's bedroom, and the indications were that she had left with the intention of returning before her mother woke.

It was a few hours after they had said goodnight that Bernadette discovered Ciara was missing. She had woken in the early hours of the morning and looked in on Ciara but the bed was empty, and when she searched the house Bernadette found the window of the downstairs room at the front had been left ajar. This was the first time her mother had discovered Ciara sneaking out of the house during the night. Ciara had once run away for a few days, but that had been nearly a year and a half ago. For hours Bernadette sat in the darkness waiting to catch her daughter when she came back in the window, but she never came home.

Ciara Breen had many things on her mind the night she disappeared. She was worried about her mother's hospital appointment the next day; Bernadette had already been to hospital to undergo cancer tests and was about to get the results. Earlier that day, at her Ógra Dhún Dealgan FÁS course, she had told her tutor, Rosaleen Bishop, that her mother had an important hospital appointment the next day. Ciara was also worried about her appearance. A problem with her gums meant the upper row of her teeth would need to be reset.

The subsequent garda investigation indicated Ciara may have been in a relationship with the prime suspect for many months. It would take years before there was enough evidence to arrest the suspect, but in time many witnesses emerged who claimed the couple often met secretly in locations around the town. Two neighbours told detectives they had spotted Ciara kissing a man in a laneway at the back of her home at Bachelors Walk. The witnesses said this had occurred sometime in August 1996, which was six months before the teenager vanished. Ciara and her mother had moved to Bachelors Walk in March '96 and the suspect was already living nearby. The incident where Bernadette had told the suspect to get away from their front door had happened sometime in the April or May.

Another witness contacted gardaí to say she had seen Ciara and the suspect together in the car park of a department store close to Bachelors Walk. The suspect told a young woman he was going out with Ciara and that she was sneaking out of the window of her home to meet him. This was many months before Ciara disappeared. A number of teenagers and young adults saw Ciara and the suspect in St Leonard's Gardens and Market Square in Dundalk. In December '96 Ciara wrote the couple's names on the wall of a handball alley while with another girl. The suspect told another man that Ciara would often sneak out of her home to meet him and he would bring alcohol for the two of them to drink in a car park.

All this information was gathered in the aftermath of Ciara's disappearance. The various accounts suggested that Ciara was in a relationship with a man twice her age. Bernadette had had immediate concerns when she saw him trying to chat up her daughter, but never suspected, until after her daughter's disappearance, that Ciara and this man were having a secret relationship.

Bernadette Breen recounted with clarity her memories of the night Ciara disappeared.

We went out for a meal to the Roma restaurant in Park Street in the town. Ciara and I were like sisters the way we would joke sometimes. And we had fun that night. Ciara really liked the actor Chris O'Donnell, and I remember she recorded him that night in *Circle of Friends*. She had marked the tape 'Ciara Breen's tape. Do not touch.' We also watched a film on Sky. *Bad Boys* was the film, with Will Smith. I was travelling to Dublin the next day for the results of a cancer test. I asked Ciara if she was worried about the results. She replied, 'Not really. Not if you aren't.' We got ready for bed and she came in and threw herself on my bed like normal, and we chatted about a few different things. I joked with her about the cancer results, saying, 'You're not going to get rid of me that easily.' She dropped a hint about her eighteenth birthday. One present that she knew she was getting was a bank book with her children's allowance money saved in it. She was very excited, wondering how much was in it. The last thing she said to me was, 'Don't read for too long. I love you.' I said to her, 'I love you too, sweetie.' I always called her 'sweetie' or 'sweet pea'. Ciara went into her own room. A few hours later I discovered she was missing from her bedroom, and her window was open.

Ciara Breen had previously fallen in with a bad crowd. In October 1995, when she was sixteen, she ran away with a friend; they crossed the border and hid in a house in Jonesborough, Co. Armagh, owned by an aunt of this friend's. Bernadette had no idea where Ciara was and immediately called the gardaí. A national appeal for information was issued. Bernadette told me that Ciara looked like a wreck when she decided to come home.

> You know the way some kids are kind of hardy – well, Ciara wasn't. She wasn't suited to running away. When she ran away to this house in Co. Armagh she didn't like it. She came home with black rings under her eyes, and she had a cold sore on her mouth. This was during a time that I was having trouble controlling her. She was about sixteen and a half, and I had about six months of trouble. She was hanging around with girls who in turn knew boys that would give any mother nightmares. There were about a dozen times that she was in trouble, and I had to ground her many times. But from about July 1996 up to when she disappeared she was fine. She wasn't mixing with those people any more, and we were getting on so well. She had seemed to settle down and had even told me that she had taken her first drink, a bottle of Ritz. She'd had two bottles, and we had a good chat about drinking responsibly. We were the best of friends.

Bernadette Breen doted on her only child. They shared much; but in the aftermath of Ciara's disappearance Bernadette knew her daughter had been keeping something from her. It would seem obvious that

Ciara left her home late that night in February 1997 to meet someone Bernadette wouldn't have approved of; but all the indications are that she intended to return to her bedroom before her mother woke the next morning.

Even the next day, having sat up most of the night waiting for her daughter to return, Bernadette thought she might be back. She left a message with Rosaleen Bishop to say that if she turned up she was to tell her Bernadette was very angry and they would talk about it after her trip to Dublin for the results of her cancer test.

I was hoping Ciara would be back by the time I got back from Dublin. My daddy brought me down to the Blackrock Clinic, and I didn't tell him Ciara had sneaked out of the house. I went in for the results, and all I could think about was Ciara; I wanted to get back to Dundalk and find her safe and well. I remember I went into the doctor and he said he was sorry to tell me that they had detected cancerous cells. I hardly heard him: I just wanted to get back to Dundalk. A few weeks later that doctor told me he thought that I was the coolest cucumber he ever told such news to, but he now understood why. Going back in the car, I told Daddy Ciara was missing.

Though Bernadette and Ciara lived alone at Bachelors Walk, they had a large extended family dotted around Dundalk. Bernadette's parents, Brendan and Marie Coburn, lived just around the corner in St Mary's Road. Bernadette also had brothers in the area. A sister lived in the US. In the late 1970s Bernadette married a Dundalk man; by the time the short-lived marriage broke up they had a baby girl they named Ciara. Ciara's father left for America and never saw his daughter. Bernadette told me that Ciara was beginning to ask more and more about her father.

We never had any contact with him from the time Ciara was very young. He left Ireland and it was just me and Ciara. But she was beginning to get curious about him. And I always told her that if she wanted to see him, or get in contact, or know more, that she could go to her granddad, my daddy, and he would know what to do. Her granddad would know how to make contact. Around the time Ciara disappeared, her father was to travel to Ireland for a wedding. But she never got to meet him.

Ciara's father arrived back in Dundalk some weeks after Ciara's disappearance to attend a family wedding in Co. Louth. He had never met his daughter, who he knew was now almost eighteen. He held out the hope that his daughter might like to see him just once. As he stepped off the train in late February he was full of expectation and trepidation. The first thing he saw at the station was a poster with a photograph of a girl and beside it the words 'Missing – Ciara Breen'.

As detectives began investigating Ciara's disappearance, and before the suspect was identified, they spoke to the girls with whom she had been mixing during her few unsettled months. Conscious that Ciara had once run away with a friend, gardaí investigated all the places she might have visited voluntarily. One detective told me there was a great degree of urgency about the search.

We knew that Ciara had run away by herself once before. But even if she had done this again, she was still a child. She was only seventeen, and we knew that she might be in danger, even if she had chosen to go somewhere. But we were also faced with a number of clear indications that Ciara had not chosen to run away this time. She didn't take any money with her from her bedroom. There was no note for her mother – and remember, she knew her mother had an important hospital appointment the next day. Every instinct told us Ciara was not hiding out somewhere. Not this time.

With the assistance of the RUC, searches were undertaken in a number of places in counties Armagh and Down, including Newry and Warrenpoint. The girl with whom Ciara had previously run away knew nothing about her fresh disappearance. She did suggest that Ciara might have had contact with a woman in Dungannon. The gardaí investigated this possibility, but it led nowhere. As detectives questioned Ciara's friends they discovered that she had recently met a young man from Kilkeel, Co. Down, at a disco in the Carrickdale Hotel. This man was eventually tracked down but he had not seen Ciara.

In the aftermath of Ciara's disappearance Bernadette stayed living in the house at Bachelors Walk until 2000. She later moved back to St Mary's Road, where she had grown up. She found it very difficult to leave the home she and Ciara had shared.

Ciara disappeared a month and a half before her eighteenth birthday. The home we lived in at Bachelors Walk was a lovely, comfortable home, close to my parents' home here. For months and months after Ciara vanished I couldn't go into her bedroom. I stayed in the house though. I wanted to keep the house going for Ciara. It was our home. But as I began to realise Ciara wasn't coming home I began to think about leaving. But I stayed in the house until what would have been Ciara's twenty-first birthday. It's just something I felt compelled to do. She was my baby. I even kept her on my VHI until she was twenty-one. I left the house on Ciara's twenty-first, on the 31st of March 2000. I came home here to care for my mam.

As the gardaí began to look at possible suspects for the abduction and murder of Ciara Breen, the name of one man began to crop up, a man in his early thirties who many were claiming had been in a relationship with Ciara. As the number of people providing information increased, a derelict house was searched in the village of Louth, six miles south-west of Dundalk and owned by a relative of the suspect, but nothing was found.

Detectives also travelled to south Co. Meath to question other initial suspects. They had received information suggesting that two men, who were cousins, had been in the greater Dundalk area at about the time Ciara disappeared. They were known criminals, and detectives from Operation Trace would also later question them about their movements at the time Jo Jo Dullard was abducted and murdered in November 1995. However, in relation to the time of Ciara's abduction and murder, the two men were able to provide alibi witnesses corroborating their movements.

As the investigation progressed, more and more people put the prime suspect and Ciara together on a number of occasions in 1996 and prior to her disappearance in '97. The suspect was apparently also making self-incriminating comments. One young woman said he had told her he knew where Ciara was; another said the suspect told her he used to throw stones at Ciara's bedroom window to get her to come out, and that he appeared to 'be crazy about Ciara'.

On 10 September 1999, two and a half years after Ciara's disappearance, the suspect was arrested by local detective Con Nolan on suspicion of the murder of Ciara Breen. Gardaí from Operation Trace were also present in the town to coordinate questioning. Although the suspect had previously told gardaí he had no information about Ciara's disappearance, it was time to put all the witness statements to him, which suggested he was lying about the extent of his relationship with Ciara.

A team of experienced detectives from the National Bureau of Criminal Investigation conducted five interviews with the suspect. During this questioning he admitted he had kissed Ciara, but said it was only on one occasion and that they had not been going out. When a witness statement was read to him, which stated Ciara had told a friend she was going to meet the suspect that night, he told gardaí, 'I'm not answering that, I'll take my chances. I'll take my chances from here.' Two of Ciara's young friends were brought into the interview room to directly confront the suspect, but he denied their accounts and said it was all lies. At 7.55 p.m. that day the suspect was released without charge. It would be another sixteen years before he would be rearrested and questioned again.

In the immediate aftermath of the man's first arrest, gardaí received even more information. Perhaps some of the witnesses were emboldened by news of the arrest, realising that Ciara's case was now being thoroughly investigated. Down the years assistance came from many different quarters, including some criminals who knew the suspect. They provided information, which stated they had seen the suspect and Ciara together or the suspect had told them he was going out with Ciara. Some witnesses said the suspect had told them he had buried Ciara, but the witnesses gave different locations for where he claimed the body was. He was alleged to have told one witness Ciara was buried beneath the floorboards of his home at Bachelors Walk, and another that she was buried near Omeath on the Cooley Peninsula.

Detectives also learnt the suspect had been in a number of previous relationships in the 1980s and '90s, including with teenage girls. A common theme in many of the relationships was possessiveness and emotional abuse. One former partner said he had once kicked her and another said he had twisted her arm. Some of the relationships involved meeting in lanes and car parks in Dundalk. The suspect also had a habit of following ex-girlfriends around when they broke off the relationships.

Several people reported the suspect's strange behaviour the night an appeal was broadcast on RTÉ's *Crimeline* programme in 1998. He had been in a pub, drinking whiskey, and was very drunk. A number of patrons told detectives that after Ciara's case was mentioned on the pub television, the suspect had said, for example, 'she's not coming back' … 'that one's gone' … 'you won't see her again'. All of this information was intriguing, but in the absence of a body or a crime scene, what was by now a murder investigation ran into the sand.

Bernadette Breen knew the identity of the prime suspect for the murder of her child. In the aftermath of Ciara's disappearance, the man's denial of ever being in a relationship with Ciara conflicted with her suspicion.

I remember one evening when Ciara was sixteen I heard her at the front door talking to someone. I heard this man's voice. He was saying to Ciara, 'Are you going with somebody?' I went to the door. I knew from the voice it wasn't a boy she was talking to. And sure enough it was this man. I chased him away from the door, telling him he was almost old enough for me, and to leave Ciara alone. I was thirty-eight years old at the time, and this man was in his thirties too; and there he was trying to chat Ciara up. And for him then to later claim that he never knew her, never met her! I saw him talking to her. I chased him from my own doorstep. I never liked the look of him. Three days after Ciara's disappearance he passed by my house at Bachelors Walk and he looked at me. My blood turned to ice. Every hair on my body stood to attention.

Among the many clear memories Bernadette had was the day the suspect was arrested in September 1999.

I was told about his arrest just twenty minutes before it appeared on the news. A local detective and a woman from Operation Trace came to the house. When they told me, my heart hit my knees. That whole day was just so difficult. And then he was released without charge.

As gardaí continued to investigate the disappearance of Ciara Breen, a number of searches were conducted after confidential information was received. A piggery on the Dublin Road just outside Dundalk was searched – that premises is now gone, with a block of apartments on its site. Gardaí knew that young people used to gather in the area after dark. Nothing was found during an extensive search of the area. Gardaí were also aware of the vast mountainside and forested areas in the north-eastern corner of Co. Louth that lie just past Dundalk and out towards Carlingford. But without an indication of where to begin, a search of such an enormous area would not be feasible.

North Co. Louth has an unenviable distinction in relation to the disappearance of several people who were murdered and whose bodies were concealed. The IRA buried four bodies in the county, three of which have since been found. The body of Jean McConville, a mother of ten, was buried at Shellinghill Beach after she was shot dead in March 1972 and found by chance in 2003. Gerry Evans was buried in bogland in Carrickrobin in March 1979 and recovered in 2010 following specific information provided by the IRA. Eugene Simons was shot dead in January 1981 and his body buried in a bog west of Dundalk. He was found three years later. One IRA victim buried in the county was not recovered. British soldier Robert Nairac was shot dead near Ravensdale in 1977 but the IRA has failed to provide information about where his body is buried.

Although a local suspect eventually emerged for Ciara's disappearance, other theories were also considered. Ciara's case was investigated by detectives from Operation Trace for a year before the man was arrested. Bernadette Breen was very upset about how she discovered Ciara's disappearance was being linked with the possibility of a serial killer.

I was never told about the setting up of Operation Trace. I remember clearly it was October 1998, and I was watching the RTÉ news at six o'clock. That's where I learnt about it – from the media. I was distraught. They were talking about all these poor girls and whether their disappearances were connected. I smashed so many cups and plates that night – anything I could find – I was so angry. To hear Ciara's name being linked with a serial killer; and for me to hear about it on television! I'm still angry about it. Even the local gardaí didn't know. One local detective arrived twenty minutes after the news report. He was too late. He didn't know about this Operation Trace either. I was given no warning about that news report. Is that right?

Ciara Breen was three weeks into an early school-leavers' course with Ógra Dhún Dealgan when she disappeared. She had put her name down many months before, and a place became available with the small group of ten or so in January 1997. She was learning how to sew and use computers, and she was doing life and social skills. It was a one-year course, certified by FÁS. Ciara had liked history and English in school but wasn't academically minded and left St Vincent's Secondary School in Dundalk at the end of fifth year. She loved working with make-up, and was thinking about the possibility of working as a beautician. She had to walk a short distance every day to the Ógra centre in Chapel Street, the old Boys' Technical School. Rosaleen Bishop, Ciara's tutor, only knew the teenager for a short time but had fond memories of her.

I remember Ciara was a quiet young girl. She was shy, and she was conscious of her teeth and that they needed some work done on them. She would put her hand up to her mouth when she'd be talking to you. She was very fond of her mother. I remember the day before she disappeared Ciara came into my office and told me her mother wasn't very well. She said she had to get some results from hospital. Ciara told me she was going to go home and put on a nice fire for her mam and tidy up the house for her, to make her feel a little better. Ciara never mentioned her dad. I wouldn't say Ciara was a streetwise kid. She wouldn't be gullible either but maybe would have a trusting nature. She was a lovely wee girl. She was very good at crafts and flower arranging, and she did T-shirt prints as well. I remember when the gardaí came in to question me and the other staff they were so thorough, they wanted to know everything – like the tone of a voice and facial expressions.

As part of her search for her child Bernadette Breen hired a private detective, but he failed to find any real leads. She even turned to psychics for help, going as far as the US to speak to a medium.

When Ciara Breen sneaked out of the house that night she was wearing a three-quarter-length leather jacket and jeans. She was also wearing a limited-edition watch, which has never been found. The watch was one of only 2,500 sold in Florida to mark the soccer World Cup held in the US in 1994. It had a square face with a green background featuring Mickey Mouse on the left-hand side, and had a black leather strap. Ciara got the watch when she and her mother were in Florida four months before she disappeared. As well as the distinctive watch, Ciara was wearing a white T-shirt from Sea World in Florida.

Bernadette told me that Ciara was an open, loving and trusting person.

> Ciara couldn't see anything wrong in anyone. She was the type of girl who fed stray dogs. She loved animals, from dogs and cats to sharks. She loved make-up, but she wouldn't wear anything that had been tested on animals. She kept a few dogs. Ciara was her own person, but she was my daughter. She was my baby.

Some of the girls Ciara hung around with during her wild period are now dead. Three died in a horrific car crash while travelling in a car being driven by a teenage boy who had no driving licence. One detective told me that down the years many young people in Dundalk had hurt themselves by falling in with the wrong crowd.

> What gets to you is that these were fundamentally good kids. But that's just it: they were kids. And they found themselves doing things that right-thinking adults would not be doing. So many of them have been hurt or killed in accidents. I met many of them during our investigation into Ciara's disappearance. They wouldn't have always seen eye to eye with the gardaí, but when it came to the search for Ciara, they really tried to help us. I'll never forget the bravery of some of those girls in giving us information about the

people they hung around with, and who Ciara might have hung around with.

For many years after Ciara disappeared Bernadette Breen kept a journal, a record of her innermost thoughts. Sometimes there were days she couldn't write at all. Bernadette fought the cancer she was diagnosed with in 1997. She lived for a further twenty-one years, and made countless appeals for information about Ciara's case. Bernadette kept a snip of Ciara's hair, and guarded it in a locket.

Bernadette always believed the local detectives involved in the search for Ciara were wonderful, but she had reservations about the wider investigations into the cases of missing people.

> I really think the government come out with things every now and then to keep the families of missing people quiet. I think there should be detectives working for maybe eighteen months or two years at a time in a dedicated unit, and then bring in fresh people. It's little things that really upset you: the fact that families learn things from the media rather than the gardaí. It just hurts sometimes. But then there are gardaí who are great. You know they really care. There is one detective who I know keeps a photograph of Ciara with him, just to remind him that it's a teenage child who is missing.

A large black-and-white photograph hung on a wall of Bernadette's home showing Ciara on her First Holy Communion day, smiling proudly in her white dress. In another room hung a large photograph of Bernadette's grandfather, James Coburn – Ciara's great-grandfather, who was a Fine Gael TD for Louth for twenty-seven years.

In 2014 there was a fresh investigation into Ciara's disappearance. The full file was re-examined, and newly appointed senior investigating officer Detective Inspector Pat Marry made a number of appeals on *Crimecall* on RTÉ. Those appeals led to significant new information, which in turn would lead the following year to the rearrest of the chief suspect, and a major search of bogland on the outskirts of Dundalk.

Some of the new information came in the form of anonymous letters to gardaí in Dundalk, which named the prime suspect as the person responsible for Ciara's murder. Coupled with other information assembled from the time of the first arrest in 1999, there was enough new evidence to seek the arrest of the suspect for a second time.

The suspect was still living in Dundalk – having moved to a nearby estate from Bachelors Walk the year after Ciara disappeared – when he was arrested on 21 April 2015 just after 7.30 a.m. by Garda Brendan Duffy on suspicion of the murder of Ciara Breen and taken to Drogheda Garda Station.

The suspect was agitated during questioning and some detectives thought he was close to tears. His solicitor was present with him at all times. The suspect occasionally requested a private consultation, and on the advice of his solicitor answered 'no comment' to all relevant questions relating to Ciara. The suspect declined to sign the notes of the interviews. He was released from custody the following day just before 7.30 a.m.

Similar to what had happened in 1999, it was in the days after the man's second arrest when even more information came into the investigation team. On 24 April gardaí received a call saying they would find Ciara's body 'in the bog at the old railway track behind the brewery'. Detectives had received many such calls down the years, nominating different spots where bodies might be located. But it was a second call, with more precise information two days later, which really intrigued gardaí. This call, from the same person, mentioned the suspect by name. The caller said the suspect had made comments suggesting that Ciara's body was in the bog at the back of McArdle Moore's old brewery close to the railway. But the anonymous caller had another piece of precise information: the suspect had been seen with Ciara close to the scene at 1.20 a.m. on 13 February 1997. This time would tie in with Ciara sneaking out of her house a short time beforehand.

As detectives followed up on the new lead, they spoke with even more people who had relevant information. One woman said the suspect had once told her you could throw someone into the marsh at Balmers Bog and they would never be found. Another witness said they had heard that the suspect had once referred to another girl and said if she wasn't careful she'd 'end up in the bog with Ciara Breen'. Another witness said the suspect had told her, 'I'll bury you in the bog where I buried the other one.' Gardaí now believed they had a location that needed to be fully searched – the only issue was that it was a large section of very difficult terrain.

The search for the body of Ciara Breen began on 18 August 2015. Balmers Bog is in a natural hollow, and four acres of a sixteen-acre site were cordoned off to be completely searched. Forensic archaeologist Niamh McCullagh from the Independent Commission for the Location of Victims' Remains was on-site to advise gardaí on how to search the area inch by inch. Parts of the search involved the Garda Sub-Aqua Unit walking chest-deep in bog water. Large sections of swamp reeds were cut away to allow a surface search. Vast tracts of bog were excavated using diggers slowly scraping the soil. A nearby river was dredged and a cadaver dog walked the land searching for any sign of remains. Female clothing and shoes were found during the search, but when later shown to Bernadette Breen she said they were not Ciara's.

As the search continued it became clear that a significant issue would hamper the work. Garda searchers began to find building rubble and rocks. Detectives would soon discover that hundreds of tonnes of hard fill had been dumped on the land many years after Ciara disappeared. The forensic archaeologist advised gardaí that the dumping had caused incalculable harm to the progress of the search and the potential to find human remains at the location.

The search of Balmers Bog ended without success on 9 September. All of the garda team were extremely disappointed and frustrated that the search had turned out to be fruitless. They knew there were three possibilities: Ciara's body was never in the bog in the first place; the body was in a different section of the sixteen-acre site; or, because of the dumped rubble, her body could not be located.

The suspect was seen walking by the site a number of times during the search. He was a free man, and quite entitled to go wherever he wanted, but detectives were puzzled. Why was he watching?

In the aftermath of the search, officers compiled a file for the Director of Public Prosecutions outlining all the new information that had come into possession of detectives in 2014 and 2015. Gardaí asked the DPP to give a view on whether there was enough evidence to bring a prosecution against the suspect for offences from withholding information to murder. The DPP replied that no proceedings should be brought in the case.

The suspect died in Dundalk in 2017 from a suspected heroin overdose. He was in his fifties. He had sixteen criminal convictions, including five for criminal damage and two for theft. He had nine motoring offences including two for drink-driving. Was he the man who murdered Ciara? A significant number of people claimed he was in a relationship with the teenager, something he denied when twice arrested. Even if the suspect was lying about the relationship, was he responsible for killing Ciara? Was it possible she sneaked out of her house to meet this man, but someone else crossed her path and attacked her? Why then did the man allegedly make incriminating statements to so many people?

In various comments the suspect allegedly made down the years, he nominated various places in Dundalk and beyond as the location he had hidden Ciara's body. If he was the killer, why was he mentioning different burial sites, none of which ever bore fruit?

One alleged comment the suspect made continues to intrigue those who have investigated Ciara's case. At one point when the suspect was asked to tell the truth about his involvement with Ciara, he reportedly said, 'If I tell you, will I be charged with murder? There's no reason to charge me with what I did.' By his actions and his comments down the years, the suspect put himself at the centre of the case.

Given the history of the investigation, detectives believe there are still people in Dundalk with more information about Ciara's disappearance. Gardaí hoped that although the search at Balmers

Bog ended without success, that search proved to people that officers would act on information that was deemed credible. No stone would ever be left unturned.

In October 2017 builders carrying out renovation work found skeletal remains buried in a back garden of a house on Mary Street North in Dundalk, a short distance from Bachelors Walk. The scene was immediately sealed off and detectives investigating Ciara's disappearance wondered if this might be the answer to the case. State Pathologist Professor Marie Cassidy visited the scene, but news soon emerged that the body could not be Ciara or any other person who had disappeared in recent times. Superintendent Gerry Curley confirmed to the expectant media that the body was at least seventy years old and that the National Museum was being contacted. While it was false hope in the Ciara Breen case, the discovery of the skeleton shows how a body can lie hidden in a suburban area for many decades.

In the aftermath of the prime suspect's death in July 2017, I interviewed Bernadette Breen on RTÉ's *Prime Time* programme. She was conscious the dead man had a family. She said that no matter what way detectives examined the case, and considered other possibilities and suspects, it always came back to one man, one suspect. In a powerful and passionate plea she looked directly at the camera and thanked all the people who had provided new information and urged people still holding information on Ciara's case to do the right thing.

Bernadette died in June 2018, following a long battle with illness. Through her faith she always said that Ciara was with God, but her daughter had no grave. Nobody could lay flowers for her.

Every day I think that's another day gone without Ciara. I always think I might get some news tomorrow. Maybe 'tomorrow' is what keeps me going. I just can't bear to think of her lying out there somewhere. Two things I definitely know are that Ciara wasn't on drugs, and she was not pregnant. But I know she sneaked out of the house to meet someone I wouldn't have approved of. I'd like younger people reading this to remember that parents don't warn about evil people just for the sake of it. Ciara was stupid once and paid the highest price possible. When I'm at my lowest I can smell her. Ciara wore White Musk, and I can still smell her. I would give anything in the world just to hear just two words again: 'Hi, Mam.'

CHAPTER 6

FIONA SINNOTT

O f all the missing women feared to have been the victims of a violent death, nineteen-year-old Fiona Sinnott is the only one who has left behind a child. Her daughter was eleven months old when Fiona vanished in February 1998. When she disappeared Fiona was living in an isolated location at Ballyhitt, four miles south-west of Rosslare, Co. Wexford. Gardaí are aware that, some time before her disappearance, Fiona had suffered a number of brutal assaults at the hands of a former boyfriend. On different occasions she was hospitalised for injuries, including a damaged jaw and twisted ankle, but discharged herself.

Despite the litany of abuse she endured, Fiona Sinnott had much to look forward to. She doted on her baby daughter, and she was planning to work as a chef. Though Fiona and her ex-boyfriend Seán Carroll had ended their relationship they remained on good terms, and their daughter spent her time between the Carroll and Sinnott families. All the indications are that Fiona Sinnott did not choose to disappear. She was looking forward to her daughter's first birthday, and her sister Diane was having her twenty-first birthday later the same month. Fiona's disappearance devastated her parents and her two brothers and two sisters.

Gardaí have two main hypotheses. Fiona may have been murdered, possibly by one or more local people; or she may have suffered an accidental death, and the person or persons who were with her panicked and concealed her body. Detectives remain convinced that there are people in south Co. Wexford who know what happened to Fiona Sinnott, and who know who is responsible.

Seán Carroll is the last person known to have seen her. He said he last saw Fiona at about 9.15 a.m. on Monday, 9 February 1998. He told gardaí he was standing in her bedroom having spent the night on a sofa downstairs. He outlined how he went up to wake Fiona before he left the house. He had stayed the night because she had been complaining of a pain in her arm the night before, and he had agreed to escort her home from the pub. He said that by Monday morning she said she was still not feeling well and that she was going to the doctor in Bridgetown, about eight miles away, and would thumb a lift over. Seán said he asked her if she'd any money and she replied that she hadn't. He told detectives he gave Fiona about £5 and headed out the door, to where his mother was waiting in her car to collect him. That is the last reported sighting of Fiona Sinnott.

The night before she disappeared, Fiona was in Butler's pub, up the road from her house. On a number of occasions that night she complained of a pain in her arm, but because of her disappearance, and the fact that she never made it to the Bridgetown Medical Centre, we will never know exactly why her arm was causing her pain or whether this pain had anything to do with her disappearance. Despite the pain, she was enjoying herself that Sunday night. She was going about her normal routine of having a drink and a chat with friends. Her movements in the last few hours before she vanished were those of a nineteen-year-old woman enjoying herself. On closer inspection, however, her life was far from perfect.

Fiona Sinnott had suffered much during her nineteen years. She met her first boyfriend when she was fifteen, and had several more relationships over the next four years. Fiona came from a loving and close-knit family, but there seemed little they could do to help her when one boyfriend became violent. She suffered several violent physical attacks. The first time she was treated at Wexford General Hospital it was for bruising to her face and jaw; other hospital visits followed when she suffered bites to her legs, and when she was beaten about the head and back. However, each time she attended the casualty department she would discharge herself, or decline to say what exactly had happened. While she never made a formal complaint against the person brutalising her, gardaí were becoming aware that Fiona Sinnott was being physically assaulted by a man from the south Co. Wexford area.

In late 1996 two gardaí sped to a house a mile outside Rosslare Harbour. Garda Michelle Power had just received a 999 call to say that a man had reportedly threatened a woman with a knife. The two male gardaí who arrived at the scene found Fiona Sinnott on the street being comforted by another woman. Fiona and the two gardaí went into a house, where the man who had allegedly threatened her was lying asleep on a sofa. He had been drinking. He awoke and held a conversation with the two gardaí while Fiona collected her belongings and left the house. The two gardaí noted the night's events in the garda log. No charges were made.

One detective believes that a pattern of abuse was unfolding but never proved.

> Here we had a young woman attending Wexford General Hospital on a number of occasions for bruising to her face, a twisted ankle, a damaged jaw. She never once told gardaí that these injuries were caused by another person. Of course we might all suspect the injuries were the result of a violent relationship, but suspicion is not enough. Fiona never pressed charges. Were it not for that incident where a man reportedly threatened to kill Fiona, we might not have looked in that direction. But even then the feeling we got from Fiona was that this fellow was going to sleep it off. No charges were pressed. I believe Fiona was physically abused by a man she was having a relationship with. But I can't prove it. And this man had no convictions for anything. He was clean as a whistle.

The feeling of many people close to the case about who might be responsible for Fiona Sinnott's disappearance is influenced heavily by an assault that took place a year before her disappearance. Detectives only became aware of the attack after Fiona vanished; but one officer said the circumstances of this reported assault disturbed gardaí investigating her disappearance.

> Fiona confided in a number of people about a particular assault she suffered at the hands of this same man, who we believe might have been responsible for her earlier treatment in hospital. We have more than one report about the nature of this assault, which is a very serious attack on a young woman. If we charged the alleged attacker he would be facing up to life imprisonment. But we can't charge him. We need Fiona.

But Fiona had ended her relationship with the man who was believed to be assaulting her. She was a quiet young woman who enjoyed the company of her friends and family, and she was the mother of a baby girl. Her future looked much brighter.

Seán Carroll sat up at the bar, smoking and drinking a pint. He and Fiona shared access to their baby, and that night their daughter was staying with Seán's parents, Kitty and Seán Snr.

At one point during the evening Fiona phoned home to her brother Séamus, asking him to come down to the pub. Séamus Sinnott, a fisherman, had just come in and was drained after a hard day's work. He declined the invitation. Later he would wonder whether Fiona was asking him to the pub because something was wrong. Had she something to tell him? Was she looking for help? This phone call is the last contact Fiona Sinnott had with any of her family. All the indications are that she was going about her normal routine that Sunday night.

As the evening wore on, Fiona's arm was still paining her. She decided she would head home to her house, about a quarter of a mile away, close to Ballyhitt Racecourse. One of Fiona's friends asked Seán

Carroll if he would walk Fiona home. He said he would. He phoned his mother to tell her Fiona was not feeling very well and that he was going to walk her home and stay the night in her house. He asked his mother to collect him the next morning at about half past nine. Fiona said goodnight to her friends and took two packets of peanuts with her for the journey home.

Seán Carroll and Fiona Sinnott started going out when Fiona was in her mid-teens. Seán was ten years older than Fiona. He was a 'biker' who had bought his first motorbike when he was seventeen. He had spent time in Australia and in London but had returned to his native Co. Wexford and worked for a time in a local factory. He had married a woman he met while working in London, but that relationship was long over. Fiona was attracted to Seán's lifestyle, and eventually they began dating. Their relationship was to continue on and off for more than three years. On 28 February 1997 Seán and Fiona celebrated the birth of their daughter and moved into a flat in George's Street, Wexford. Although they later split up, they were on good terms and so, when Fiona's friend asked Seán to escort Fiona home that Sunday night, he didn't hesitate.

Fiona Sinnott was the youngest of five children. Caroline, the eldest, was nine years older; in between were Séamus, Norman and Diane. Sadly Caroline passed away in 2017, aged just forty-seven; another tragedy to hit a family that has suffered such heartbreak. Caroline once told me:

> I know Fiona is dead. Fiona was such a curious, nosy person. If she was away by herself she would have to be in contact. She wouldn't be able to stay away. She couldn't bear it. I know something awful happened to her and she was put somewhere. You don't just disappear. Fiona didn't have a penny on her. But there is no clue – nothing.

Fiona Sinnott's two older sisters were passionate about her. Both women campaigned for years for answers. The Sinnott family have carried out numerous searches themselves, including excavations in Co. Wexford, all without success. Diane described her memories of Fiona.

I last spoke to Fiona that Sunday night when she rang from the pub in Broadway. She was looking for my brother Séamus to go down to her. It was a quick conversation. Our nickname for Fiona was 'Fifi'. Fiona and I were very close. She wanted to be a chef; she could make the most delicious pastries. She loved all types of music: she loved the Cranberries; Dolores O'Riordan was her favourite singer. She loved partying: she was a real party-bopper. It's the not knowing what happened to Fiona that is the worst thing.

After saying goodnight to friends, Seán and Fiona left Butler's pub late on the Sunday night. The walk to Fiona's home was a short distance along a quiet road. Seán would later tell how the journey was slow, with Fiona taking her time because of the pain in her chest and arm. He said that along the way they smoked and chatted and ate the peanuts Fiona had bought. Seán said that as soon as they got to the house he asked Fiona if she wanted a cup of coffee. She said she didn't and that she was going to bed. Seán set the alarm on his watch for nine o'clock, having arranged with his mother to collect him. He went to sleep on a sofa.

Seán said he woke at nine the next morning. He went into Fiona's room and woke her; they spoke briefly, and Fiona said she was going to the doctor in Bridgetown. Seán gave her some money and left; his mother had just arrived to collect him and drove him home to Coddstown, two miles west of Broadway. He later told Garda Jim Sullivan that Fiona was awake and in bed when he last saw her. This is the last reported sighting of Fiona.

It was nine days after that reported sighting of Fiona Sinnott that gardaí became aware that she was missing. It was not uncommon for Fiona – like many teenagers – to head off somewhere with friends and perhaps stay with them. On a previous occasion she had travelled to Cork to try to sort out differences in a relationship she was in. Although she hadn't contacted her family or friends by mid-February, alarm bells did not ring. By arrangement, her daughter was being cared for at that time by Seán and his parents. Some of Fiona's family thought she might have travelled as far as Wales to see someone; but it gradually began to dawn on everyone that something was wrong. Fiona didn't phone home to her family in Bridgetown; she didn't phone either of her sisters, not even Diane, whose twenty-first birthday was fast approaching; and she didn't make contact with the Carroll family to collect her daughter to buy her a new outfit for her first birthday. It took nine days for everyone to think that something very bad had happened – nine days during which the person or persons responsible for Fiona's disappearance were able to cover their tracks.

Pat Sinnott reported his daughter missing on 18 February 1998. He walked into the garda station in Kilmore Quay, where he met Garda Jim Sullivan and told him he was concerned about his daughter Fiona. He told him that the last time any of the family had spoken to Fiona was on 8 February. On hearing that she hadn't been seen in over a week, Garda Sullivan phoned the gardaí at Rosslare Pier to alert them also. Word quickly spread that Fiona Sinnott had vanished.

Detectives in Rosslare and Wexford began to examine what was known about Fiona Sinnott's last movements. All her friends and family were interviewed, and people from around Broadway were also questioned. One detective said the condition of Fiona's house was unusual.

The house was spotlessly clean. This was unusual for Fiona. Her family told us that she was not the most house-proud of people; but the house was very clean. And considering that Fiona was complaining of a pain in her chest and arm before she disappeared, we doubted whether she might have cleaned the house. We searched the house for clues, for any sign of anything that might tell us what happened to her, but we found nothing.

The area from where Fiona Sinnott vanished is a quiet townland just west of Ballyhitt Racecourse. Four miles to the north is Rosslare Harbour, with daily ferries to Wales and France. Four miles south is Carnsore Point, the south-eastern tip of Ireland. An extensive land and water search was organised, and the normally quiet area around Broadway became the focus of intense garda scrutiny as every possible witness was tracked down and questioned. When it was established from Seán Carroll that Fiona had intended hitching a lift from Broadway to Bridgetown, all possible witnesses were found and questioned. No one had seen Fiona Sinnott either standing on the road hitching a lift or in a car travelling to Bridgetown. She never attended the doctor that Monday.

Over the following months gardaí carried out extensive searches of land in Co. Wexford, but no trace of Fiona Sinnott was found. One of the areas immediately examined was Lady's Island Lake, a large lake a quarter of a mile south of where Fiona was last seen: it is almost two miles long and a mile wide at its southern base. Only for a thin stretch of land, known as Grogan Burrow, the lake would be part of the sea. The burrow stretches from near Kilmore Quay eastwards to Carnsore Point, and helps to form two large lakes: Tacumshin Lake, which lies two miles from where Fiona disappeared, and Lady's Island Lake, which is just a short walk from the house. Extensive searches were carried out at each lake, with garda divers searching both stretches of water as well as the small islands in the middle of each. One detective recalled that the search of Lady's Island Lake took almost a month.

We actually drained the lake. Not totally dry, but enough to be able to search in just a few feet of water. It was a massive operation. We had already searched the lake and found nothing, but we were conscious that here was a large stretch of water just a short distance from where Fiona disappeared. So we decided we wanted to be as sure as sure could be. What we did was we cut a hole in the sand of the burrow, using a JCB, and drained much of the lake water into the sea. We were able to comb the lake. If anything was there we would have found it. We found nothing.

From the time of the first report of Fiona Sinnott's disappearance staff at the ferry terminal at Rosslare Harbour were alerted and issued with a description. Through Interpol, the police at Fishguard, Pembroke, Cherbourg and Le Havre were also alerted about the disappearance of a nineteen-year-old mother. Through interviews with Fiona's friends the gardaí were able to establish that Fiona had met a Welsh lorry driver in Rosslare Harbour two nights before she disappeared.

On Friday, 6 February 1998 Fiona Sinnott and a number of her friends travelled by minibus from Broadway to the Tuskar House Hotel in Rosslare to attend a pool tournament. During the evening Fiona met a Welsh lorry driver, Gary James. At the end of the night, when the bus was heading back to Broadway, he called out to Fiona and invited her into his lorry. She agreed and got in. Sometime later a man started banging on the lorry, shouting, 'Come out of there, Fiona.' Fiona and Gary peered out of the lorry and saw a man who Fiona recognised. She stayed in the lorry, and the man who was shouting outside eventually walked off.

In March 1998 Gary James made a statement to the gardaí about his recollections of that night. He told them that the next morning he had driven Fiona to Kilrane, a village a mile outside Rosslare Harbour in the direction of Broadway. He had not seen her again.

As the search for Fiona Sinnott continued, her daughter had her first birthday. Though she was missing her mother, the little girl had many loving relatives to help her enjoy her celebration. On her father's side she had her grandparents, Seán and Kitty Carroll, and her aunts Yvonne and Sharon. On her mother's side were her other proud grandparents, Pat and Mary Sinnott, and her aunts Caroline and Diane and uncles Séamus and Norman.

As time wore on, the Sinnott and Carroll families would see less and less of each other. Fiona and Seán's daughter would be cared for by the Carroll family. Later it would be arranged that Pat and Mary

Sinnott would see their granddaughter in a hotel for about an hour every fortnight.

Everyone is proud of Fiona and Seán's daughter. One treasured photograph of her at an art competition, which was published in the *Wexford People* some years after Fiona vanished, shows a little girl having fun with her classmates at primary school: a little girl doing ordinary things; a little girl whose mother never got the chance to see her daughter grow up.

In June 1998 senior detectives held a conference with members of the National Bureau of Criminal Investigation (NBCI) in Dublin. The investigation into the disappearance of Fiona Sinnott had yielded nothing in the way of solid information on her whereabouts. However, as happens when a trawl for any information is undertaken, facts about other alleged criminal acts had come to the attention of gardaí. One detective told me that after a detailed discussion it was decided that six men in south Co. Wexford should be arrested and questioned about suspected drug-dealing in the county.

> It's the kind of stuff that goes on in every rural area. There are local people who know where to source drugs. It's usually small-time stuff, but the fact that this was happening close to where Fiona Sinnott disappeared could not be ignored. So we decided to lift them. We were legitimately questioning them about drugs in Co. Wexford, but you never know who might be keeping another secret.

A team of experienced detectives from the NBCI travelled to Co. Wexford to question the six men, who were arrested at different places and taken to Wexford Garda Station. Among them was a man who was a suspect in Fiona Sinnott's disappearance. He had no previous convictions, but aspects of his character, and certain allegations made against him, had made him a suspect. He was questioned at length over two days by two sets of detectives. The gardaí who took part in the questioning were involved in many of the most important criminal investigations of recent times: two of them were among those who would later question John Crerar, who was subsequently convicted of the murder of Phyllis Murphy in 1979.

These senior gardaí were questioning men believed to be involved in relatively small-scale drug-dealing. One local garda noted:

The irony would have been lost on the boys we were questioning. But we weren't leaving this to chance. One of them might have known something about Fiona, but it was for them to tell us. We couldn't come out and just ask them. They were not being held in connection with Fiona's disappearance. We hoped one of them might know something and come clean. We still wonder if one of them might know something. These fellows would have been aware of covert means of travelling around the countryside, without drawing attention to yourself. If anyone had seen anything that Monday, or any other day, we thought those fellows would have seen it. But we brought in the best interviewers we had, and we got nothing.

One of the young men questioned later died of a drug-related illness. He had known Fiona Sinnott, as they were from the same general area; he would occasionally give her a lift if he was heading her way. One person who knew both believes this man may have known something about Fiona's disappearance.

He seemed to be edgy whenever anybody would mention Fiona. He seemed to take her disappearance quite hard. But it's only afterwards that you start to analyse like this. The poor man was into drugs in a bad way, and that's what cost him his life. Maybe it was the drugs that were causing him to act edgy – perhaps that's a more likely answer. But we just don't know.

Fiona Sinnott's parents, Pat and Mary Sinnott, met in Co. Donegal. Pat was a fisherman from Co. Wexford; Mary lived in the fishing village of Killybegs. Caroline Sinnott smiled as she told me how her father met his wife-to-be in Killybegs.

> Dad met Mam when he was working in Donegal. His brother met one of Mam's sisters, and they're married now as well – two Wexford brothers married to two Donegal sisters. Mam and Dad went on their honeymoon to Dublin, and they settled here in Wexford. They had five children and then a number of grandchildren, but with Fiona's disappearance were left missing one of their own children and it really hurt them. When the monument for missing people was unveiled in Kilkenny, we all went up.

Pat Sinnott died in 2004 without ever knowing what happened to his youngest daughter. The following year six people were arrested in Co. Wexford and questioned about Fiona's case. The three men and three women were all questioned at garda stations in the county. The Sinnott family hoped there might finally be a breakthrough, but within days all those arrested had been released without charge.

In June 2017 the Sinnott family was hit with further tragedy when Caroline Sinnott, Fiona's eldest sister, died in Wales where she had been living. Caroline is now laid to rest in Co. Wexford with her father. The rest of the Sinnott family desperately want to find Fiona to lay her to rest with her father and sister.

As part of their campaign for answers, the Sinnotts have conducted two searches of their own at locations in south Co. Wexford. In April 2015 the garden of a cottage at Kilrane near Rosslare was searched after information was obtained linking a suspect in the case to the property in 1998. Two sniffer dogs were deployed by Joe Blake of the group Trace Missing Persons Ireland. A septic tank was searched by Fiona's uncle Gerry, and sections of land were excavated to a depth of six feet, but despite a six-week search nothing was found.

Then, in August 2018, a one-day search was conducted at a property at Drinagh, closer to Wexford town. Foundations of a property had been laid in early 1998, and again there was information that a suspect in the case had links to the property at that time. Sonar equipment was brought into the kitchen of the house and although an anomaly was detected in the flooring, it was not believed to be a body. A path directly outside the kitchen was also examined, but nothing was found.

A year after the disappearance of Fiona Sinnott, suspected serial killer Robert Howard was found to be living in Co. Wexford. Detectives have investigated Howard's movements and have tried to trace where he was when a number of women disappeared in Leinster in the 1990s. However, it appears to be pure coincidence that Howard was living close to where Fiona Sinnott had lived the year before. Gardaí established Howard was most likely living in England at the time of Fiona's disappearance, and there is no evidence that he travelled to Co. Wexford before he was identified by gardaí in the county in 1999. By the time Howard was detected in Wexford he was suspected of murdering a teenage girl in Co. Tyrone in 1994. He also had convictions for rape and sexual assault, and his victims included young children and an elderly woman.

What is now clear is that in 1999 Robert Howard arrived in Barntown, Co. Wexford, 10 miles north of where Fiona Sinnott was last seen, having travelled to Rosslare by ferry from Britain with his partner and other family members. Some detectives believed he was visiting a convicted paedophile who was renting a property in the area. By 1999 Howard had been run out of Northern Ireland by people who suspected he had murdered fifteen-year-old Arlene Arkinson. Howard had also felt the heat of garda attention in Dublin and Monaghan, as well as police forces in Glasgow and London, and he was frequently changing his address and travelling by ferry between Ireland and Britain.

There was no sex offenders register in place in Ireland when Robert Howard was at large. Frustratingly, Howard was free to move about as often as he wished. When gardaí in Co. Wexford became aware that this suspected serial killer was in the area in 1999, they paid him a visit. They informed Howard that they knew who he was and that they would be monitoring his movements. Robert Howard left Ireland a short time afterwards, returning to England, where two years later he abducted and murdered fourteen-year-old Hannah Williams in London. Her body was found at a cement works in Kent the following year. Howard died in prison in 2015. Though the extent of Robert Howard's crimes continue to be examined by gardaí, the PSNI and police in Britain, it appears that he was not in Co. Wexford at the time of Fiona Sinnott's disappearance.

In June 1998, four months after Fiona Sinnott's disappearance, the man who is alleged to have assaulted her on a number of occasions met with gardaí. During their discussion this man, who is from south Co. Wexford, was asked directly whether he knew anything about Fiona's disappearance. He replied that he 'couldn't talk about it'. One detective asked him, 'Why can't you talk to us about Fiona?'

'I've nothing to say,' he replied.

More questions met with a similar reply. 'Have you anything to do with Fiona's disappearance?'

'I've nothing to say.'

'It would be better to come clean about this …'

'Lads, I can't talk about it.'

'Why can't you talk about it?'

'I've nothing to say … I've nothing to say.'

'Are you concerned about her disappearance?'

'I've nothing to say.'

One line of enquiry the gardaí believe may still be a valid one is that the person responsible for Fiona Sinnott's disappearance may have had assistance from one or more other people. It has long been wondered whether the person responsible might have summoned help after the crime had been committed, and perhaps there is someone who got caught up in something they didn't realise was a crime until it was too late. Perhaps someone was asked to help move Fiona from one place to another, or to hide certain evidence, or to provide an alibi.

As part of this line of enquiry the gardaí identified a number of people living in Co. Wexford who it was felt might have something to hide. These people denied any involvement when they were questioned. Detectives dug up a septic tank on private land during this stage of the investigation, and part of the foundations of a house were also searched, but nothing was found. These searches were separate to the ones conducted by the Sinnott family in later years.

Caroline Sinnott told me that she and the rest of the family think that more than one person may know the secret of what happened to Fiona.

> We believe we know the person who might be responsible for the disappearance of Fiona. We've often wondered if this person might have had assistance from another person in south Co. Wexford. This other person might have been brought into it even after Fiona had been abducted or hurt. Someone knows something; someone has a guilty conscience. There are people in the county of Wexford who know what happened to our sister.

In the weeks before Fiona Sinnott went missing she confided in one person that she wanted to change aspects of her life and essentially to take more responsibility for herself and her baby. However, there was nothing to suggest that she was under any threat from anyone. Her only recent trip to the doctor was for a bout of tonsillitis the month before she disappeared. A farmer in the area later came forward to say that he saw Fiona holding her arm and looking distressed on the weekend she disappeared. Whatever was causing the pain in her arm as described by this witness, and by Fiona's friends in the pub that fateful night, has never been established. Had she been assaulted? Was it some kind of accidental injury she had suffered? Has it anything to do with her disappearance?

The disappearance of Fiona Sinnott is only one of a number of upsetting incidents to occur in the general area of south Co. Wexford. In June 2001, 35-year-old Alan Wright from Tomhaggard, four miles from where Fiona Sinnott disappeared, died after taking a heroin overdose. He had travelled with two friends to Crumlin in Dublin, where they bought heroin; he died as they were driving back to Co.

Wexford. The death traumatised his family and shocked the local community, unused to such distressing events. Coupled with the sinister disappearance of Fiona Sinnott, this area has suffered greatly in recent years.

One indication that certain people in south Co. Wexford have information about Fiona's whereabouts is a series of unexplained attacks on a memorial plaque, marking what would have been Fiona's thirtieth birthday, which was stolen in September 2008. The plaque contained a tribute to Fiona from her family that read: 'We cannot get over losing you no matter how we try. We will always keep you in our hearts until the day we die.' The plaque was placed on an old wall at Broadway, close to Butler's pub, and was to be officially unveiled the following day. However, when Fiona's family arrived early the next day they found the plaque had been removed from the wall and taken away. Although shocked and saddened, the family was grateful that Hughes Memorials were able to provide a replacement plaque and the ceremony went ahead, with former garda diver Tosh Lavery helping to unveil the replacement plaque, which was blessed by local priest Fr Brendan Nolan.

A large group of local people turned out to support Mary Sinnott, and her remaining children Caroline, Séamus, Norman and Diane, at the unveiling, but it was clear that someone local had stolen the original plaque. The obvious question was why? Was it someone whose conscience was troubled, who didn't want to be reminded of what they knew about Fiona's case?

Gardaí conducted house-to-house enquiries but did not find the original plaque, and did not identify who the thief was. Their investigations took another turn when, some months later, the replacement plaque was pulled from the wall. Considerable force would have been necessary to remove the second plaque in Broadway, but someone had used their bare hands, or some device, to destroy the only public memorial to a missing local woman. Again, whoever was responsible was never identified.

Undeterred, the Sinnott family commissioned a third plaque in 2018 to mark what would have been Fiona's fortieth birthday. This time the family put the plaque at a location at Kilmore Quay closer to the family home, rather than Broadway. This third plaque was not subsequently attacked or damaged. In February 2018 the Sinnotts held a special mass in Kilmore Quay marking the twentieth anniversary of Fiona's disappearance. All gathered reflected on the sad fact that Fiona is now missing longer than she was alive. All those present knew the answer to Fiona's disappearance lay somewhere local.

At Wexford Garda Station filing cabinets are filled to the brim with witness statements, questionnaires and 'job-sheets' that the investigation into Fiona Sinnott's disappearance has generated. A job-sheet is what is used when a piece of information has to be followed up to establish whether it might or might not be true. Some enquiries have involved liaison with police in Wales, England and France. The possibility that Fiona's abductor might have taken her by car or lorry on the ferry from Rosslare has not been ignored, and Interpol was issued with Fiona's description almost as soon as she was reported missing. However, frustratingly, because she was not reported missing until nine days after she was last seen, detectives fear that the trail had grown cold by then.

Gardaí also spoke to a married man from Co. Wexford who was rumoured to be romantically linked with Fiona. This man, a self-employed businessman, emphatically denied the rumour. The interest of gardaí was sparked when it was learnt that the man had travelled by ferry to Britain at about the time of Fiona's disappearance, but this line of enquiry led nowhere.

The loss of Fiona Sinnott is not the first misfortune to be visited on the Sinnott family. Fiona's father, Paddy was one of fourteen children. One of his brothers, Fintan, drowned in 1977 aged twenty-one, while responding to an emergency call. In a terrible irony, it turned out to be a false alarm; but Fintan, who had rushed to give whatever assistance he could, drowned in the first few moments. The loss of Fintan was something the Sinnott family could understand in a certain way and eventually come to terms with; but the loss of nineteen-year-old Fiona is an agonising mystery that has devastated the family. There are no answers, no body, nobody brought to justice and no explanation.

In 2017 a cold-case review of Fiona's disappearance led to one new line of enquiry being publicised. Gardaí were now seeking information about four unidentified people seen locally between midnight and 12.30 a.m. on the night Fiona walked back to her home with Seán Carroll. A witness reported seeing a man and woman having a dispute and two other men, in their late teens or early twenties, standing nearby. Those four people have never been identified, and detectives continue to appeal to them to come forward.

In 2017, as part of a full cold-case review, Fiona's rented house was forensically re-examined. Advances in forensic science now allow for crime-scene blood stains or other evidence to be detected, even decades later. Although the fresh examination did not immediately lead to any breakthrough, detectives believe that developments in forensics may yet help identify a crime scene. Fiona's disappearance continues to be actively investigated by Wexford gardaí.

In the years since Fiona disappeared the Sinnotts' hopes have been raised by the discovery of a number of bodies in Co. Wexford, but on each occasion it was soon established that each body was not Fiona. In January 2007 a woman walking her dog spotted skeletal remains at Kaats Strand, north of Wexford town. At low tide, and due to natural erosion at the strand, parts of a skeleton had become visible in the black mud. When the body was later analysed it was established the body was female, and naturally Fiona Sinnott and many other missing women were immediately considered as a possible match. However, further forensic testing found that the body was around 200 years old. The best theory is that the woman drowned in the nearby river Slaney and over decades her body was covered over by mud, as the tide ebbed and flowed. The case demonstrated how a body could rest beneath silt and mud for centuries before being found.

More recently, the body of a woman was found in a ditch near Ferns in January 2019. Investigations established the body was most likely that of an Italian woman who had been spotted in Co. Wexford about a year before. It's thought the body may have been in the ditch for close to a year before it was found. Once again the discovery was made by someone out walking their dog, and once again it illustrates two things: bodies can lie above ground without being discovered for months and sometimes years, but most bodies left above ground will eventually be found.

Fiona Sinnott was the second-last woman to disappear in Leinster in the 1990s. Seven months after she vanished, garda authorities decided to set up a special investigation to see if six missing women cases might be linked. Fiona's is the only such disappearance in the Co. Wexford area; the closest other missing woman case is 20 miles away in Waterford city, where Imelda Keenan disappeared from her home in January 1994. Despite the best efforts of the gardaí, no trace of Imelda has been found. She was last seen shortly after leaving her home in William Street, Waterford. Though her details were also privately analysed by detectives from Operation Trace, there was no firm evidence that she might have been the victim of a crime. While her disappearance is no less painful for her family, from an investigative point of view gardaí do not believe that Imelda Keenan's disappearance is linked to Fiona Sinnott's, and indeed they don't believe Fiona's disappearance is related to any of the other missing women cases. In Fiona's case there was a clear history of violence against her by one person who was known to her, and this is where a degree of suspicion still lies.

In December 2016 Diane Sinnott spoke publicly at the National Missing Persons Day event. The Sinnotts have attended this annual event every year since it was established in 2013, travelling from the south-east corner of the country to Dublin. Diane said the gathering of families of missing people was a great support to her mother Mary.

It's the one time a year that she can talk to people who are on the same emotional rollercoaster as her, people who know exactly how she feels, other people who are living the same nightmare.

Diane outlined how the family had physically and emotionally done everything they could to find Fiona, and she pledged they would continue to do so.

> We will never give up hope that one day our phone will ring with the words we have waited for all this time – 'we have found Fiona'. Her life has to account for something. It's too much to expect families to wait this long for answers. Stress has a way of manifesting itself physically in the body and we believe our dad died of a broken heart not knowing where Fiona was.

Operation Trace was unable to establish any links between Fiona Sinnott and any of the other missing women, or with any known convicted offenders who might have attacked women. Long ago Caroline Sinnott told me the answer in Fiona's case was different.

> We don't think that there's a link between Fiona and any of the other missing women. We don't think that a serial killer was hanging around Bridgetown. But you don't just disappear. We're fed up with bits and pieces. We'd like to see Fiona found and rested.

Caroline recounted in clear detail an evening some years before Fiona disappeared that she said should make everybody think.

> I remember looking at the news about when Jo Jo Dullard disappeared, and we were all talking about it and saying just how terrible that must be for her family. But sure you don't think much about it afterwards. Then it hit our doorstep.

CHAPTER 7

DEIRDRE JACOB

F ive months after the disappearance of Fiona Sinnott, another young woman went missing in Leinster. The circumstances of Deirdre Jacob's disappearance are deeply disturbing. Deirdre was eighteen years old when she vanished in broad daylight from the gate of her home at Roseberry in Newbridge, Co. Kildare, on Tuesday, 28 July 1998. This time the gardaí response was immediate. Within hours a massive search was under way; but no sign of the missing teenager was found. In the more than two decades since that day, Deirdre's parents, Michael and Bernadette, have campaigned vigorously for any information in relation to her disappearance. For twenty years Deirdre was classified by gardaí as a missing person, but in August 2018 detectives announced that, following a review of the case, the disappearance of Deirdre Jacob was now the subject of a murder investigation.

It was a dry summer's afternoon on 28 July 1998 in the bustling Co. Kildare town of Newbridge. Children were enjoying the long school holidays. A general feeling of well-being from the continuing good fortune of Kildare footballers in the Leinster championship was evident in the conversations that would have been heard around the town. But in total contrast to this almost perfect summer scene, something awful was about to happen to an eighteen-year-old woman that would ensure the people of Newbridge and beyond would forever remember this day with shock and sadness.

Deirdre Jacob was enjoying her summer holidays at home with her parents and younger sister. She had recently completed her first year of college in London. Deirdre wanted to be a teacher, and was studying at St Mary's College, Strawberry Hill, in London along with a large contingent of Irish students. She had been home to Newbridge earlier in the year doing a work placement, teaching at the primary school where she herself had studied. But now Deirdre had the summer to relax, catch up with friends and family, and prepare for the next year's study in London. Always active, she was also going to take up a part-time job in Newbridge during August.

Deirdre knew Newbridge like the back of her hand. She grew up in the family home at Roseberry, within walking distance of town. Her parents were both Kildare people. Deirdre had walked or cycled the route from her home into Newbridge hundreds of times. She was a fast walker with a long stride. That Tuesday afternoon she had errands to run in town so she set off for Newbridge around midday. Her parents had already left for work.

We know Deirdre made it into town because she spoke with her grandmother there. Four business premises also captured her on CCTV. While no one saw Deirdre walk into town, seven witnesses would later see her walk towards her home that afternoon, including one who saw her close to the gate of her home at around 3 p.m. That was the last reported sighting of Deirdre Jacob.

On the weekend before she vanished Deirdre stayed with two friends in Kingscourt, Co. Cavan. She returned home on the Monday evening and was in the best of spirits. She had a lie-in on that Tuesday morning but eventually got up because she had things to do. She needed to post money to a friend in London as a deposit to secure accommodation for second year of college. She also wanted to see her grandmother in the town.

The hours and minutes before Deirdre disappeared did not betray anything out of the ordinary. If she was being watched or stalked it was not immediately apparent on the CCTV footage that gardaí would later analyse. However, the current murder investigation does hold

Mother of two Antoinette Smith was abducted and murdered in July 1987. (*Courtesy of Lisa and Rachel Smith*)

Marie Kilmartin was abducted and murdered in December 1993. (*Courtesy of Marie's daughter Áine*)

Annie McCarrick, who vanished in March 1993. (*Courtesy of Nancy McCarrick*)

Annie with
her mother
Nancy. (*Courtesy
of Nancy
McCarrick*)

Annie enjoying the
St Patrick's Day parade in
Dublin, one week before she
was murdered. (*Courtesy of
Nancy McCarrick*)

Jo Jo Dullard, who was abducted and murdered in November 1995. (*Courtesy of the Dullard family*)

Jo Jo in her bedroom in Callan. (*Courtesy of the Dullard family*)

Jo Jo (centre) with her sisters Mary (far left), Nora (second from right) and Kathleen (far right) and three nieces. (*Courtesy of the Dullard family*)

Fiona Pender was seven months pregnant when she was murdered in August 1996. (*Courtesy of the Pender family*)

Fiona on a visit to Buckingham Palace in London. (*Courtesy of the Pender family*)

Fiona worked as a model for a company in Tullamore. (*Courtesy of the Pender family*)

Ciara Breen was seventeen when she was murdered in February 1997. (*Courtesy of Tom Conachy*)

Fiona Sinnott was nineteen when she disappeared in February 1998. (*Courtesy of the Sinnott family*)

Fiona was the mother of a baby girl. (*Courtesy of the Sinnott family*)

Deirdre Jacob was eighteen when she disappeared from the front gate of her home in July 1998. (*Courtesy of the Jacob family*)

Eva Brennan vanished in south Dublin in July 1993. (*Courtesy of the Brennan family*)

Imelda Keenan was twenty-two when she vanished in Waterford city in January 1994. (*Courtesy of the Keenan family*)

Mary Boyle (left) with her brother Patrick and twin sister Ann, pictured shortly before her disappearance in March 1977. (*Courtesy of the Boyle family*)

Mary playing outside her grandparent's home in Cashelard, near Ballyshannon, in July 1975. (*Courtesy of the Boyle family*)

Exact replicas of the cardigan and wellington boots worn by six-year-old Mary Boyle on the day she disappeared. (*Courtesy of An Garda Síochána*)

Philip Cairns, who was abducted near his home in Dublin in October 1986. (*Courtesy of the Cairns family*)

Images taken in 2019 of Philip Cairns' schoolbag, which was left in a laneway one week after the schoolboy disappeared. (*Courtesy of An Garda Síochána*)

Marioara Rostas was eighteen when she was taken from a Dublin street, shot dead, and her body buried in a forest. (*Courtesy of the Rostas family*)

Marioara's brother, Dumitru Jnr, and her father, Dumitru Snr, visit the location in Co. Wicklow where her body lay concealed for four years. (*Courtesy of An Garda Síochána*)

One of the garda team searching the forest in 2012 for Marioara's body. (*Courtesy of An Garda Síochána*)

out hope that whoever murdered Deirdre may have been captured on CCTV that afternoon in Newbridge. Only a few seconds of that footage has ever been released but there is a lot more, only seen by detectives until now, which has been digitally enhanced in recent years. Time will tell if that footage holds an answer.

At 2.20 p.m. that afternoon Deirdre entered the AIB on Main Street in Newbridge where she collected a bank draft. She then walked the short distance across the road to the post office and posted the draft to her friend in London. Both the bank and the post office were busy but the queues moved quickly. Deirdre came out of the post office and by chance met an old school friend. They had a quick chat at the traffic lights and then the two women went their separate ways. Deirdre was carrying her black CAT bag on her right shoulder. The last CCTV footage captured Deirdre walking down past the Irish Permanent bank in the direction of her home. It was shortly after 2.30 p.m. Within half an hour Deirdre Jacob would be abducted.

Because she knew Newbridge so well, Deirdre might have taken any one of a number of routes to get back onto the Barretstown Road as she headed home. She could have walked straight down the main street and then turned left onto Canning Place, which runs parallel to the river Liffey. Alternatively she could have taken one of a number of zigzag routes, all roughly the same distance, and any one of them would have brought her out onto the road towards home with the river Liffey to her right. Deirdre's ultimate journey would bring her past Newbridge College, and onto the Barretstown Road, with her home a ten-minute walk from there.

No witness ever came forward to say they had seen Deirdre heading down the main street for the bridge and turning left, or going through any of the side roads off Main Street and then linking up with the road for home. Did the killer spot Deirdre as she walked out of Newbridge and follow her? There is no proof of this, but it is a natural question.

As Deirdre walked the ten minutes or so along the winding Barretstown Road, the first five people to see her knew who she was. The familiarity of a good community meant those witnesses either knew her by name or knew she was one of the 'Jacob girls'. A cyclist heading into Newbridge passed Deirdre as she headed out towards home. Next, two people chatting on the footpath exchanged pleasantries with Deirdre as she walked past them. A man doing renovation work upstairs in his home looked out the window and saw Deirdre pass him by, heading up left towards her home. Deirdre was now just a few minutes from her house.

At a point on the Barretstown Road the housing developments on Deirdre's left gave way to countryside. At a spot known as the bog cross the footpath on this side of the road ended, and Deirdre crossed over to the other side of the road. There was no footpath on that side either, but it was easier to navigate and Deirdre was now facing the traffic as she walked on. Three people, up a side road to the left, saw Deirdre walking past the bog cross. From that point on, the road curves and bends. Back in July 1998 there were some individual houses on both sides of the road, but today there are many more along this stretch of the Barretstown Road.

The last few moments of Deirdre's walk took place along a relatively busy but winding country road. One motorist heading into Newbridge drove by Deirdre as she approached her house. This woman was the second-last witness to see Deirdre. She didn't know Deirdre but would later recall that the young woman she saw matched her description.

Deirdre Jacob was five feet three inches in height and a slim build. She had grey-green eyes and dark hair. That day she wore a navy Nike top, blue jeans and blue Nike runners. And as she walked closer to home she still had her CAT bag on her right shoulder.

The last person to see Deirdre was a young woman who was a passenger in a car heading along the Barretstown Road towards Newbridge. Moments earlier Deirdre would have crossed back over the road, heading towards the entrance to her home. Knowing her habits her family say she would have done this directly outside her house. The gate of the Jacob home is set in off the road. As the passenger in the car travelled along she looked to her right and saw a young woman standing at the gate of the Jacob home. The sighting lasted just a few seconds, and would only become significant once Deirdre was reported missing. This is the last sighting of Deirdre; she is just a few feet from the gate of her home. She was never seen again.

There are two possibilities: the murder of Deirdre Jacob was either opportunistic or it involved a degree of planning. If it was opportunistic it is still possible that the killer arrived on the scene shortly after Deirdre, or was in the area as she arrived near her home. If the murder involved some degree of planning, Deirdre was followed out of Newbridge, or the killer lay in wait, knowing she would be travelling back out the Barretstown Road after going to Newbridge. One thing is sure: the attack on Deirdre was committed by a stranger who used the large hedgerows and other natural covering on the Barretstown Road to commit an abduction in broad daylight.

When the scene was later examined, there was no sign of a struggle at the gate of the Jacob home, nothing to indicate the horror that had unfolded that afternoon. There were no belongings dropped on the ground. Deirdre's CAT bag was never located.

When gardaí later canvassed witnesses, there was nothing to indicate precisely what had happened. There was no scream, no screeching of brakes, no sound of the slamming of a car or van door – nothing to suggest that a would-be killer had abducted Deirdre.

When Deirdre's parents arrived home later and found their daughter wasn't there, they were immediately concerned. Deirdre was the kind of teenager who always let her family know where she was. She was dependable in her movements. Heading off somewhere without telling someone just wasn't Deirdre. She didn't have a mobile phone and would have said in advance if she was planning to go somewhere. Michael and Bernadette rang the landlines of Deirdre's friends but none had seen her. Very quickly her parents contacted gardaí.

A search began within hours of Deirdre's disappearance. The search was exhaustive, with roads, lanes, hedges, fields, bogs, rivers and ponds subjected to a thorough examination.

As gardaí began a trawl of CCTV in Newbridge they and Deirdre's family made contact with all her friends, both in Ireland and in London. Nobody had heard from her. As hours became days it was clear her bank account had not been touched. Huge tracts of land were searched across Co. Kildare. While the disappearance was firstly classified as a missing person, detectives were conscious that Deirdre might have been abducted. They sought to establish the whereabouts of known violent men who had either served prison sentences or who were on bail. But nothing jumped out, no specific lead.

Gardaí were of course conscious that Jo Jo Dullard had been abducted in south Co. Kildare over two and a half years earlier. That crime had taken place in darkness, while Jo Jo was hitchhiking. Yet Deirdre had disappeared in broad daylight and at the gate of her home. Detectives also considered an unsolved abduction and murder when, nineteen years earlier, 23-year-old Phyllis Murphy had last been seen alive at a bus stop in Newbridge just before Christmas 1979. Her body was found hidden four weeks later in the Wicklow Gap. By July 1998 her killer had not been brought to justice. And the disappearance of Annie McCarrick in March 1993 was also unsolved. She had disappeared in the middle of the day, last seen on a bus to Enniskerry, Co. Wicklow. A question already being asked before Deirdre Jacob disappeared was now being openly discussed. Could any of these disappearances be linked?

Seven days after Deirdre disappeared, a garda reconstruction of her last known movements was shown on RTÉ news. A friend of Deirdre's played the role of Deirdre and recreated her journey into the bank and post office and then out the Barretstown Road. Deirdre's father Michael appealed for anyone with information to come forward. It was one of numerous appeals the Jacobs would make over the following decades.

There were two routes Deirdre's attacker could have taken after committing the crime. He could have driven back towards Newbridge, or he could have continued out on the Barretstown Road – a more likely scenario, given the remote locations the road quickly enters. Deirdre's home is on the side of the road where traffic heads out of

Newbridge. It would have been more plausible for the attacker to have driven out on that road rather than to try and cross over traffic and head back towards a more populated area. If the attacker did drive further away from Newbridge, he would have passed Newbridge Golf Club on the left and arrived at a difficult turn merging with traffic at a junction on the Thomastown Road. The car or van would have had to stop at this point and then turn onto a road, which to the west brings you towards Kilmeague and Robertstown, and to the east to the N7 Dublin–Limerick road. The attacker could have driven farther east through Naas and into any of the back roads of Co. Wicklow. Every conceivable escape route continues to be analysed by gardaí.

Frustratingly, the garda investigation would be sidetracked by a false sighting of Deirdre by a man who made anonymous phone calls and wrote letters to newspapers and radio stations claiming to have given a woman matching Deirdre's description a lift from Co. Kildare to Carrickmacross in Co. Monaghan on the day she disappeared. This man wasted months of garda time as they tried to establish who he was, and if the information was true. The Jacob family also publicly appealed to the man to come forward with more information. Michael and Bernadette went to Co. Monaghan to see if Deirdre might have travelled there and did an interview on local radio, appealing for help. The fact that Carrickmacross was only 10 miles from Kingscourt where Deirdre had stayed with friends the weekend before her disappearance made everyone hopeful that the caller was genuine. But sadly it was all a hoax. The man was eventually identified by gardaí and arrested on suspicion of wasting garda time. But no charges were brought: this man had suffered the loss of his young daughter in a horrific road accident and detectives did not believe he had concocted the story out of malice. But the whole episode was a drain on resources and ultimately hampered the search for Deirdre.

For twenty years Deirdre's case was classified as that of a missing person. Her case was included in the list of cases investigated by Operation Trace, which was set up by gardaí in late 1998 to try and establish if any of the cases of women missing in Leinster might be linked. Indeed, Deirdre's disappearance, and the shocking nature of it, was the catalyst for the garda initiative to be put in place. In hindsight such an initiative should have been in place long before that. Many other disappearances prior to Deirdre's might have been linked.

In 2018 detectives in Kildare began re-examining the entirety of the Deirdre Jacob file. A number of gardaí were involved in what would eventually become a full murder investigation. Brian Sutton was the newly appointed chief superintendent in the district. He had been involved in a recent reinvestigation into the disappearance of thirteen-year old Philip Cairns, who vanished while walking to school in south Dublin in 1986. Although that cold-case review had not led to the solving of the case, it had unearthed new witnesses and new information. Sutton's arrival in Co. Kildare coincidentally came in the aftermath of Michael and Bernie Jacob deciding that they needed to make public their frustration at the lack of action in the case. At the National Missing Persons Day event in Dublin in December 2017 Michael Jacob made an impromptu speech, praising the memorial event they were attending but asking a pertinent question in relation to all missing persons cases. Directly addressing both a deputy garda commissioner and the Minister for Justice Charlie Flanagan – who were attending the event – Michael highlighted the fact that little progress was being made in a large number of long-term missing persons cases, and in some cases no progress at all. 'Is that good enough?' he asked.

In gathering every piece of information about Deirdre's case, Brian Sutton spoke with retired Assistant Commissioner Tony Hickey about the work he and his Operation Trace team had done. He also spoke with Christy Mangan who, as former head of the Garda Cold Case Unit, had overseen a complete examination of Deirdre's case. A detective in Kildare station was appointed senior investigating officer and began assembling a team of gardaí to collate and chart every piece of information on the twenty-year investigation. Garda John Butler was put in charge of the newly established incident room. Inspector Séamus Rothwell, who had worked on the case from day one of the investigation, and had been the point of contact for the Jacob family for many years, informed the family that Deirdre's case was being completely re-examined.

In July 2018, to mark the twentieth anniversary of Deirdre's disappearance, Michael and Bernadette made another public appeal, which led to new information. Added into the wealth of information already collated, gardaí now had an important decision to make. The twenty-year investigation was extensive. Over 2,500 witness statements had been taken during that time. Over 3,200 lines of enquiry had been followed up. Every 'proof of life' enquiry that had been conducted by detectives in Ireland and beyond had turned up negative. It was now considered inconceivable that Deirdre had chosen to go missing. All possible sightings of a woman matching Deirdre's description had been followed through to the end, and, added to all the information gardaí now had about the movements of people in Newbridge in July 1998, there was no credible view other than that someone had caused harm to Deirdre. Detectives were now prepared to officially reclassify Deirdre Jacob's case as a murder investigation. A full incident room was set up. If ever gardaí identified a suspect, they could arrest him on suspicion of murder.

As detectives pursue the murder investigation they have liaised with police forces in many other countries to find people who were in Newbridge that day in July 1998. Witnesses are being tracked down across the world. The CCTV footage from various business premises that has been recently enhanced is helping with this work.

Michael and Bernadette Jacob still live in the family home in Newbridge. They moved into their house just before Christmas 1976. Deirdre was born three years later. Deirdre is now missing longer than she was alive. Her loss has affected her family and friends and the wider community in both visible and invisible ways. Deirdre was a normal, happy teenager, home for the summer, with a bright future ahead of her, walking in broad daylight in her home town. And somehow, a killer crossed her path. Anyone with information on Deirdre's case is urged to contact gardaí at the incident room in Kildare station at 045 521222.

CHAPTER 8

OPERATION TRACE

Within days of the disappearance of Deirdre Jacob, senior gardaí were once again considering that there might be a serial killer targeting women in Ireland. This had been debated previously; from the disappearance of Annie McCarrick in March 1993, to the case of Fiona Sinnott in February 1998, at least five women had been abducted either from the roadside or from their homes at various places in Leinster. Two other cases of women who had vanished in the 1990s might be suspicious: Eva Brennan had disappeared in Dublin in July 1993, and Imelda Keenan vanished in Waterford in 1994.

Also on the minds of detectives were three murder cases, where women had been abducted, murdered and their bodies concealed: those cases were the unsolved murders of Antoinette Smith, Patricia Doherty and Marie Kilmartin. With the disappearance of eighteen-year-old Deirdre Jacob, that made eleven cases in eleven years: women who were either missing or murdered. While some of the cases were believed to be isolated events, others appeared to be random incidents, which might involve the same attacker. A number of senior detectives realised that something had to be done.

By the end of 1998 a specialist six-member garda team had been hand-picked in an attempt to establish whether any of the cases were linked. For the first time, a special computer system was developed to cross-reference information on thousands of convicted sex offenders. The investigation would bring gardaí into contact with some of the country's most violent men. At the back of everyone's mind was one question: was there evidence to suggest a serial killer was active?

In the immediate aftermath of Deirdre Jacob's disappearance, detectives wondered if there could be a link with the case of Jo Jo Dullard, the 21-year-old woman who was abducted and murdered in November 1995 and who was last seen in Moone, Co. Kildare – 15 miles from Newbridge. The close proximity of the disappearances of two young women, both last seen on a roadside in Co. Kildare, was something that could not be ignored. Though the two women disappeared at different times of day – Jo Jo Dullard was abducted as she hitched a lift at around midnight, while Deirdre Jacob disappeared in broad daylight at the gate of her home – detectives were privately wondering whether the same person might be responsible. Had the abductor and murderer of Jo Jo Dullard changed his modus operandi? Was the disappearance of Deirdre Jacob the work of the same opportunistic attacker? Or was there no link between the cases at all? Was there more than one random attacker roaming the roads of Co. Kildare and beyond?

Certainly, gardaí had always feared that whoever took the life of Jo Jo Dullard would strike again. Indeed some detectives wondered if the killer might have struck in previous years, before he murdered Jo Jo. Whoever was responsible for the abduction and murder of Annie McCarrick in the Wicklow Mountains in March 1993 had never been caught. Could the person who killed Annie have killed Jo Jo too? Furthermore, could they be responsible for other abductions and murders?

Gardaí also thought of the three cases of women murdered between 1987 and 1993, and their bodies concealed, only to be found months later. The murder of Antoinette Smith, last seen getting out of a taxi in

Rathfarnham in July 1987, seemed to be a random and opportunistic crime. There was also the unsolved murder of another mother of two, Patricia Doherty from Tallaght in south Co. Dublin, last seen alive in December 1991; her body was found in June 1992, also buried in the Wicklow Mountains. And while there was evidence to suggest that another woman, Marie Kilmartin, was lured from her Port Laoise home in December 1993 by someone who may have known her, whoever strangled her and put her body in a bog drain many miles away had never been caught.

Then there were the cases of three missing women in each of which individual suspects had been identified, but the question had to be asked – what if those suspects were not the people responsible? Though it was considered unlikely, what if a serial attacker was responsible for murdering Fiona Pender from Tullamore in August 1996, Ciara Breen from Dundalk in February 1997 and Fiona Sinnott from Co. Wexford in February 1998? What about missing Dublin woman Eva Brennan, who disappeared in July 1993, four months after Annie McCarrick was murdered. Was she a forgotten victim of a random attacker? There was also the case of Imelda Keenan, who had vanished from Waterford city in January 1994. Despite extensive searches, by autumn 1998 there was still no sign of the 22-year-old.

At a meeting in the Garda College in Templemore in August 1998, one garda superintendent, who was approaching retirement, took a senior officer aside and said to him:

> I'm not the type to be alarmist, but we have to consider there might be a person or persons actively targeting women. If there is a serial killer out there, we have to find him, and also, we have to let him know we're here. Remember Shaw and Evans.

This was a reference to two Englishmen who in 1976 abducted and murdered two women at random, one in Co. Wicklow and the other in Co. Mayo. The senior garda said he would bring the concerns to the attention of the Garda Commissioner as a matter of urgency. So it was that, twenty years after the last serial killers to terrorise Ireland were put behind bars for the rest of their lives, gardaí were once again faced with the distinct possibility that a serial killer or killers might be at large in Ireland.

Detectives privately knew that the disappearances of Annie McCarrick and Jo Jo Dullard would fit the profile of random attackers. But what about the other missing women? A top-level conference was held at which it was decided that six specific cases of missing women, all feared to have been the victims of violent abduction, should be cross-referenced to see if there were any similarities.

In September 1998, less than two months after the disappearance of Deirdre Jacob, Commissioner Pat Byrne announced the establishment of a special garda operation to investigate the cases of six missing women. Operation Trace would be under the command of Assistant Commissioner Tony Hickey from the Garda Eastern Region, from where the missing women had vanished. Hickey had previously directed the team investigating the murder of journalist Veronica Guerin and was still working on that case when he hand-picked a team of detectives. The task of the operation was to trace, review and collate the evidence around the disappearances of Annie McCarrick, Jo Jo Dullard, Fiona Pender, Ciara Breen, Fiona Sinnott and Deirdre Jacob.

Of paramount importance to the operation was the setting up of a computer system that could analyse and cross-reference every scrap of information, every suggestion and innuendo about each case. Detectives were hoping to find a common name of a suspect in at least two of the cases, someone who was in the area at the time of two disappearances but had seemed to be in the clear; or perhaps a vehicle spotted in the area of two or more of the disappearances. As the establishment of Operation Trace was announced, there was a degree of optimism among gardaí that something positive was about to emerge.

Assistant Commissioner Hickey selected an experienced superintendent to oversee the day-to-day running of the Operation

Trace team, which would be based in Naas, Co. Kildare. Superintendent Jerry O'Connell had worked with Hickey on the Veronica Guerin murder investigation and on a number of other murder cases in the 1980s and '90s. The other members were Inspector Mark Kerrigan, Detective Sergeant Maura Walsh, Sergeant Pat Treacy, Detective Garda Marianne Cusack and Detective Garda Alan Bailey. Between them the six gardaí had decades of experience in investigating serious crime, including murder cases and missing persons cases. Mark Kerrigan was a former murder squad officer who was based in Carlow. Maura Walsh was working with the NBCI at Harcourt Square, Dublin. Pat Treacy worked with the murder squad and had investigated the disappearance of Philip Cairns and the murder of Patricia Doherty. Marianne Cusack was a member of the National Drugs Unit and had been involved in a number of serious cases, including the prosecution of the prominent Dublin criminal 'Dutchy' Holland. Alan Bailey was attached to the Bridewell Garda Station in Dublin, where he had been involved in preparing the book of evidence in nearly every recent murder case in the north Dublin area.

Jerry O'Connell, now retired, told me that every member of the Operation Trace team brought some individual expertise or knowledge to the operation.

Among the six of us we had detectives who were experienced interviewers, and we had men and women who had experienced previous major criminal investigations. We also had a mixture of ages, and we had gardaí who had worked in both towns and cities. In Pat Treacy, for example, we had someone who had worked on previous missing persons cases, such as Philip Cairns. I myself had worked on the investigation into the murder of Antoinette Smith, whose body was found in the Dublin Mountains in April 1988, nine months after she had disappeared. We had detectives experienced in tackling organised criminal gangs. Although we were looking at six specific cases of missing women, we were all bringing our collective experience of other major cases with us.

The compilation by computer of information about specific crimes for cross-referencing purposes had never been done before in Ireland. Gardaí wanted to choose a program that was 'non-judgemental', whereby the information on each disappearance would be treated in the same way and in turn might throw up connections that otherwise might not be found. In each of the six missing women cases there were no witnesses to any abduction and no crime scene. The task of trying to establish any possible links between them would be painstaking. In choosing a suitable computer program, gardaí looked at countries where such cross-referencing of cases was already in existence. Jerry O'Connell and Alan Bailey travelled to meet English police at the National Crime Facility at Bramshill, outside London, and learn about the Home Office Large Major Enquiry System (HOLMES). Gardaí visited the FBI's Research Centre at Quantico in Virginia to learn about the Bureau's Violent Criminal Apprehension Program. Gardaí also looked at a system used by the Canadian police, the Violent Crime Linkage Analysis System (ViCLAS). This was introduced in the mid-1980s to identify and track the movements of serial violent criminals, including rapists and suspected murderers.

Crucially, certain aspects of the Canadian system dealt specifically with solved and unsolved sexual assaults, and with missing persons where there was a strong possibility of foul play. After studying the different programs available, gardaí decided to adapt aspects of the Canadian model to form their own Offenders, Victims and Incidents Database (OVID).

The OVID system allowed detectives on Operation Trace to collate information about three distinct and crucial areas of their investigation: all known sexual and violent offenders, all known victims of attacks by such people, and information on all reported violent incidents, including attempted abductions. Every scrap of information on each of the six missing women was also compiled and assimilated in the search for any kind of link.

Within weeks of the setting up of Operation Trace the detectives who had worked on the original investigations into the disappearances of Annie McCarrick, Jo Jo Dullard, Fiona Pender, Ciara Breen, Fiona Sinnott and Deirdre Jacob met the Operation Trace team at Naas Garda Station. Over a full day the Trace team was briefed to bring them up to date on each of the cases, including any recent developments. One detective who helped to brief the Operation Trace team said there was an optimistic mood at the conference.

> None of us were upset or anything like that at these new detectives coming in to look at our work. It's not like that, anyway: the missing women are what's important, not office politics. We were all happy to cooperate with Trace, and we all actually felt that a fresh pair of eyes would be quite welcome after all this time. Sometimes you might be so close to a case that you can't see the wood for the trees. And we were all thinking that maybe this computer analysis of the cases might do the trick. The OVID system was used to compile a list of all known sexual and violent offenders dating back to the early 1980s. It included hundreds of convicted rapists and dozens of men jailed for murdering women; it also extended to men convicted of exposing themselves in public and men who stole underwear from clothes lines. The list covered everything that might label a person as a sexual deviant. The names of many men who had no previous convictions were also nominated for inclusion. In the weeks after Operation Trace was set up gardaí received hundreds of phone calls from members of the public identifying people they thought might be serial killers. All these names were examined, and if there was any suspicion the name was put in the database. Within a short time OVID contained the names and details of more than 7,500 people.

The publicity generated by the establishment of Operation Trace led also to a number of women contacting the team directly. These were women who had never made a complaint but had been the victim of sexual assaults, or attempted assaults, or attempted abduction. Some had been beaten or sexually assaulted by former boyfriends; some had been attacked by other people known to them; others had been attacked by strangers. Detectives found themselves meeting women who had never come forward before with their chilling stories of sexual attacks. Each victim said she was coming forward not necessarily to bring criminal complaints herself but to try to help find any of the missing women.

While many phone calls received were anonymous, a number of people with a professional involvement also contacted the Operation Trace team with their concerns about certain individuals. Some gardaí from various parts of the country rang the Trace team nominating suspects. Some officers said they had little on which to base their suspicions, other than a hunch.

In addition, the Operation Trace team did an extensive trawl through the cases of the six missing women. When the operation was established, in September 1998, there had been no arrests in connection with the disappearance of Annie McCarrick, Jo Jo Dullard, Ciara Breen, or Deirdre Jacob. Three women and two men had been arrested in April 1997 in connection with the disappearance of Fiona Pender, and a prime suspect had been identified in Fiona's case, but no charges had been brought. While no one had been directly arrested in connection with the disappearance of Fiona Sinnott, a number of people who gardaí hoped might have information were held in June 1998 and questioned about other crimes, including drug-dealing in south Co. Wexford. All had been released without charge.

At the back of the minds of the detectives working on Operation Trace was the hope that the computer might throw up a link that would lead to an arrest and in turn to the discovery of one or more of the missing women.

While the Operation Trace team were beginning their work at Naas Garda Station, gardaí investigating the most recent disappearance had been misdirected by a man who had anonymously contacted newspapers and radio stations claiming he might have given Deirdre Jacob a lift from Newbridge to Co. Monaghan. It would be early 1999 before the man was identified and it was established that his story was false. A number of hoax callers contacted gardaí in the weeks following the launch of Operation Trace. Each phone call and each tip-off had to be investigated fully, but it was a source of frustration to detectives that some people were simply making up stories to get attention. In the process they were wasting valuable garda time.

Among the many names entered into the OVID system was a suspected killer with multiple convictions for rape and sexual assault. Originally from Wolfhill in Co. Laois, Robert Howard was by then in his mid-fifties, and responsible for vicious attacks both in Ireland and England. He was the one and only suspect in the murder of missing fifteen-year-old Arlene Arkinson, last seen in a car with Howard in Co. Tyrone in 1994. When Arlene accepted a lift from Howard that night, she had no idea the man behind the wheel was a serial rapist, who at that time was awaiting sentence for sexually abusing another teenage girl. She wouldn't have known Howard had raped a 79-year-old woman in Youghal, Co. Cork in 1973 or that in the late 1960s he had attempted to sexually abuse a child and rape a woman in separate attacks in England.

In 1973 when he first moved to Youghal he used an alias – Leslie Cahill – and got a job in a local factory. Nobody in Youghal had any idea that a dangerous man with convictions in England was living among them. The circumstances of Robert Howard's crime in Youghal in 1973 were particularly shocking and upsetting. After breaking into a local woman's house, he had stuffed cotton wool into his victim's mouth to stop her crying out for help. After raping the woman he fled to Dublin, but was tracked down by good garda work and jailed for ten years. At his sentence hearing, the judge heard a psychological report describe Robert Howard as a 'dangerous psychopath'. A list of previous convictions was read out, outlining how Howard had spent much of his teenage life in custody for robbing houses throughout Ireland, before travelling to England where his crimes escalated to sexually assaulting children and women.

By the mid-1990s gardaí throughout the country were aware of Robert Howard. An internal garda bulletin alerted officers that

Howard travelled extensively throughout Ireland and England and 'picks up lone hitch-hikers or befriends young females in pubs, nightclubs and amusement arcades'. He was listed as a suspect in attempted abductions of children in places as far apart as Bray, Co. Wicklow and Crossmolina, Co. Mayo. A garda report circulated to stations throughout the country alerted officers that Howard was a 'smooth-talking, plausible type, this man is regarded as a dangerous sex offender posing a serious threat'. An English police report from the mid-1990s described Robert Howard as 'particularly surveillance conscious'.

Robert Howard was free and roaming Ireland and Britain from the time of his release from Mountjoy Jail in 1981 until his arrest in London in 2002 for the murder of fourteen-year-old schoolgirl Hannah Williams. Howard lived near Hannah and befriended her. He lured her to an unknown location, where he choked her to death with a rope that was still around her neck when her body was discovered in Kent more than a year later. When Howard died in prison in 2015 he was serving a life sentence for Hannah's murder.

With his multiple criminal convictions, Robert Howard was typical of many sex offenders whose details were included in OVID. However, what was unique about him was that by 1998 Howard was suspected of murdering fifteen-year-old Arlene Arkinson and burying her body somewhere in either Co. Donegal or Co. Tyrone. He used the border between the Republic and Northern Ireland to try and stay one step ahead of various police forces. He often travelled by ferry to Britain, and would melt away into the anonymity of city living in Glasgow or London. He was always on the move, and although detectives in Britain and Ireland knew he was the main suspect in the Arlene Arkinson case, Robert Howard was still able to evade the watch of all police forces to abduct and murder Hannah Williams.

Among the unsolved murders that gardaí from Operation Trace also looked at was that of Phyllis Murphy, who was abducted in Newbridge in December 1979 and whose body was recovered in the Sally Gap in Co. Wicklow in January 1980. Whoever had raped and murdered Phyllis had never been brought to justice, and may have attacked other women. However, what only a handful of gardaí knew when Operation Trace was set up, was that a review of Phyllis' case was already underway that would soon see the killer caught and convicted, twenty years after he raped and murdered the young woman in Kildare.

News of the dramatic breakthrough in the case was given to Detective Inspector Brendan McArdle of the Garda Technical Bureau on the afternoon of 24 June 1999. At that time McArdle was part of a search at Templeton Beach in Co. Louth where the IRA said it had buried the body of mother of ten Jean McConville who was abducted from her Belfast home and shot dead in 1972. As he stood on the coastline at the Cooley Peninsula, Brendan McArdle spoke by phone with a scientist at a laboratory in England that had been involved in crucial forensic testing in relation to the murder of Phyllis Murphy.

Two years earlier, in 1997, McArdle had begun reinvestigating the Phyllis Murphy case, knowing there was now a new process for extracting DNA profiles from small semen or blood samples taken from historic crime scenes. Semen stains had been recovered from the body of Phyllis Murphy in 1980, but at that time only the blood group of the attacker could be identified. Although Phyllis' naked body lay undiscovered for four weeks, amazingly the trace evidence left by her murderer was still on her body when it was examined by State Pathologist Professor John Harbison in January 1980. At that time Professor Harbison carefully used twelve cotton buds to take swabs from Phyllis' body, and the swabs were placed in sealed containers.

For almost two decades gardaí knew the cotton bud swabs contained potential crucial evidence that could catch Phyllis' killer, but the science had not become advanced enough to allow for a full DNA profile to be extracted during the 1980s or the early to mid-1990s. However, by 1997, it was becoming clear that the time was right to re-examine the case. News was emerging in forensic circles of a major breakthrough, known as the PCR (Polymerase Chain Reaction) method, whereby small amounts of body fluids could be used to generate full DNA profiles.

In March 1998 McArdle brought the cotton bud samples to a specialist laboratory in Oxfordshire. The scientists there told him they had previously managed to get DNA profiles from tiny semen samples, but none had been as old as the ones the detective had brought from Ireland: then, a month later, scientist Matthew Greenhalgh rang Brendan McArdle to say they had managed to get a full DNA profile.

The next stage in the investigation involved applying the same science to 'blood stain' cards. These were blood samples provided by a number of men during the original investigation in 1980 – the blood had been dried onto special cards and kept safe all those years by Garda Christy Sheridan at Naas Garda Station, and later Garda Finbar McPaul at Kildare Garda Station. The call that Brendan McArdle received in June 1999 outlined that the PCR method had got a hit on one of the blood samples. It was a direct match with the semen left on Phyllis' body.

The semen was a match to a blood sample provided in 1980 by John Crerar. It would later emerge that Crerar had been asked to give a blood sample all those years ago because a garda had fortuitously written 'Treat this man as a suspect' on a sheet of paper. Brendan McArdle didn't know anything about the man who was now the prime suspect in a cold-case murder. Given all the amazing elements of the case, when a fellow garda asked McArdle at Templeton Beach if Crerar might still be alive, the detective replied, 'I've no doubt but that he is alive.'

Early on Tuesday, 13 July 1999, Detective Garda Mark Carroll from Newbridge and detectives Dominic Hayes and Bernie Hanley from the NBCI arrested 51-year-old John Crerar, a married father of five, at his workplace in Co. Kildare. Crerar blanched as a two-decades-old crime came back to haunt him. He didn't say a word, but gave a sharp intake of breath, as if he had been punched in the chest. Later that day he gave a DNA sample, which matched the blood sample given nineteen years earlier and the semen recovered from Phyllis' body. Although he would plead not guilty, a jury would ultimately unanimously convict John Crerar of murder, accepting the forensic evidence that there was a one in a billion match between John Crerar's DNA and the DNA found on Phyllis' body. A man who, in the original investigation, had given John Crerar a false alibi for the day of Phyllis' murder changed his story, saying he had lied, believing he was simply helping a friend who had not been at work when he should have been. In October 2002 Crerar was jailed for life, and is serving his sentence in Arbour Hill Prison.

Detectives from Operation Trace coordinated the questioning of Crerar, prepared the book of evidence and kept the valuable exhibits safe. Crerar's movements were later examined in relation to the disappearance of the missing women in Leinster. Gardaí also examined the unsolved case of Kathleen Farrell, a 52-year-old single woman who was found murdered at Little Curragh in Co. Kildare on 12 March 1972. Kathleen had worked as a cinema cashier at the Tower Cinema in Kildare town. She was fully dressed when her body was found lying in furze. Kathleen had been manually strangled, and died as a result of asphyxia. Her killer was never caught.

One detective said the solving of the murder of Phyllis Murphy led indirectly to progress being made in other cases.

> You should see the amount of calls we get when some breakthrough happens in a case. The conviction of John Crerar has shown not only detectives but the general public that hard work does pay off, and that the guilty people will never be allowed forget their evil deeds, whether it's a year or ten years or twenty years or more before gardaí come knocking on their door. Solving the murder of Phyllis Murphy has added much impetus to the investigations into the missing women in Leinster. And that was a clear case of showing that someone giving a false alibi will be found out. There are other people out there of course who have given alibis for friends, or sons, or husbands, and they know it is wrong.

One difference between Phyllis Murphy's case and those of Antoinette Smith, Patricia Doherty and Marie Kilmartin, is that Phyllis' killer left her body above ground and covered in furze. The freezing cold temperatures as a new decade dawned in 1980 meant that forensic evidence on Phyllis' body was preserved. The fact that the killer or killers of Antoinette Smith and Patricia Doherty buried the victims in bogland greatly lessened the chance for any forensic materials to be maintained. Similarly, whoever put Marie Kilmartin's body into deep bog water also destroyed many opportunities for forensic advancements to assist the case.

Within weeks of the discovery of Marie Kilmartin's body, two Co. Laois men were arrested and detained for questioning. Both were held for twelve hours but were released without charge. In comparison, there were never any arrests in the cases of Antoinette Smith and Patricia Doherty. Detectives working at the Operation Trace headquarters in Naas entered all the information relating to the murders of Antoinette, Patricia and Marie in the OVID system, as well as detail on the murder of Phyllis Murphy – which would soon be solved. There were no common features between the cases that would suggest that the cases were linked. The private feeling of many gardaí is that the murder of Marie Kilmartin is not linked to other unsolved cases, but that the murders of Antoinette Smith and Patricia Doherty may be linked.

Gardaí are satisfied that Antoinette Smith did not know the men who murdered her. Detectives have long feared that the same pair might have struck again, perhaps abducting Annie McCarrick or Jo Jo Dullard, or that one or both of these killers may be responsible for unsolved sexual assaults in the greater Dublin area. However, the Operation Trace team did not turn up any concrete evidence linking Antoinette's case with any of the missing women.

As well as examining unsolved murders that might fit the profile of a serial killer, detectives from Operation Trace considered whether there were any other missing women who might have fallen prey to a random attacker. It was later felt that two cases not included in the original six of Operation Trace should be thoroughly analysed: 22-year-old Imelda Keenan and 39-year-old Eva Brennan.

Eva Brennan was last seen alive on Sunday, 25 July 1993, when she left her parents' house at Rathdown Park, Terenure, Dublin. Eva walked down towards her own apartment at Madison Avenue in Rathgar. She was not seen again. When it was established by the following Tuesday that no one had seen Eva her family broke into her apartment but there was no sign of her. Gardaí are satisfied she arrived safely back to her apartment from her parents', as a raincoat she had been wearing was in the apartment when it was later checked; but her handbag, keys and bus pass were missing. There were no reports of Eva getting on a bus that Sunday.

Her brother Paul and sister Eileen both told me Eva was a creature of habit and would never have simply gone off somewhere on a whim. She regularly attended mass, and was a member of a prayer group. She was very close to her parents and siblings. Another of Eva's sisters, Collette McCann, who passed away in 2015 was a passionate advocate on behalf of missing people and a support to many other families. She said Eva's family had carried out most of the searches themselves. She said she feared Eva was the victim of a random attack.

> You don't just disappear; you don't just vanish. And if you do something to harm yourself, how do you hide your own body? You have to look at other things going on at the time to really think about what might have happened. Eva disappeared just twelve weeks after Annie McCarrick was abducted and murdered. Eva could very well have gone for a walk that Sunday afternoon, and before she knew anything a car had stopped and she'd been attacked. When I initially asked a senior officer why Eva's case wasn't part of Operation Trace he said something like 'It's not my jurisdiction.' Eva's a missing woman, last seen on a Sunday afternoon in a well-populated suburb of south Dublin. Surely that's a matter of concern for any right-thinking person. Eva's remains are most probably in the Wicklow Mountains. I just wish gardaí could do more to find her and the other missing people.

The other disappearance also factored into Operation Trace was that of Imelda Keenan who vanished on Monday, 3 January 1994 from Waterford city. The 22-year-old was living with her fiancé at a flat at William Street in the city. The couple had become engaged in 1989, but there was no date set for the wedding. The plan was to get married in Rome.

Imelda told her fiancé she was going to the post office to collect her dole payment. She washed her hair, gave her partner a cup of tea, did her make-up and headed out. She said she wouldn't be long, and mentioned she had to get cat litter. She headed out the door at 1.30 p.m. but didn't take her bag with her. She was wearing leopard-print ski pants, a round-neck white jumper and a waist-length denim jacket.

A woman who knew Imelda saw her walking across William Street. The witness was driving from the Quay into William Street and Imelda stopped in the middle of the road to let the car pass. That is the last reported sighting of Imelda.

The nearby river Suir was searched at the time and again in the mid-2000s. Locals say that the vast majority of people who enter the river are later found: that belief was proven, for example, in the case of Meg Walsh, a mother of one who was murdered in October 2006. The body of the 35-year-old was found two weeks after she was last seen alive. Meg's body had not travelled far in the water and had surfaced while a huge search for her was underway.

Imelda Keenan's family have spent the last quarter of a century trying to find her. In December 2018, Imelda's brother Gerry spoke at the National Missing Persons Day event, saying he believed some people in Waterford must have information on what happened to his sister. He urged people to come forward. One curious aspect of Imelda's disappearance is that the Monday she disappeared was a Bank Holiday. She had told her fiancé she was going to collect her dole payment, but the post office wouldn't have been open that day. Did Imelda get as far as the post office before realising it was closed? Did she remember while on the journey that it was a Bank Holiday, and then change her plans? Did someone cross her path at some stage who caused her harm? There are so many questions, but no clear answers.

Detectives working on Operation Trace assembled a list of known violent men who would be capable of either abducting or killing a woman. They looked at double killer Michael Bambrick, who was caught in 1995 when he confessed to gardaí that he had killed his wife Patricia McGauley in September 1991 and another woman, Mary Cummins, in July 1992. Both women were killed at Bambrick's home in Ronanstown, west Dublin. He later dismembered their bodies and hid the remains elsewhere in west Dublin.

Gardaí also examined the history of the few convicted rapists given the maximum sentence of life imprisonment for their crimes. Over a year before Operation Trace was established, Thomas Stokes was convicted of raping a woman who was working as a prostitute on the night that Stokes and an accomplice, Adrian Power, abducted her in Dublin city and held her captive in the Wicklow Mountains during a two-and-a-half-hour ordeal.

Stokes was the leader of the two-man abduction team. By the time he carried out the horrific attack on the young woman in December 1994, he had amassed a number of convictions both in Ireland and England for crimes including indecent assault, threatening to kill, and arson. Whenever he was arrested for his various crimes he claimed he was being victimised because he was a member of the Travelling community.

Thomas Stokes was apprehended for the abduction and rape because he left a used condom close to the scene where he had raped his victim. Hair from the victim and fibres from her clothes were also found inside Stokes' car. The victim described how she had been raped in various ways by Stokes. His accomplice was later given a ten-year sentence.

What was of interest to detectives from Operation Trace was that Stokes had links to Co. Kildare, and travelled extensively throughout Leinster and indeed the whole country. While officers were considering if Thomas Stokes might have anything to do with any of the unsolved crimes they were investigating, the Trace team got word that Stokes wanted to speak with them. Stokes was offering to help with one case that he himself could not be responsible for, as he was in jail at the time. He indicated he could use his contacts, influence and knowledge to assist officers, but never came through with this information.

Another violent man was David Lawler, a married man living in Blanchardstown at the time. In the early hours of 22 December 1995 he randomly murdered 41-year-old Marilyn Rynn. Marilyn was almost home when Lawler attacked her from behind and dragged her into Tolka Valley Park where he strangled her to death. Marilyn's body was found sixteen days later and DNA from her body was matched to Lawler, who was later jailed for life.

Until his arrest, Lawler had worked for Telecom Éireann as a van driver, and his work would have involved some travel. Having lived in Baltinglass until his teens, Lawler would have known the forests and woods of west Co. Wicklow. He is intelligent, an avid reader, interested in astronomy and economics, and spends much of his time in prison doing cryptic crosswords.

Another violent man who was put on the OVID list was Philip Colgan, who in late 1991 committed two separate rapes in Dublin. In the first incident Colgan broke into the home of a 79-year-old woman and raped her. Days later he went into Dublin city where he met a young Spanish woman who he convinced to go back to his home in Donaghmede with the promise that there was a party there. But there was no party, and Colgan raped the woman. He was later caught and given an eight-year sentence. Colgan was assessed by Operation Trace when detectives established he had been out of jail by the time Deirdre Jacob disappeared. However, no evidence was found linking him to the case. But Colgan's crimes were about to escalate and in 1999, at this stage released from prison, Colgan murdered Layla Brennan, a young woman he abducted in Dublin city, and whose body he concealed in the Wicklow Mountains. Colgan was brought to justice when he confessed the murder to his wife, a teacher he had met while in prison, who was aware of

Colgan's double rape conviction but wrongly believed her husband was a reformed character.

Operation Trace was established in 1998 but it wasn't until 2006 that detectives became aware of Robert Quigley as a very violent man. In November 2006 Quigley, a 26-year-old from Tallaght, posed as a hackney driver and parked along Harcourt Street where he picked up a fare, a young woman who believed she was getting into a taxi. Quigley had an aerial fitted on the roof, which made his Vauxhall Cavalier look like a hackney. The woman fell asleep on what she believed was her journey home, only to wake up in the car in the Wicklow Mountains with her captor smoking a cigarette in the driver's seat. Quigley turned violent, pulling at the woman's hair, putting his hands around her neck and tearing at her clothing. Another car passed and Quigley panicked and drove on before pulling in a short distance away, where he then began beating the woman with a bat. Miraculously she managed to open the passenger door and escape. Quigley took off in the car. He was later arrested in Tralee, from where he had travelled to commit the attack, and jailed for eight years. Quigley is one of a new generation of violent men to use the Wicklow Mountains to commit attacks.

One woman, who at the time was serving a prison sentence for robbery, contacted gardaí soon after Operation Trace was set up to say she had information that might be of assistance with particular reference to the disappearance of one missing woman. Detectives were conscious they were dealing with a person who was a convicted criminal, and that any such person might be looking for something in return, such as temporary or early release. One detective told the woman that if she had any information at all that could ease the suffering of one family she had a duty to help. The woman said she did want to help and that she was trying to better her own circumstances and do the right thing. She took gardaí to a location in Co. Kerry where she said she thought there might be evidence that would assist them. Unfortunately she was unable to pinpoint an exact site that could be searched.

Nine people were questioned by detectives from Operation Trace in connection with the disappearance of Jo Jo Dullard. Several people in the Waterford area were arrested and questioned about crimes including the abduction and murder of Jo Jo Dullard. Others were also arrested throughout the country and taken to Naas Garda Station to be questioned – including one with a previous conviction for a violent sexual assault – but all were subsequently released without charge.

As detectives continued to assimilate and enter vast amounts of data into the OVID system, several violent convicted criminals contacted gardaí claiming to have information about the missing women. Over the following months detectives would find themselves in communication with criminals in Ireland, England and Canada who claimed to know something about one or more of the cases. Frustratingly, just like the hoax calls, each of the criminals seemed to have concocted an elaborate story of lies, a figment of their disturbed imagination. Yet the gardaí are acutely aware that people who make up stories about abducting and murdering women are capable of acting out such violent deeds. One of them was a teenage criminal from Athlone who would later be jailed for a most shocking crime.

When he first contacted detectives from Operation Trace, the young man was serving a prison sentence and was also being treated at the Central Mental Hospital in Dundrum. He claimed he knew a man who was responsible for at least one of the disappearances and he named two sites where he said gardaí might find evidence. Officers searched land near Clara in Co. Offaly and Creggan bog just outside Athlone but found nothing. The information provided by the teenage criminal was no longer considered credible.

However, this young criminal proved he was capable not only of fantasising about evil deeds but of carrying them out. In the early hours of the morning of 30 June 2001, and recently released from prison, he abducted at knifepoint a seventeen-year-old who had travelled into Athlone to buy chips. He sat behind the terrified boy on his parked scooter and forced him to drive first to Moate, then to Clara and eventually to Creggan bog, off the Athlone–Dublin road.

The boy was forced to push his bike out of view of the roadside and was then frogmarched further into a remote part of the bog. The criminal ordered his petrified victim to take off his runners and his football jersey, which was used to gag him. His hands were chained behind his back with the chain from the scooter, and his feet were tied together with the laces from his runners. The criminal then pushed his victim into a bog hole, and pushed the scooter in on top of him. As the boy fought to keep his head above the water his attacker said to him, 'Goodbye, and good luck.'

Sergeant Seán Leydon and Garda Brian Lee were on patrol around Athlone that night when they noticed the teenager loitering on the street. The young man was well known to both officers, and they were aware that he was back on the streets after serving a prison sentence in Dublin. As they approached him to assess what he was doing out so late at night he said to them, 'I've done it this time. Now you'll believe me.' Within seconds the young man confessed that he had left a teenager bound and gagged in a bog hole.

The criminal brought the two gardaí to the scene, where they found the victim struggling to keep his head above the water. The gardaí managed to pull the teenager to safety. One of the criminal's first questions when he was arrested was 'How long will I get for this?' In July 2002 the criminal was jailed for twelve years for false imprisonment, reckless endangerment and assault. His young victim was too upset to give evidence in court.

This episode reminded gardaí that while some people who contacted Operation Trace might have concocted stories because they were attention-seekers, there was still the possibility that some of them might one day try to act out their sick fantasies.

Another extremely violent man who contacted the Operation Trace team with false information was a convicted child serial killer in Canada. The first time detectives came across the name Clifford Robert Olson was in late 1998 when a sergeant at Baltinglass Garda Station in Co. Wicklow answered the phone to find himself speaking directly to Olson. Because Olson had assisted Canadian police in recovering some of the bodies of the children he had murdered in the early 1980s, he had certain priveleges in prison, including access to a phone. From his prison cell in Québec, Olson had managed to obtain access to information about the garda operation to find Ireland's missing women. He concocted an elaborate tale, saying that a now deceased friend of his, Colin Miller, had murdered five women in Ireland.

Detectives at first kept an open mind about Olson's claims, but eventually they ruled out his 'information' as nothing more than twisted fantasy. The fact that Olson was serving a life sentence for murdering eleven children in Canada in the late 1970s and early '80s had at first made gardaí take notice. His own crimes had caused waves of panic in the Vancouver area before he was caught and jailed in January 1982.

Clifford Olson claimed he knew where to find the bodies of five missing women. He said they were buried in Co. Kildare but he wanted to be brought over to Ireland to find the bodies, something gardaí were not prepared to contemplate. One detective said Olson wasted a lot of their time.

Olson learnt about our operation through the internet and newspapers, and then he tried to get in the middle of it. He's tried it before with other countries as well. He claimed he could get us photographs of the locations where bodies were buried, but he would have to be brought over. Can you imagine us flying this serial killer over from Canada on a whim? He tried it on with police in Seattle and Hawaii, and in England too, claiming he knew information about murders and other crimes. He led us a merry dance for a little while, but because he had killed at least eleven children we were taking great notice of him; but he was lying all the way.

Detectives with Operation Trace went to meet a prisoner in Britain who also contacted them with information about missing women in Ireland. As with the conversations with the young Athlone criminal and with Clifford Olson, the 'information' this person had amounted to nothing. While this man was already known to gardaí by the time Operation Trace was set up, other violent men had not yet come to their attention. Although the name of Larry Murphy from Baltinglass, Co. Wicklow, is the most prominent of those who have been convicted of abducting and raping women in recent times, other men have been put behind bars for similar crimes, and one thing they all have in common is that they had no previous convictions. But for the courage of the rape victims in coming forward with their harrowing tales, coupled with the dogged determination of detectives in pursuing them, these criminals would still be as clean as a whistle.

In September 2000 nineteen-year-old Daniel Moynihan from Raheen East, Rathmore, Co. Kerry, set out in his car posing as a hackney driver. He headed for Killarney, where he began driving around. In the early hours of the morning two young women got into the car, thinking it was a hackney cab. Moynihan drove one woman to her intended destination and then set off towards where the other young woman wanted to go. However, instead of driving to the woman's home he drove to an isolated spot, where he raped her. He later brought her to another place, where he attacked her again. When he was arrested he told detectives he was glad he was caught and had 'wished to be found out'. He was later jailed for twelve years after admitting two charges of raping the woman, with the final two years of the sentence being suspended because he had pleaded guilty.

Another violent young man was Thomas Callan from Shanmullagh, Carrickmacross, Co. Monaghan. He was twenty-one when he abducted a seventeen-year-old girl, who he put in the boot of his car in Carrickmacross in June 1999. He drove the terrified teenager to a secluded area outside the town, where he sexually assaulted and tried to rape her. It would later emerge that this was not the first time Callan had tried to abduct a girl. In February 1999 he approached a fourteen-year-old girl in Carrickmacross and tried to take her to an isolated spot, but she managed to flee. In May 2001 Callan was sentenced to ten years' imprisonment for his attack on the seventeen-year-old and to four years for falsely imprisoning the fourteen-year-old. As he passed sentence, Mr Justice Paul Carney remarked that this was the second case in a month in which he had to sentence a violent man who had abducted a woman and put her in the boot of his car. The other man was Larry Murphy.

From the time he was apprehended in February 2000 detectives have wished they could get into the mind of someone like Larry Murphy. In August 2010 Murphy walked out of Arbour Hill Prison having served three-quarters of a fourteen-year sentence for abducting, repeatedly raping and attempting to murder a Carlow woman in February 2000. The now separated father of two left Ireland soon after his release. He lived for a time in Amsterdam and also in Spain, but more recently has been living in London, and also spends time in Scotland.

On the night of Friday, 11 February 2000, Murphy approached a woman in a car park in Carlow town and punched her in the face, fracturing her nose. The woman was immediately stunned, bleeding and in great pain. Murphy bundled the woman into the boot of his car and drove from Carlow to Athy, and from there to near his home in west Co. Wicklow. Twice, in both Athy and the forest at Kilranelagh, Co. Wicklow, he pulled her from the boot and raped her in the vehicle. He then pushed the woman back into the boot and tried to murder her. Only for her fighting back and managing to get her legs out and onto the ground, Murphy would have succeeded in suffocating her with a plastic bag. The arrival on the scene of two hunters, who just happened across the attempted murder, also helped save the victim's life.

To this day we don't know what Murphy planned to do with his victim if he had killed her. Did he have a location in mind where he would bring the body? As Larry Murphy pleaded guilty to the charges against him, the victim in the case was spared the ordeal of giving evidence, but the guilty pleas also meant that the public never got to hear details relating to Murphy's statements to gardaí.

After his arrest Murphy quickly admitted he had raped the woman, but he also described the violent attacks as 'sex' and 'making love'. He admitted the attack began when he had hit his victim and forced her into her car, before transferring her to his car in the same car park in Carlow. He said he had originally travelled to Carlow that night to visit two men but decided to stop off to buy a bag of chips. He said he was walking to a chipper when he saw the woman walking towards him.

During the attacks that Murphy committed that night he spoke to his victim, and told her a mixture of fact and fiction. He said he was 'Michael from Dublin' but gave her correct information about his young children. If anyone had looked into his Fiat Punto before the attack that night they would have seen a child's car seat in the back. It was there for a genuine reason, but perhaps it could also be used to mask the criminal intent Murphy actually had.

On the day Murphy pleaded guilty he fainted in the packed courtroom. Yet when he walked out of prison ten years later on 12 August 2010, he was self-assured, unfazed by the huge media presence awaiting him. He actually took a taxi that day to Coolock Garda Station to complain about being harassed by the media.

Perversely, authorities had no choice but to help Larry Murphy prepare for a new life. While in prison he applied for, and was granted, a new driver's licence. A man who used a car as a location of confinement and entrapment, a location for rape and attempted murder, was given a new driver's licence. There was no law to state that a rapist who abducted his victim and drove her to two different counties during the prolonged attack should not be allowed drive another vehicle.

Detectives investigating the disappearance of women in Leinster have studied Murphy's modus operandi in an effort to find new leads. Like Daniel Moynihan in Co. Kerry and Thomas Callan in Co. Monaghan, Larry Murphy had no previous convictions and therefore did not feature in the OVID database when it was set up by Operation Trace. He simply wasn't on the garda radar in the 1990s at all. The difference between Larry Murphy and Moynihan and Callan was that Murphy was seemingly a happily married man, while the other two were single. Murphy was thirty-five when he carried out the heinous crime for which he was convicted. He was twenty-eight when Annie McCarrick disappeared in March 1993; he was thirty when Jo Jo

Dullard disappeared in November 1995. He was forty-five when he was released from prison in 2010 and left Ireland.

Some depraved people have used the cases of missing women to terrorise other women. One man was jailed for three years in 2001 for subjecting at least nine women to a reign of terror by threatening them over the phone and sending them obscene packages. He picked on single women and widows and threatened them that they would meet the same fate as Annie McCarrick and Jo Jo Dullard. One woman reported receiving a letter with faeces on it. Another received a newspaper headline, 'Theory of serial killer rejected'. Gardaí pursued the stalker for five years before he was caught near the house of one of his victims. Detectives, conscious of the man's references to missing women during his reign of terror, conducted a thorough examination of his previous life. No information could be found to suggest that he had ever met any of the missing women.

Detectives investigating the disappearance of women in Leinster were mindful that a killer might have travelled from Britain or elsewhere to commit crimes in Ireland. One man suspected of murdering a woman near Norwich and burying her body was found living in Co. Cork. He was later extradited to England. And a triple killer, Philip Smith, who murdered three women in Birmingham in three separate attacks in 2000, had previously lived for a time in the Irish midlands. These were just two cases of a number of violent British men known to have spent time in Ireland.

Conversely, there are violent Irishmen who were jailed in Britain who are also of interest to detectives investigating cases of missing Irish women. One such criminal is now deceased Dublin man Martin Stafford, who was given a 33-year prison sentence in England for the murder of a woman whose body has never been found.

Michelle Gunshon was staying at a bed and breakfast in a Birmingham pub when she vanished in December 2004. The mother of three had travelled to Birmingham where she'd been working as a security guard at a major clothes exhibition at the National Exhibition Centre. Michelle had no idea that Martin Stafford – who was working as a glass collector at the pub – was a convicted rapist from Dublin who had previously held a woman at knifepoint and served a seven-year jail sentence for the attack, which occurred in Dublin in 1997. The rapist often travelled back and forth by ferry between Ireland and England.

Michelle Gunshon vanished from the pub in Birmingham and was never seen again. The subsequent police investigation uncovered CCTV footage of Martin Stafford driving Michelle's Ford Escort following her disappearance. He would later be convicted of murdering Michelle and also of the crime of preventing the burial of a body. Stafford refused to say what he did with Michelle's body. He died in prison in 2015, just three years after being given a life sentence.

Martin Stafford's crimes did not end with the murder of Michelle Gunshon. Before he was brought to justice by English police for that crime Stafford had returned to Dublin, where in 2005 he raped a woman who was working as a prostitute. Stafford held his victim captive for ten hours at a disused railway carriage at Heuston Station. He was later extradited to England to face trial for Michelle Gunshon's murder; he was found guilty and jailed for life.

Due to a peculiarity with the law, Martin Stafford was never formally questioned about the murder of Michelle Gunshon. Under extradition law, a person can only be extradited from one country to another for the purpose of being charged. This means a ludicrous situation exists whereby Martin Stafford now stands convicted of the murder of Michelle Gunshon due to overwhelming forensic and CCTV evidence, yet police could not formally arrest him and question him regarding the whereabouts of Michelle's body.

In one of the most shocking murders in recent times, Graham Dwyer groomed a vulnerable woman over a period of years and then lured her to a location where he stabbed her to death. In August 2012 Elaine O'Hara, following Dwyer's instructions, parked her car at one end of Shanganagh Park in Shankill, south Co. Dublin and walked a considerable distance to the shoreline to meet him. Dwyer then took Elaine up into the Wicklow Mountains, stabbed her to death in a forest and left her body hidden. By manipulating Elaine into parking her car near the local cemetery and then walking towards the shoreline, Dwyer ensured that many people would later think there was nothing suspicious about Elaine's disappearance and that she might have taken her own life. Instead the truth was almost unbelievable. Graham Dwyer, a married man living in Foxrock and a successful architect, was living a secret life whereby he liked to stab women while having sex with them. He had made contact with Elaine O'Hara some years previous on a bondage and sadomasochism website and began to manipulate a very vulnerable woman.

The chance discovery by local men in Co. Wicklow of bondage items found dumped in a reservoir, coupled with the curiosity of local Garda James O'Donoghue who later entered the water and discovered further items, including mobile phones, ensured that the story would eventually emerge of how Dwyer murdered Elaine O'Hara. Naturally, Graham Dwyer's movements have been examined at the time various women disappeared. He was only unmasked as a vicious and cunning killer when Elaine's body was found in 2013.

In the late 1990s and early 2000s the work of Operation Trace involved both a reassessment of the original investigations and the following up of new lines of enquiry. More than 5,000 people were interviewed and 4,000 statements taken, leading to more than 7,000 lines of enquiry. Detectives looked at every conceivable motive that might link some or all of the cases; the different months in which the women disappeared, the days of the week and the times of day. Even the phases of the moon were assessed and logged to see if any link might be established. Searches were carried out in Leinster, Connacht and Ulster, some of them at the request of the families of the missing women. Sniffer dogs trained in Britain were used to search fields and bogs. Detectives used metal probes, which they stuck deep into the ground at the various sites; these were then assessed by the sniffer dogs to see if anything suspicious might be buried there. But nothing was found.

Several graveyards were examined to establish if any bodies might have been hidden there. In the investigation into the disappearance of two of the missing women – Fiona Pender and Fiona Sinnott – the idea had already been raised that the bodies of the women might have been hidden in graveyards, but detectives could find no evidence of this.

By December 2001 Operation Trace had established no clear links between any of the cases of missing women. With all conceivable lines of enquiry examined, the six gardaí on the Operation Trace team had begun to be reassigned to their original duties. The investigations into each of the missing women continued at individual garda stations. Detective Alan Bailey remained as the Operation Trace coordinator, and when the Garda Cold Case Unit was established in 2007, he was one of the first to be selected for the new unit. Another detective in the new unit was Sergeant Noel Mooney, who had close links with profilers in the FBI and Canadian Police. Mooney was involved in introducing new computer software entitled ViCLAS (Violent Crime Linkage Analysis System), which was once again modelled on the Canadian system of the same name. Although ViCLAS, just like its predecessor OVID, did not establish any links between missing women cases, the system did help to establish commonalities in unsolved rape and sexual assault cases.

Officially known as the Serious Crime Review Team, cold-case detectives under the direction of firstly Detective Superintendent Christy Mangan, and later Detective Superintendent Walter O'Sullivan, would over time look at all the missing women cases. They provided detectives in Bray with recommendations regarding the unsolved murder of Antoinette Smith, and did similar work for detectives in Tallaght investigating Patricia Doherty's murder. In 2018 detectives from the Garda Cold Case Unit assisted officers in Kildare in completely reviewing the Deirdre Jacob case, work which saw the case being reclassified as a murder investigation. Most recently, cold-case detectives were planning to review the investigation into the disappearance of Annie McCarrick.

After Operation Trace was set up in September 1998, women did not disappear in Leinster at the same rate. One detective believes there could be a number of reasons for this.

To put it at its most simple, if there is a serial killer, or if there was a serial killer, he may just be lying low; he could be in prison serving a sentence for other crimes; he could have travelled abroad and is now living elsewhere; or he may be dead and has taken his evil secrets with him. The same analogy can apply to any of the cases, whether it's a serial killer or a once off 'crime of passion' killer.

One detective who worked on Operation Trace pointed out drawing assumptions about any of the cases is hazardous.

As it stands, we have three individual prime suspects in relation to the suspected abductions and murders of Fiona Pender, Ciara Breen and Fiona Sinnott. And we have a number of suspects in other cases. But suspicion is one thing, proof is something entirely different.

Detectives who have investigated the cases of the missing women are conscious that having a prime suspect does not mean the case is solved. There is always the possibility that the prime suspect, while capable of killing, might not in fact have committed the crime. The gardaí are mindful of one case from the 1970s in which a young woman had a row with her boyfriend and stormed off. A short time later she was abducted and murdered by a complete stranger. At first detectives looked at her boyfriend as a suspect, based on the ill-feeling between the two of them on the night the woman disappeared. From a prosecution point of view the boyfriend had a motive and opportunity. It was more than two months before the killer was caught, and the utterly distraught boyfriend was cleared of any suspicion.

There was also a case in the early 1980s in which a young woman was murdered by a married man she had met only that day. By sheer coincidence she had earlier been in the company – unknown to her – of another sexual deviant. At first gardaí thought this man was the killer, but after a number of months they established that he wasn't and that it was the 'upstanding' man she had met later that day.

When the Operation Trace detectives began to be reassigned in December 2001 many gardaí privately felt the detectives should have been left to continue their work full-time. There was always the possibility the computer system was about to show a link between two or more of the disappearances. Perhaps the next piece of seemingly innocuous information to be given to a garda might unlock the mystery of where the bodies of the women lay. Other gardaí argue that all possible leads had been exhausted, and it was pointless to leave the detectives in a room in Naas Garda Station with no more leads to work on.

The commitment of the gardaí who worked on Operation Trace could never be called into question. All of them worked long hours, often in their own time, in an effort to bring closure for the families of the missing women. Members of the Operation Trace team had many other successes in their careers, solving many murders and other serious crimes; but Operation Trace did not achieve what the public wanted it to achieve. Was it a failure? Certainly it failed to establish links between any of the cases of missing women in Leinster, but it is also possible that none of the cases have anything to do with each other and the fact remains that the tens of thousands of pieces of information gathered by OVID have failed to show any corroborative evidence.

The real debate, which continues to this day, is that many detectives feel Operation Trace was established far too late, and that something similar should have been operational soon after Annie McCarrick and Jo Jo Dullard's disappearances, and therefore before Fiona Pender, Ciara Breen, Fiona Sinnott and Deirdre Jacob disappeared. Perhaps new witnesses could have been identified in the cases of Jo Jo, and Annie, and Antoinette Smith and Patricia Doherty before the various trails went cold.

One detective says he feels Operation Trace would have come across many of the killers during the specialist garda work, but they need witnesses to come forward.

I think we have most of the names of the killers at this stage, but we just need that little bit extra: we need a wife or girlfriend to break the false alibi they have given to the killer, or we need a neighbour who saw what they thought was a body in someone's car or garage. We need something like that, something tangible to match with the names we have circled as suspected killers who are either at large or behind bars for other attacks.

In May 2018 a man abducted a woman in a random attack at Kilcroney Road, Enniskerry, Co. Wicklow. Three children and an adult witnessed the man force the woman into his Nissan Qashqai. The witnesses made an emergency call from a mobile phone and gardaí immediately responded to the call. An analysis of CCTV footage from a bus that was travelling in the village that evening identified the full registration number of the abduction vehicle. Gardaí used their technology software to conduct a quick vehicle registration check and the name and address of the owner of the vehicle was soon established. Gardaí also held a press conference within twenty-four hours of the abduction, making a major appeal for the public's help in finding a specific vehicle. News outlets immediately published details of the garda appeal online. This technology was not available when women disappeared in the 1990s.

Sadly, the victim was murdered soon after she was driven away from Enniskerry, and her body was hidden in an isolated spot in south Co. Dublin. Her body was found two days after the abduction. The attacker had already been shot dead by a garda in a car park at Cherrywood. Gardaí from the Serious Crime Review Team naturally checked out the abductor's details to see if there were any links to the cases of missing women, but nothing was established. However, yet again, the perpetrator was found to be a family man, married with young children.

It was the abduction and murder of Deirdre Jacob in July 1998 that sparked intense public concern and led to the establishment of Operation Trace. As well as a massive search by local gardaí of bogland, rivers, fields and roads around Co. Kildare and beyond, it was hoped that the Operation Trace team might provide a computer-generated lead that would bring the teenager home. Deirdre was a dependable young woman who was always in contact with family or friends. The eighteen-year-old disappearing from the gate of her home in broad daylight is one of the most audacious and cruel crimes Ireland has known. The response time of gardaí to this disappearance could not be faulted; the young woman was reported missing within hours of her disappearance, and extensive searches began the same night. This garda response was far faster than any of the other missing women cases and yet not a shred of evidence was found on the roadside.

For whatever reason, this was to be the last such unexplained disappearance of a young woman in the 1990s, and a similar rate of disappearances did not occur in the 2000s.

CHAPTER 9

MARY BOYLE

Mary Boyle is Ireland's youngest missing person; but her case is one of the oldest. Long before the disappearance of thirteen-year-old Philip Cairns in 1986, or the disappearance of women in the Leinster area in the 1990s, something terrible happened to little Mary Boyle. Six years old, going on seven, she vanished in March 1977 at Cashelard, near Ballyshannon, on the southern tip of Co. Donegal. What happened to the little girl who was last seen eating a packet of sweets? It's a heartbreaking question that would torment her parents, Ann and Charlie Boyle, her twin sister, Ann, and older brother, Patrick. It's a case that affected many gardaí who worked on the original investigation, all of them now retired.

There are only two possible explanations for Mary's disappearance. Did a desolate patch of marshy ground swallow up the little girl? Or is there a more sinister answer, was she abducted from the quiet Donegal countryside that Friday afternoon? Whatever the reason for her disappearance, why has no trace of her been found over forty years later?

Mary Boyle disappeared seven years after the murder of ten-year-old Bernadette Connolly, who was abducted 30 miles away in Collooney, Co. Sligo. Bernadette's body was found four months after her disappearance in a bog drain in Co. Roscommon. Mary Boyle and Philip Cairns remain Ireland's only long-term missing children.

There has only ever been one arrest in connection with Mary Boyle's disappearance. In 2014, thirty-seven years after Mary vanished, a man was taken from prison in Port Laoise to be questioned on suspicion of kidnapping Mary. The man was a convicted paedophile, whose crimes had become more apparent in recent years. He had been a soldier in 1977 and had been stationed at Finner Camp near Ballyshannon. Detectives established the man had links to Cashelard and would have known the remote area well. There was much publicity surrounding the arrest, but the man denied any involvement in Mary's disappearance, saying he could not remember anything about Mary Boyle. Enquiries revealed that the man was supposed to have been confined to the barracks at the time Mary disappeared because he was actually facing a charge of indecently assaulting a child earlier that year. There was nothing to prove whether or not the man was absent without leave from Finner Camp on the Friday afternoon that Mary disappeared. It appears that the man was never considered a suspect in the 1977 investigation. Detectives involved in his arrest in 2014 considered him a viable and credible suspect because of witnesses, medical reports, and the man's previous history of sexual assault. After extensive questioning in October 2014 the man was released from garda custody and returned to prison. He has since completed his sentence for abusing two boys, and maintains he did not attack Mary Boyle.

There are many hypotheses as to what happened to Mary Boyle, or who might be responsible. Even Mary's family has different opinions on how to progress the investigation. Her sister Ann has called for an inquest, but their mother Ann does not want an inquest, saying she needs to believe that Mary is still alive. Mary's mother lives in north Co. Donegal, as do her granddaughter and great-grandchildren, but in 2005 she tragically lost her husband Charlie in a drowning accident.

Mary Boyle's uncle and godfather Gerry Gallagher is the last known person to see Mary. It was about 3.30 p.m. on the afternoon of Friday, 18 March 1977, and he was carrying a ladder back to the house of his neighbour, Patrick McCauley, in the quiet countryside of Cashelard, three miles north-east of Ballyshannon. His little niece followed at a distance, her black wellington boots occasionally getting stuck in the mud along the isolated laneway between the Gallagher and McCauley houses. The walk was only about 450 yards but was over marshy ground. No cars could travel along this laneway. Its main use was as a shortcut between the Gallaghers and their nearest neighbours.

Gerry Gallagher chatted with his niece as they walked, but the conversation was stilted, because he was carrying a heavy ladder and Mary couldn't keep up with her uncle's big strides. About 70 yards from the end of the journey, Gerry, with the ladder over his shoulder, made his way through mud up to six inches deep. Mary, who was only three feet eleven inches tall, hesitated. She pointed over her uncle's shoulder and asked him if he was going up to that house in front of them. He said he was, and he saw her turn back in the direction of his own house, from where they had begun their short walk. He turned to continue his journey. Mary Boyle would not be seen again.

Mary Boyle was three months short of her seventh birthday when she disappeared. She was a bubbly character, a chatterbox, always smiling for photographs. When she disappeared she was wearing her favourite lilac-coloured hand-knitted cardigan, and her brown jeans were tucked into her black wellington boots. Mary was born on 14 June 1970 at the Sorrento Maternity Hospital in Birmingham to Ann and Charlie Boyle, both natives of Co. Donegal. Shortly after Mary's arrival her twin sister, Ann, was born.

I first met Ann and Charlie Boyle in 2002 in their home in Burtonport on the west coast of Co. Donegal. This is the home they were in the process of building in 1977 when they lost their little daughter. In one way Mary was in the house, smiling down on visitors from a large photograph above where Charlie sat. It's a photograph of the three Boyle children, the twin sisters and their brother, Patrick, taken just before March 1977.

Though Ann and Charlie Boyle were both natives of Co. Donegal, they met and married in Birmingham. Ann grew up on a farm at Cashelard, near Ballyshannon, where Mary was to disappear years later. Charlie Boyle was an island man, from Owey Island, one of the many small islands that dot the western coast of Co. Donegal. He left school at fourteen, and in the late 1950s, hearing tales of money to be made on building sites in England, he left Owey and his beloved Co. Donegal to make his living among the large Irish community in Birmingham. One of his five brothers was already in Birmingham, and Charlie soon got work as a builder. At a dance in Birmingham he met Ann Gallagher from Cashelard, and in 1967 they were married. Two years later Ann gave birth to their first child, Patrick, and on 14 June 1970 Mary and Ann were born.

Looking back on their time in Birmingham, Ann and Charlie Boyle found it sad and ironic that a conscious choice they made about their family's future was to lead inadvertently to a terrible event in their home country. Charlie told me it was his choice that the family should return to Co. Donegal.

> There was this drugs problem developing in Britain in the early 1970s. Birmingham had been good to us, but we wanted our children to be safe, and to have a good future. Ann actually wanted the family to go to America, but I wanted to go home. I love the sea, the water; I missed it so much when we were in England. I'd been away from Ireland many, many years before I met Ann. And so we brought the family home to Donegal.

In 1972 they said goodbye to their friends in Birmingham and brought three-year-old Patrick and the two-year-old twins home to Co. Donegal. Five years later, Mary Boyle would disappear.

On 17 March 1966, while Ann Gallagher was living in Birmingham, one of her older brothers, Patrick, aged thirty-two, was killed in a tractor accident at Cashelard. It was the third tragedy to hit the Gallagher family. Another of Ann's brothers had died when he was only three months old, and one of her sisters had also died at a very young age.

After returning from Birmingham, the Boyle family first settled on Owey Island, from where Charlie had left for England two decades before. He began working as a fisherman, and the Boyles fitted in perfectly in the close-knit island community. There were fifteen or twenty people on the island at this time, with the mainland towns of Anagaire, Cionn Caslach and Burtonport just a short distance away. Owey Island gave the Boyle children a wonderful open playground of streams, fields, old walls, hidden nooks and crannies, all within a short distance of their home. Ann told me that while living on Owey Island, Mary was the most cautious of the three.

> There was a small river on Owey Island where Patrick and Ann would run across a small pathway to get to the other side of the river. The pathway was a couple of feet wide, but Mary was so cautious that she lay on the pathway and crawled from one side to the other. She was very careful when out playing, but she never wanted to be left out either.

The family later moved a few miles to the mainland, first living in Burtonport, then Belcruit, near Cionn Caslach, while they began building a house in Burtonport. In March 1977 the future was bright, and Patrick, Mary and Ann were all in primary school and full of wonder and adventure. The three children naturally became excited when they were told they were going to visit their Granny and Granddad Gallagher, Uncle Gerry and Auntie Eva and cousins Gregory and Gerard in Cashelard. Early on St Patrick's Day 1977 the five set off in the family car from Belcruit down the coast through Dungloe, the Glenties, Donegal town, on to Ballyshannon and up to Cashelard.

Ballyshannon lies at the southern tip of Co. Donegal. The seaside resort of Bundoran is a couple of miles south-west; Finner Camp, along the coast just west of Ballyshannon, is another prominent feature. Cashelard is three miles north-east of Ballyshannon, close to the border town of Belleek, Co. Fermanagh.

The Gallagher house in Cashelard is on a hill, with access by a narrow winding laneway. Today the property is in ruins. It's now owned by Gerry Gallagher who lives with his family elsewhere in the county. The nearest neighbours are still the McCauleys. Their house is not visible from the Gallagher house but is up to the right, over a wall and up the isolated laneway between both homes. Beyond the McCauleys' house, also out of view, is the road that leads one way to the border and Belleek, and the other way to Cashelard and Ballyshannon.

On the afternoon of 18 March 1977 Ann Boyle, her sister-in-law Eva Gallagher and her mother, Lizzie Gallagher, were in the kitchen. Charlie Boyle was chatting with his father-in-law, Patrick Gallagher. Mary's twin sister and her brother were playing outside with their cousins Gregory and Gerard to the left of the house, towards the forested area about 30 yards away. Gerry Gallagher was doing odd jobs at a ditch in front of the house.

Ann Boyle broke down as she recounted her memories of that terrible day.

> We had travelled down to Cashelard on 17 March 1977 for a memorial mass for my brother Patrick. We stayed over in the house in Cashelard where I grew up. My mother and father were living there, and my brother Gerry, and his wife, Eva, and their two sons, Gregory and Gerard. In the early afternoon of Friday, 18 March 1977 we had our dinner in the house. I remember clearly we arranged it that the adults sat at one table and the kiddies sat at another table beside us. So we had our dinner; and the children went outside and we were clearing up after dinner. The kids were playing out to the left of the house as you go outside the door. We could hear their voices. I remember my father saying something like 'Are those kids all right?' I was sweeping the floor and I remember he said it again. I said, 'I'll check. I'll look out.' I looked out and could see Paddy and Ann and Gregory and Gerard in a field. I asked them if they'd seen Mary, and one of them said, 'We haven't seen her since dinner time.' Immediately I had this terrible feeling.

What happened over the next couple of moments was a scene of utter panic. Ann Boyle knew immediately that something was wrong.

Once the kids said they hadn't seen Mary, I went back into the house in a terrible state. Charlie said to me that he was sure she would be found in a minute. But I just had this feeling. I said to my mother that if she had a blessed candle in the house she should light it. I got some holy water and shook it out around the house as well. Then I thought of the well close to the house. I ran out there to make sure Mary hadn't fallen in there. There was no sign of her there. I started shouting, screaming her name. I remember telling my brother Gerry and his wife, Eva, that Mary was nowhere to be seen. Gerry immediately ran off in the direction of our nearest neighbours, the McCauleys. I was in a total panic. I remember Daddy saying to me, 'Stop that shouting, Ann. The neighbours will hear you.' But I just knew something was terribly wrong. I just had this feeling. The others thought that perhaps Mary was around somewhere and would be back shortly. Then Gerry arrived back at the house from the McCauleys' and said Mary had followed him when he was leaving the ladder back to the McCauleys. Gerry had retraced those steps to the McCauleys' house, but Mary was nowhere to be seen.

In the panic that engulfed the family after it became apparent that Mary was missing, Gerry had run back immediately towards the McCauleys' house. When he couldn't find her he ran back to the house and told Ann and Charlie that Mary had followed him earlier that day when he was bringing the ladder back to Patrick McCauley. It was a story he was to relive again and again.

After finishing his dinner, Gerry Gallagher had gone outside and picked up a ladder from the front yard to bring back to his neighbour. He set off over a wall and over a rough, hilly pass of marshy ground, along a broken track that acted as a shortcut to his neighbours' house. Mary saw her uncle head off with the ladder. Her brother, sister and two cousins were playing nearby, but Mary wanted to go on a walk. Eating sweets her aunt Eva had given her, Mary chatted with her uncle as she followed him, her black wellington boots getting more muddy as she continued on her adventure. It was about 3.30 p.m.

About 70 yards from the McCauleys' house Gerry and Mary had come upon the particularly muddy patch in a laneway. It was at this point that Gerry saw his niece turn back in the direction of her grandparents' home. In 2000 Gerry Gallagher was interviewed on a *Cracking Crime* programme on RTÉ. Standing outside the old, now derelict Gallagher home, Gerry remembered how he and Mary had been talking as they walked. 'We were chatting, I don't know what it was about. And she quit speaking, I looked around, and she was heading back towards the wall.'

After Mary had turned back, Gerry said he continued on with the last leg of his journey, and stayed about twenty minutes chatting with Patrick McCauley until around 4 p.m.

Ann Gallagher had grown up in the same house, and so she knew the surrounding area like the back of her hand. Once she realised that one of her daughters was missing, and despite her panic, she was able to think of the likely danger areas if Mary had wandered off.

> I immediately thought of Lough Colm Cille, which is some distance from the back of the house. I ran down there in a total panic. I remember there were men out on a boat on the lake and I called out to them to see if they had seen a wee girl. They said they hadn't, and that a man had just asked them the same thing. I saw Gerry: he had thought of the same thing and had gone down to the water too. I asked the men if they could contact the gardaí for us. We had no phone in the house. The men said they would call the gardaí in Ballyshannon.

The two men Ann Boyle spoke to that afternoon did not hesitate in contacting gardaí. This was the era before mobile phones and there were not many landlines in this part of Co. Donegal; the nearest was about half a mile away. One of the men, P.J. Coughlin, knew a lot of local people. He made his way to a phone and contacted gardaí in Ballyshannon. Garda records show the call being made at about 6.30 p.m., some two and a half hours after Mary was last seen by her uncle Gerry.

The two men in the boat on Lough Colm Cille that day were to become important witnesses in the garda investigation. Fishing on the still lake that afternoon, P.J. Coughlin and his friend had their eyes peeled and were listening intently for any sudden or unexpected movements: they would have been the best witnesses to spot anything out of the ordinary. But there is an issue about what exactly P.J. Coughlin told gardaí when the search for Mary began.

In 2016 P.J. Coughlin told *Irish Daily Star* journalist Michael O'Toole that just ten minutes before Mary's uncle Gerry had raised the alarm with him that afternoon in 1977, P.J. had seen a red Volkswagen Beetle drive away from the area. P.J. said he had told gardaí about the red car in 1977 but the information hadn't been recorded in his original statement. The 1977 statement records that P.J. heard a car driving from the area in the direction of Belleek at around 5 p.m. that day, but could not describe the car. There is also no mention of the car being identified as a red Volkswagen. When P.J. gave a further statement in 2002, during a cold-case review, he told officers about seeing a red car that day. In his newspaper interview in 2016 P.J. said he recounted to 'half the town about the car over the years'. He suggested one reason that mention of the car hadn't been recorded in his original statement was because some detectives in the original investigation already had a suspect in mind. The man P.J. was fishing with at Lough Colm Cille that day says that he didn't see any car that afternoon.

The current garda team investigating the case have acquired detail from border checkpoints in the area that day. There is information about a red car recorded in a log, but it is not a Volkswagen Beetle.

From the moment Mary was reported missing on the evening of 18 March 1977, Inspector P.J. Daly at Ballyshannon Garda Station took charge of the investigation. When the alarm was raised there were still some hours of daylight left. Conscious that the Boyle and Gallagher families had checked the main likely areas that Mary might have wandered off to, the gardaí immediately took a decision to call in an army helicopter from the nearby Finner Camp to help in the search. With the helicopter hovering over the mountainside, dozens of gardaí and local people and twenty soldiers combed the countryside around the Gallagher house. A drama festival was under way in nearby Ballyshannon, and those involved, hearing that a little girl was lost or missing, came up to Cashelard to give a hand. Across the border the RUC were alerted. As the hours went by, Ann and Charlie Boyle had terrible thoughts of their daughter lying injured somewhere close by. As dusk turned to night, flares were set off into the air to light up the sky and assist the search.

In Ballyshannon Garda Station a discussion took place between a number of officers. Studying a map of the area, and piecing together the information from Gerry Gallagher and Patrick McCauley, they saw there was a slight chance that instead of heading back towards her grandparents' home, Mary might have turned back again in the direction her uncle had been walking. If Mary had done that, she could have walked on past the McCauleys' house and onto a quiet roadway. Gerry and Patrick had been standing and talking at a shed. It was possible Mary could have walked past them without them noticing her. It was a theory that was studied in March 1977 and it's a theory that Mary's mother Ann believes may be the answer. In 2017 Ann walked the roadway with me and pointed out a location towards the front of the McCauley property where one of Mary's aunts had found a sweet wrapper during a search. The small bit of paper had been caught on briars beside the road. Frustratingly, once recovered, the wrapper hadn't then been kept safe, but Ann Boyle believes it might have been from the sweets that Mary was eating that day – her aunt Eva had earlier broken a roll of sweets in two and given Mary one half.

If the sweet wrapper was Mary's, it meant she didn't walk home as her uncle believed she was going to, but had instead followed him, and then walked through the McCauley property out onto the road. Gerry and Patrick had spoken for about twenty minutes before Gerry headed back to his own home.

Ann Boyle told me that one person involved in the search in 1977 had seen small footprints close to the McCauley property on the laneway linking to the Gallagher property, but these had then been walked over as people arrived to search for Mary. The footprints were farther on from the point that Gerry Gallagher said his niece had turned back. If those footprints were Mary's they strengthened the theory that Mary had doubled back and followed her uncle and then walked to the road, which led one way to Cashelard and the other way to Belleek.

At the time of Mary's disappearance, the IRA was active in south Co. Donegal and Fermanagh. While most of the IRA attacks in the first three months of 1977 were in Belfast and Derry, one British soldier was killed in a bomb attack in Newtownbutler, Co. Fermanagh, and an RUC member was shot dead in Lisnaskea just five days before Mary disappeared. The ongoing violence meant that border checkpoints were more thorough, but the IRA was still able to find ways to traverse the border. It was clear the IRA was one group with eyes and ears in different places, and gardaí wondered if any IRA member might have spotted anything out of the ordinary on the day Mary disappeared, but no relevant information was ever forthcoming.

Also, it would seem logical that the British army would have been involved in reconnaissance activity, recording detail of the movement of vehicles and people around the border area of Co. Fermanagh. The RUC would also have generated documentation about the border, including paramilitary and smuggling activity. No information of relevance to Mary's case was every passed to Irish authorities.

On hearing the first details of Mary Boyle's disappearance, and knowing the layout of the countryside, gardaí feared the worst. If she couldn't be found after a few hours' search over what was a relatively small area, perhaps she wasn't lying injured; perhaps she had been taken against her will. It was against this background that at 6 a.m. on

19 March 1977 the search was extended for miles around Cashelard. A further twenty soldiers were despatched from Finner Camp to assist gardaí. Busloads of relatives and friends of the Boyles travelled down from the north of Co. Donegal to help walk dozens of acres of land. And so began six weeks of searching miles upon miles of rough harsh terrain, cutting back scrub and gorse.

The landscape around Cashelard is dotted with lakes, rivers, streams, ponds, bog holes and drains. All were searched in March and April 1977, and indeed many have been searched again since then. Nothing was ever found. As well as garda divers, other divers came to lend a hand in the search. The Sligo Aqua Club, Ballyshannon Canoe Club and Bundoran Inshore Rescue Team searched the lakes and rivers. As well as Lough Colm Cille they searched nearby Lough Uinsinn, Lough Aghvog, Lough Nagolagh, Lough Meenasallagh and Lough Atierna. It was exhausting work, but the divers were spurred on by the thoughts of a little girl lying alone somewhere, and her inconsolable parents hoping against hope.

Tosh Lavery was a member of the Garda Water Unit. He says the search was thorough.

> At that time there was no such thing as specialist search units. You had gardaí, the army, civilians, all walking the land, and when any deep holes were found myself and others in the Water Unit went to the spot, and we'd get into water-filled holes, sometimes standing up to your neck and we'd search the holes. We got into many bog holes, we searched through muck and slurry. I don't ever believe that Mary fell into a hole, because if she did we would have found her.

Lavery also searched a number of lakes, including Lough Colm Cille. He recorded in a garda notebook how he swam repeatedly back and forth across the lake in a methodical fashion. The water was clear, he spotted bottles and broken crockery on the bottom, but there was no sign of the little girl.

Local Alsatians were deployed as sniffer dogs in the search from the second day. It would have taken too long to transport sniffer dogs up to Co. Donegal from the Garda Dog Unit in Dublin. Gardaí say that every river and lake was searched in the immediate locality. Every search that could be done was done.

In the days immediately after Mary Boyle's disappearance, Ann and Charlie Boyle were hoping that perhaps Mary might have wandered off the beaten track on her way back to her grandparents' house. And then they considered that perhaps someone had picked her up wandering on the road and was just minding her. Journalists descended on Cashelard and RTÉ news filmed those who were searching the land, and also interviewed Ann. Visibly upset, Ann said the family were now thinking someone had picked Mary up. Reflecting back on that time, Ann told me she has many vivid memories of the following few weeks, but the memories are all jumbled together.

> We stayed in Cashelard, and the house was packed tight with people. Charlie would be out helping in the search, and another brother of mine, Michael, was heavily involved in the search. I just felt so sad. Mary wouldn't have known the area. Cashelard was my home. Mary wouldn't have known where she was. Patrick and Ann were so upset. It was to affect Ann for a long time afterwards – her twin sister gone. It was such a sad time for us, but we had such support from people. People came from as far as Co. Mayo and Co. Down to help search for Mary.

Within days, as the search of the Cashelard countryside was yielding nothing, some gardaí decided to take a somewhat unorthodox approach. Conscious that Mary and her twin sister Ann were close, and with all other avenues yielding nothing, local detectives Martin Collins and Aidan Murray arranged a reconstruction. Aidan Murray recounted the tale.

What we decided to do was to bring Mary's twin sister, Ann, on the same journey that Mary had taken, under the pretext of doing an errand or something like that. We thought that because they were twin sisters, and because we knew they were very close, that perhaps Ann might do whatever Mary had done, and might lead us to Mary. Maybe something would catch her eye and she would walk this way or that way. We had gardaí dotted around the laneway, so she was never in any danger. Martin Collins walked with Ann towards the McCauleys' house, and at about the same location that Mary disappeared he said something like, 'Oh, Ann, I've forgotten such-and-such; could you run back to your nana's and get it for me?' So Ann turned back to walk the same walk that Mary had walked, over marshy, bumpy land. Now we were keeping a very close eye on Ann, but we were lying low, out of sight, trying to see if, being a twin, Ann might do the same as Mary had done, whatever that was. As she started to walk back towards her grandparents' house she couldn't see the house. There are some hills and trees in this area. At one stage she stopped and seemed to sway, not knowing where the house was. Was it over this little hill or that one? But she got her bearings and got back to the house. It was worth a shot, but nothing came of it.

The effect of Mary's disappearance on her twin sister and her brother was immediate and deeply saddening. Ann, especially, became much quieter. Her twin sister had been the chattier one; often Mary would speak for Ann. Mary, Ann and Patrick had been on endless journeys and adventures in the fields and laneways around their homes on Owey Island and in Cionn Caslach and Burtonport. Now one of the three members of the gang was gone. Some weeks after Mary's disappearance, Ann made her First Holy Communion. There should have been two Boyle girls enjoying their special day. It was a day dominated by great sorrow.

During March and April 1977 the land around Cashelard and Ballyshannon was combed for clues. Hundreds of questionnaires were circulated in the Ballyshannon area. Five hundred people helped gardaí climb Behy Mountain and surrounding mountainous terrain around the Gallagher home.

The gardaí also investigated whether any strangers had been in the area of Cashelard that Friday afternoon. While there had been visitors in the general area, no one was seen up near the Gallagher home. The people who were attending the drama festival in Ballyshannon that weekend were also questioned, and their movements were traced, but nothing came of this either.

To put it at its simplest, there are only two possible explanations for the disappearance of a little girl on a quiet afternoon in Co. Donegal. Either she was abducted or she wandered into a part of the countryside where she accidentally met her death.

Gardaí say they searched every inch of the surrounding countryside. One detective, in explaining the extent of the search, recounted a distressing tale of how the body of a boy had been found in the north-west many years before.

We had been searching the bogland for Mary, and we searched the water. We covered every inch of the mountain. And then a senior officer remembered how a body of a young boy had been found in a tree. Yes, in a tree. This young fellow had disappeared maybe forty years before. It turned out he had been climbing a tree and had fallen into a hole in the tree. The poor lad was identified by a medallion he wore. But it made us think: we're looking down all the time, what about looking up? Even though Mary was only seven years old, and wouldn't have been capable of climbing a tree in her wellies, we hadn't been looking above our heads. We checked every tree. Nothing was found. But it just shows you. Sometimes you need to take a step back and think: are there any areas we're not covering? I think we searched every inch of the area around Cashelard. If Mary was close to her home, I really believe we should have, and would have, brought her home.

In 2017 detectives Frank Tracey, Tony Keane and Frank Lambe from the Garda Serious Crime Review Team began working with local detectives in Co. Donegal to completely review the case. Chief Superintendent Walter O'Sullivan from the Garda Cold Case Unit outlined the work that was ongoing at the incident room in Ballyshannon Garda Station to try and get a breakthrough in Mary's case.

> Our review seeks to establish all human activity within a 500-yard radius of where Mary was that afternoon. Searches at the time and down the years have been intensive, thorough and systematic. Areas have been searched and researched and no trace of Mary has been found. It is reasonable to assume that Mary's disappearance is associated in some way with criminality, and that a sinister hand was to play in her disappearance.

The crucial question is who might be responsible for Mary's disappearance, and there are many differences of opinion on that matter. Some people believe the answer is local to Cashelard, and a certain group are fixated on one person as the possible culprit. However, other people including Mary's mother Ann say the original garda focus was far too narrow and far too local.

> I don't know what went wrong with them but the guards would be far more aware of things nowadays. At the time, I asked the gardaí to check outside of the area because Mary could have got to the road, and I believe she did get to the road. We asked them to look at the ferry sailings, to look at the boats, to look at images from the boats, and they were too late by the time they went looking for it.

One detective who worked on the case said gardaí investigated the movements of local men who would have been known as potential suspects.

There were at least six what you'd call perverts in the area, around the Donegal–Sligo area. These were fellows who'd be known to be unstable, and would have had convictions or been accused of sexual attacks, mostly against women. None had ever gone as far as abduction, but we of course checked them out. We ruled them out early on. But I suppose these were only the fellows we knew about. At the back of our minds was the case of that poor girl Bernadette Connolly in Sligo in 1970. They never got to charge anyone for that abduction and murder, and we wondered if the same fellow was at work in Mary's case.

Bernadette Connolly was ten years old when she was abducted while cycling near Collooney, Co. Sligo on 17 April 1970. She was running an errand for her mother, collecting a parcel of fish from a neighbour's house, when she disappeared in broad daylight. Her bike was later found propped up in a ditch. Bernadette's body was found at Limnagh Bog in Co. Roscommon on 6 August of that year. She had been murdered. Her killer was never caught. In a cold-case review conducted in very recent years gardaí focused their attention on an English paedophile, Bob Reynolds, who had been travelling in the west of Ireland at the time Bernadette was murdered. Detectives visited Reynolds in prison in Peterborough to discuss Bernadette's case, but there was no breakthrough. Reynolds died in prison in 2013. There is nothing to suggest he was in Co. Donegal when Mary disappeared, although his movements in the 1970s continue to be investigated.

Mary's sister Ann later married Seán Doherty from Gweedore and the couple moved to the midlands. In recent years Ann Doherty has taken part in a number of marches as part of the 'Justice for Mary Boyle' campaign. In 2016 she joined hundreds of people who walked from the centre of Ballyshannon to the local garda station. The previous year she attended a Dublin garda station and made a statement to detectives about her sister's case, and also visited TDs in Dáil Éireann. Speaking outside the Dáil she said she believed she knew what had happened to her sister and that she knew who was responsible for her sister's disappearance.

Talk about who might be responsible for the disappearance of Mary Boyle has been fuelled by the belief of some of the detectives and uniformed gardaí involved in the original investigation. One former officer said he was convinced he knew who was responsible, and that the man had become very upset when being questioned as a witness in the aftermath of Mary's disappearance, crying and saying he didn't harm Mary.

But the current team of garda investigators are considering other possibilities. A huge reinvestigation began in 2011 with the entire case being re-examined under the direction of Detective Superintendent John O'Reilly. A team of detectives at Ballyshannon Garda Station pored over all the original statements and identified new witnesses and new lines of enquiry. One lead emerged when it was established that a man recently convicted of sexually abusing two boys had strong links to Cashelard. The man was now in his early sixties and in 1977 had been a member of the Defence Forces, stationed at Finner Camp. There were suggestions that in the late '70s the man would wander alone cross-country. He was also known to the Gallagher family. Gardaí studied fresh witness statements and assessed medical and psychological reports about the man. He seemed a credible suspect.

In October 2014 the man, now aged sixty-four, was taken from the Midlands Prison in Port Laoise to Mullingar Garda Station where a team of detectives interviewed him on suspicion of kidnapping Mary Boyle in 1977. The man denied any involvement in Mary's disappearance. During the course of the day a large group of journalists gathered outside the garda station, and Assistant Commissioner Kieran Kenny spoke to the assembled reporters, confirming details of the arrest and urging anyone with information regarding Mary's disappearance to contact the team reinvestigating the case.

The man being questioned was later released from garda custody and returned to prison. A much hoped-for breakthrough in the case did not emerge. Information gleaned from the Defence Forces suggested that the man might have been confined to Finner Camp on a disciplinary matter on 18 March 1977, at the time of Mary's disappearance. There was no documentation to prove either way if the man had been at the barracks that Friday afternoon but detectives involved in the cold-case review established that a number of now retired soldiers believed the man might have been under orders to stay at the barracks. If the man wanted to leave the barracks, it would have been easy for him to simply walk out. What really brought the focus onto this man was the fact that the disciplinary matter in question was the suspected indecent assault of a child two months earlier. He had been charged at the local district court. Amazingly, it seems that in 1977 the man was not considered a major suspect in Mary's disappearance. Whether or not the soldier was at Finner Camp when Mary vanished was not established. His was the only arrest in the search for Mary Boyle, and it happened thirty-seven years after she disappeared.

In 2017 I met Mary's mother Ann at the old family home in Cashelard. Also with Ann was her granddaughter Mary Duffy, who was named after her missing aunt. Mary told me how it would mean so much to her and her granny and everyone to know what happened to Mary. As we stood outside the derelict Gallagher family home, full of such life in March 1977, Mary described how sad she felt.

I never met Mary but I've heard so much about her, the type of girl she was. When you're here you feel the sense of loss because this is the last place she was seen. It's so sad to see the way it's gone to ruin. At one point this was a booming family home with much activity in it and to see it derelict now is very sad.

Ann Boyle urged anyone with information to go to the gardaí. Although critical of the original garda team who she believes were too narrow-minded in their investigation, Ann is very supportive of the current garda team who she says are investigating the case with an open mind.

I have begged to know for over forty years what happened to our Mary. She was a wee angel. And it was Charlie's wish to know, poor man, and he died before he knew. It would be very important to me to know before I die.

In 2005 Charlie Boyle died in a drowning accident in waters close to his home at Burtonport in north Co. Donegal. A quiet and decent man, a loving husband and father and grandfather, he found it difficult to speak publicly about the frantic search for his daughter that he had been involved in during late March and into April 1977. Photographs taken by media at the time show the torment on both Ann and Charlie's faces.

A serial killer, who is now dead, was once considered a suspect in the disappearance of Mary Boyle. After an extensive investigation in the 1990s gardaí considered if Scottish man Robert Black might have been working in Northern Ireland on the day Mary disappeared. It was 1994 before Black was brought to justice for murdering three girls in the 1980s, and he was later convicted of murdering a fourth young girl.

In recent years a group of people who favour a Co. Donegal man as a suspect have been critical of those who linked Robert Black with Mary's case. This criticism ignores the fact that two gardaí attended a high-level police conference in Britain relating to Black in 1994, and that for over a decade afterwards many detectives believed Black should at least be questioned about his whereabouts in 1977. In fact, Robert Black was indeed finally questioned, when gardaí met him at Maghaberry Prison in Co. Antrim in May 2013. Black told detectives involved in the current reinvestigation of Mary's case that he had no knowledge of Mary Boyle and had never been to Co. Donegal.

The reason Robert Black had been considered in relation to Mary's disappearance is because at the time of his death in 2016, Black was serving multiple life sentences for murdering four girls and kidnapping two others. In May 1994 Black was convicted at Newcastle Crown Court of murdering three girls over a five-year period and hiding their bodies in northern England within a 26-mile-wide area dubbed the 'Midlands Triangle'. Black murdered eleven-year-old Susan Maxwell from Northumberland in 1982, five-year-old Caroline Hogg from Edinburgh in 1983 and ten-year-old Sarah Harper from Leeds in 1986. He was also convicted of kidnapping a fifteen-year-old girl in Nottingham in 1988. Black was convicted after the jury was told of a previous conviction for sexually assaulting a six-year-old girl in 1990 and of circumstantial evidence that put him and his van at the scene of each of the abductions.

In 2011 Robert Black was found guilty at Belfast Crown Court of the murder of nine-year-old Jennifer Cardy in Co. Antrim in 1981. Jennifer was abducted as she cycled her bike in the village of Ballinderry. Her body was found in Co. Down two weeks after her disappearance.

After Black's conviction for murdering Jennifer Cardy, I spoke with some detectives who had investigated his crimes. They told me that despite him now being convicted of a fourth murder, and this time on the island of Ireland, they did not think Black was responsible for Mary Boyle's disappearance. Members of the PSNI visited Cashelard and walked the land, assessing the geography. The area seemed too remote for Black to be a suspect. All his proven crimes had occurred close to motorways to allow for a quick getaway. They told me that Black was now actually in the frame for a fifth murder – he was now the prime suspect in the murder of missing thirteen-year-old Genette Tate who vanished in Devon in 1978 – but nothing garnered during the investigation into the Jennifer Cardy murder had advanced the Mary Boyle case at all. Some members of the PSNI who successfully prosecuted Robert Black for murdering Jennifer Cardy in Co. Antrim also feel that Black may not be the answer in Mary Boyle's case. According to them, abducting a girl from a mountainside in Co. Donegal just doesn't fit his profile.

Evidence from Robert Black's employer also seemed to lessen the chance the killer was in Ireland in March 1977. Black had worked as a delivery driver for a poster company, and travelled long distances throughout Britain and Northern Ireland. However, gardaí involved in the current reinvestigation of Mary's case have in recent years established that petrol receipts and a wages book from Black's employer suggest he was more likely in Britain when Mary disappeared. The wages book shows Black received a £50 bonus that week, which was the rate that was paid for driving to Northern Ireland for a delivery. However, that payment could also reflect two journeys to Scotland or the north of England, where the rate was £25 per journey. More importantly, there are two petrol receipts that indicate Robert Black was travelling towards Scotland on 16 March, two days before Mary disappeared. One receipt shows petrol was purchased along the M6 motorway, and another shows a purchase on the M1 in England. There is no receipt to show any petrol purchase in Northern Ireland in March 1977. Indeed, it seems from the company records that Robert Black only began delivering posters in Ireland in 1980.

Talk about Robert Black and Mary's case was fuelled in the 1990s by stories from people who were convinced they had met Black in Co. Donegal in the late '70s. People claimed to have seen him in Anagaire and Dungloe in 1976 and 1978. By 1998 Inspector Michael Duffy wrote to Garda Headquarters seeking permission to question Black. The inspector hadn't received a reply by the time he retired soon afterwards. It was well over a decade later when gardaí finally did get to speak with Robert Black in prison, but not only did he deny anything to do with Mary's disappearance, he said he had never been in Co. Donegal. Detectives formed the view that Robert Black was quite possibly responsible for murdering other girls in Britain in the 1970s, but it seemed less and less likely he was involved in Mary's disappearance. His death in prison in 2016 meant he took many dark secrets with him.

Many of those who are critical of any mention of Robert Black in relation to Mary's case are fixated on a man they believe is the prime suspect in the case. This fixation led to suggestions that there had been political interference in the original garda investigation. More recently detective Martin Collins told a local newspaper there had been no such political interference, and his former colleague Aidan Murray swore an affidavit to that effect too. The matter was fully investigated by the current team investigating Mary's disappearance, and there is absolutely no evidence whatsoever to support the claim of political interference.

In 1978, a year after Mary Boyle disappeared, her grandfather Patrick Gallagher – Ann's father – died. Ann told me that within a short time the home she had grown up in became derelict.

> Daddy died in 1978. He was so upset at Mary's disappearance, and then we lost him. Mammy later came to live with us in Burtonport. She was supposed to stay two weeks, and she ended up staying nine years. She had Alzheimer's when she died. My brother Gerry owned the house in Cashelard, but he closed it up in 1981. He and Eva and the kiddies moved a short distance away.

When I met Ann and Charlie Boyle at their home in Burtonport in 2002 there was a bustling atmosphere in the house. They were now proud grandparents, and as we spoke about their lost daughter, their grandson Ultan, Patrick's son, played with jigsaws spread out on the sitting-room floor. Both Mary Boyle's siblings are now married with children.

In 2017 when I revisited Ann at her house there was a different feel. It was still a welcoming home, but now without Charlie. Ann was very upset as she told me how she had received hate mail the previous Christmas. One particularly distressing letter had been written by someone pretending to be her missing daughter.

> There had been some terrible stuff on social media, and then at Christmas and in the New Year I got hate mail, and I was frightened because the stuff in those letters was something else, it threatened my life, and it frightened the life out of me. One was a Christmas card and the other was a letter, and one was written as if it was from wee Mary. I mean, my God, someone pretending they were Mary. That made me ill. I don't think any mother should

be put through that. It's enough to lose your wee girl, a wee girl I doted on, I adored the ground she walked on.

Ann's granddaughter Mary also described the upset the vile material had caused. 'Nanny's been afraid in her own home and no one should be made to live like that,' she said. 'It is horrible.'

While many people use social media for responsible publicity surrounding Mary's case, some were using the online anonymity to post hurtful comments, hijacking the case as a means to criticise gardaí, politicians, media and some of Mary's loved ones. A man from Co. Donegal was identified as the prime suspect for sending the threatening mail to Ann Boyle. Forensic tests made for a strong case against him but he died before he could be brought to court. Whether he was acting alone or as part of a group was never established.

Extensive searches have taken place in the south Donegal area in the years since Mary Boyle disappeared, some as a result of anonymous information provided to local gardaí. In November 1995 members of the Garda Sub-Aqua Unit spent a week trawling a lake near Cashelard, but found nothing. In September 1996 a patch of bogland in Cashelard was searched after a request from the Boyle family. A mechanical digger was brought in and a quarter of an acre of swampy bogland, about half a mile from the old Gallagher home, was drained. In an intensive two-day search, nothing was found. In 2016 another search was undertaken locally, also to no avail.

Gardaí also suspect that the body of a fifteen-year-old Co. Tyrone girl may lie in the area between Ballyshannon and the Co. Tyrone border. Arlene Arkinson from Castlederg, Co. Tyrone, disappeared in August 1994 after attending a disco in Bundoran. During searches for her body in the late 1990s around the Pettigo area of Co. Donegal gardaí were also privately hopeful that some trace of Mary Boyle might turn up. Nothing was found, but detectives know that any effort to excavate any land around south Co. Donegal may inadvertently turn up a lead in either case.

The investigation into the disappearance of Mary Boyle continues. Amid claim and counterclaim, theory and opposing theory, a six-year-old girl is still missing, now away from her family for more than forty years. Gardaí are in close contact with Mary's mother; Garda Sandra McGinty is the liaison officer, and she and Ann are now good friends. Detective Inspector Shay O'Leary now oversees the work that is continuing on Mary's case.

Sergeant John Kennedy retired in 2002, one of the original team to investigate Mary Boyle's disappearance and the last of that team to leave the force. At the time of his retirement he and Superintendent John McFadden met Ann and Charlie Boyle in Burtonport to assure them that although the original garda team were all now retired, the investigation into Mary's disappearance was still at the top of the agenda of the gardaí in Co. Donegal. File no. C31/32A/77 will remain open until Mary Boyle is found.

A memorial to Mary Boyle was unveiled in Cionn Caslach, Co. Donegal, in June 2000. Mary's mother said that the time was right for the memorial.

> We knew about the memorial to missing people that was being planned for Kilkenny. It's a great idea, but it's just a bit too far for us to get to. So I started to wonder about setting up some memorial closer to home. Now we've a lovely little grotto at Cionn Caslach. I didn't want anything too big. This is just right.

The memorial features a small statue of a guardian angel, a plaque bearing a photograph of Mary Boyle, and the inscription: '*Faoi choimirce an aingil choimeádaí go raibh tú*. Mary Boyle, who disappeared from her family on 18 March 1977.'

Ann and Charlie Boyle both told me that it was the not knowing that was the worst thing.

Newspapers report on Mary's disappearance and they mention certain things and draw conclusions. But nobody knows the real answers. Until Mary is found, who knows anything?

Ann's great-grandchildren are a big part of her life; picking them up from school, spending time with them. From an early age the children knew about Mary. When Ann thinks of Mary she wonders if someone picked her up that day and brought her to a different country.

I have to live this way. Did someone pick her up? Is Mary alive in some other country? I've all those thoughts in my head, always. I couldn't imagine her dead. I couldn't cope with it, I wouldn't have been able to cope.

In Burtonport Ann recounts vivid memories of a girl who was almost seven years old, a chatterbox, a wonderful daughter.

Mary was a very jolly little girl. She'd be outside and she'd come in and wash the dishes, and she'd take the turf in for the fire, and she'd be chatting away about school, and what had happened that day. She'd tell me about her day. She was a wee angel, Mary was.

CHAPTER 10

PHILIP CAIRNS

I n October 1986, in a Dublin suburb, a thirteen-year-old boy vanished while walking to school. It was just after lunchtime, and Philip Cairns was making his way back to Coláiste Éanna in Rathfarnham, Co. Dublin, where he had recently started first year. He never arrived. Somewhere on the fifteen-minute walk from his home in Ballyroan Road, Philip Cairns was abducted.

Despite a massive investigation, Philip Cairns has never been found. There is another dimension to this distressing case – an extraordinary event that continues to both baffle and intrigue everyone involved in the search for Philip. A week after Philip was snatched from the roadside, his schoolbag was left in a laneway a short distance from his home. Was it dumped there by Philip's abductor hurriedly trying to get rid of evidence? Or was it more likely left there by a young person who had found it on the day Philip disappeared, but was then too afraid to come forward? Or was it left there by someone related to the abductor, who continues to keep their secret?

The abduction of Philip Cairns continues to shock a country where child abductions are extremely rare. Philip Cairns' disappearance happened nine years after the disappearance of six-year-old Mary Boyle in Co. Donegal, and twelve years after eleven-year-old Thomas Spence and thirteen-year-old John Rodgers disappeared while waiting for a school bus in Belfast.

Philip's disappearance from a busy road in a Dublin suburb is still deeply disturbing to the gardaí who originally worked on the case, and to those who continue to work on it. It is a source of constant anguish for Philip's family. His father, Philip Snr, passed away in 2014 still wondering what happened to his son. Philip's mother Alice still lives at the family house on Ballyroan Road, and Philip is also missed by his four older sisters Mary, Sandra, Helen and Suzanne and his younger brother, Eoin. The Cairns family have endured more than three decades without any answer as to what happened to Philip. On many occasions there have been media reports suggesting detectives were on the brink of a breakthrough, only for the investigation to hit another brick wall. There have been many theories and lots of speculation, most of it well intentioned. However, more recently, an irresponsible social media campaign by some self-appointed experts in the case, which was critical of gardaí and mainstream media, caused great distress to the Cairns family who feared it might potentially hinder some witnesses coming forward.

It was after one o'clock on the afternoon of Thursday, 23 October 1986. Philip Cairns sat at the kitchen table in his home in Ballyroan Road and began doing his maths homework. He had a few minutes to spare before heading back to school. The lunch break at Coláiste Éanna was from 12.45 to 1.45 p.m., and the walk to school would take him about fifteen minutes. Also in the house were Philip's sister Suzanne and his granny, May, who lived with the Cairns family. Philip's mother, Alice, was also at home but was getting ready for a trip to town with his sister Helen, who had a toothache that needed treatment.

Philip gathered the books he'd need for his afternoon classes and got ready to head back to school. He had religion, geography and maths that afternoon; having started secondary school two months before, he was beginning to learn by heart what classes he had each day. He went to talk to his granny and then went back to another room to get his schoolbag. From the hallway he called out, 'Cheerio, Gran. I'm off,' and pulled the front door shut behind him. Within minutes, he would be abducted from the roadside.

Nobody saw Philip leave his house to go back to school that afternoon. It was an ordinary day in the Cairns house, and Philip was following his normal routine of coming home for lunch. To this day Alice cannot remember whether she left for town before or after Philip left for school. The fact that little can be recalled about that lunchtime is precisely because it was so ordinary. But sometime around 1.30 p.m. that afternoon, along the curving Ballyroan Road in Rathfarnham, or on a side road close to the school, Philip Cairns was abducted.

All through that Thursday afternoon no one would realise Philip was missing. His family thought he was in school, while at Coláiste Éanna his teachers assumed he was at home because of illness or a family emergency.

When Philip didn't come home from school that evening his family began to worry. He was a dependable boy and followed a particular routine. His father was not very worried at first, thinking Philip might be out with new friends from school. Starting in secondary school is a daunting time for any teenager, but Philip was beginning to find his feet. It was only when his mother arrived back from town that the first feelings came that something wasn't right. She was met by her eldest daughter, Mary, who said to her: 'Philip isn't in. He didn't come home from school.' Concerned, Alice called to the house of Enda Cloke, Philip's best friend in school, hoping he would be there, but he wasn't. She then checked at the school, where a teacher told her that Philip had never returned that afternoon. It was then that everyone realised that something serious had happened.

At 6.30 p.m. a garda at the desk at Rathfarnham Garda Station received a phone call from Paddy Cloke, Enda's father, who was also a garda. That conversation was to set in train an investigation, which continues to this day.

In the decades since their living nightmare began that October day in 1986, the pain suffered by Philip's loved ones has never diminished. For the Cairns family there are ongoing feelings of hope, frustration and sadness. The fact that a boy could be abducted from a busy Co. Dublin road, and never be found, is a matter of terrible concern for all parents; for the parents of the missing boy, it became an agonising and unrelenting mystery.

Alice and Philip Cairns Snr told me they knew their son was abducted by an unknown attacker. However, they also pointed out that everything else after that was just speculation. When I interviewed them in their home in Ballyroan Road tears welled up in the eyes of both parents when they thought of the boy they lost. With clarity, Alice recounted her memories of the day that changed their lives for ever.

Once I arrived home and heard Philip hadn't come home, I went around to his friend Enda Cloke, but Philip wasn't there. I contacted the school, and found out he hadn't been there in the afternoon. Another friend of Philip's was Gareth, who also lived a short distance away; but Philip wasn't there either. We called in the gardaí immediately. I remember it was getting dark quite early by the end of October, and the weather was quite bad that night. An inspector called down from Rathfarnham Garda Station and said that because of Philip's age, and the weather, they were putting out a full alert, contacting all gardaí immediately. And then the full-scale search began.

The disappearance of Philip Cairns is a mystery that continues to haunt both the Cairns family and the gardaí, who have often feared that the same violent person might strike again. At whatever point Philip Cairns was snatched on the walk back to Coláiste Éanna, the road would have been quite busy. It was a fluke that the abduction most probably happened just seconds before and after other cars and pedestrians travelled past the same spot, or just moments before or after someone went in or out their front door, someone who, but for a few seconds, could have been a crucial witness. Or perhaps there actually is a witness, someone who did see a neighbour or a motorist acting suspiciously, a person who has kept what they saw secret all these years. Certainly, if you walk from Philip's house towards Coláiste Éanna, the first thing to strike you is the volume of traffic. Rarely a minute goes by without a car travelling along the road that links the residential areas of Templeogue and Ballyboden. The large semi-detached houses on each side of the wide road would also have provided a vantage point for a potential witness to Philip's abduction. But no one has come forward to say they saw Philip being dragged into a car, or speaking to anyone on the roadside.

The Cairns family have lived on Ballyroan Road since the late 1970s. Photographs of Philip making his First Holy Communion and his Confirmation have a prominent place in the sitting room. Alice showed me a St Brigid's Cross that Philip made in school a short time before he disappeared; it now has pride of place in the hallway of the house. Alice told me Philip was a quiet and conscientious pupil.

He enjoyed his time in primary school and was very good at arts and crafts. When it came to essays and written tests, Philip would shine. He played a bit of sports, including hurling, and I remember he joked that he didn't know if he'd play for Dublin or Kilkenny – because I'm from Kilkenny. Philip had settled into secondary school and had good friends. He also had interests outside of school and would play out in the garden with his friends and his brother. Everything was normal when this happened.

Philip Cairns was born on 1 September 1973. For the first five years of his life the family lived at St Columba's Road, Drumcondra, Dublin. They then moved to Rathfarnham, to the south of the city. When Philip disappeared in October 1986 his four sisters – Mary, Sandra, Helen and Suzanne – were aged from twenty to fifteen. His only brother, Eoin, was a year and two months younger than Philip, and the two boys were very close. The loss of their brother deeply affected all five remaining siblings. Eoin was in primary school when Philip vanished; he later went to the same secondary school that Philip should have been in.

The intensive and exhaustive search for Philip Cairns began on the night he disappeared. Never in living memory had gardaí investigated the case of a boy snatched from the roadside in such circumstances, and the case remains the only such abduction in the Republic of Ireland. In 1974 two schoolboys, Thomas Spence and John Rodgers, vanished while waiting for a bus to school one November morning in Belfast. The case was never solved, and was hampered by the fact that the boys disappeared from a Republican area on the Falls Road, and the subsequent RUC investigation had been quite limited. There is nothing to suggest that the case of Thomas and John was linked to Philip's, but whoever abducted the boys in Belfast also struck in broad daylight on a busy street, and similar to what happened on Ballyroan Road in October 1986, apparently nobody in Belfast in November 1974 saw a thing. John Rodgers and Thomas Spence are still missing.

As they began their investigation in Rathfarnham gardaí were conscious that, assuming Philip was abducted sometime around half past one that afternoon, the person responsible had seven or eight hours in which to cover their tracks. House-to-house searches began in the immediate area, and gardaí in nearby Terenure and Tallaght were alerted. In the days immediately following Philip's disappearance, lanes, rivers, ponds, fields and parks were searched throughout south Co. Dublin in an increasingly desperate effort to find the missing boy. The searches took place in terrible weather, as the remnants of Hurricane Charlie brought howling winds and heavy rain. However, despite the weather, hundreds of volunteers, gardaí and members of Civil Defence conducted extensive searches in the Wicklow Mountains, situated a couple of miles south of Rathfarnham.

Initially, there was the possibility that Philip had wandered off somewhere by himself, but that possibility fizzled out within days. With the numerous searches by hundreds of gardaí and volunteers, it quickly became apparent that Philip had not chosen to disappear.

Philip Cairns was five feet tall, with dark-brown hair. When last seen he was wearing dark grey trousers, a dark grey V-neck jumper, his grey school shirt, a grey jacket with black shoulder corners and black lace-up shoes. He was carrying his grey schoolbag. None of Philip's clothing has ever been found; but a week after he was abducted something extraordinary took place, something that has never been explained but may yet shed some light on what happened to Philip Cairns. On the evening of Thursday, 30 October 1986, in a laneway a few hundred yards from his house, Philip's schoolbag was found.

It was 7.45 p.m. when two teenage girls, Catherine Hassett and Orla O'Carroll, were walking through the dark, curving laneway that serves as a shortcut between Anne Devlin Road and Anne Devlin Drive, and spotted a schoolbag lying on the ground close to a telegraph pole. They picked it up, looked inside, and quickly discovered that it belonged to Philip Cairns. Shocked at their discovery the girls ran to Rathfarnham Garda Station, where Detective Garda John Harrington was that evening working on other leads in the search for Philip. He took the bag and arranged for it to be searched thoroughly, while still keeping open the hope of gaining some scientific evidence from it.

John Harrington, who is now retired, says the schoolbag holds the key to this case.

The discovery of Philip's bag one week after his disappearance is the best clue we've ever had. The bag was only in the laneway for a short time before it was found by the two girls. That laneway had been thoroughly searched before the bag was discovered, and nothing was found. And dozens of people had passed through the laneway even on the day the bag was found and they didn't see anything. Also, it was drizzling quite heavily that night, but the bag was relatively dry. Whoever left it there did so just a short time before the girls walked through just before eight o'clock that night. So the bag was deliberately left in that laneway one week after Philip disappeared. The questions remain: who left it there? Why did they leave it there? What more do they know?

Whoever left Philip's schoolbag in the laneway did so when it was dark and quiet. The laneway is only about a hundred yards long, and is bordered on each side by high walls behind which are back gardens of nearby houses. Whoever left the bag dropped it at a spot where the laneway curves, so they would not have been seen from either entrance as they dropped it. The identity of the person who left the bag has never been established. That person holds information that is crucial to establishing what happened to Philip Cairns.

There are a number of hypotheses that detectives believe could explain why the bag was left as it was. Philip Snr believed his son dropped the bag when he was abducted, and it was then picked up, perhaps by a young person.

> I think Philip was dragged into a car, and in the struggle that ensued he dropped his schoolbag. Maybe some teenagers found the bag and took some of the books out to sell them to make a bit of money for cigarettes, or a disco. Could it be more than coincidence the bag was left in the laneway just hours after all the children were called back into Philip's school?

On the morning of Thursday, 30 October the boys in Coláiste Éanna were supposed to be enjoying their midterm break, but they had all returned to the school voluntarily, with their teachers, to be addressed by the detectives investigating the case of their missing fellow pupil. The detectives who spoke to the boys were friendly and approachable, but the arrival of gardaí in a classroom must still have been somewhat disturbing. Hours after the boys were quizzed by the gardaí, Philip's schoolbag was found in the laneway.

Philip Cairns' father's belief that the schoolbag was found by other schoolchildren on the day Philip was abducted is one that holds currency with a number of detectives involved in the case. One believes that if the bag was left in the laneway by an innocent person, they could still help in finding Philip Cairns.

> Say the bag was dropped on the road when Philip was attacked and some young kid or kids picked it up. With all the publicity and all the garda activity, that kid may have kept the bag hidden at home. They may have then dumped the bag in the laneway, or

maybe one of their parents or brothers or sisters dumped the bag for them. If this is the case, that person or persons still hold so much information that they may not even know they have. They were a child when they did this, and the natural instinct of a child is not to get in trouble. That child is now an adult, and needs to act like an adult. If they could tell us exactly where they found the bag, then we have our crime scene and, believe me, we would begin to make progress. That person is now definitely an adult; they may even have children of their own. I'm convinced that person is tormented every single day by this whole case.

This schoolbag is almost unique in investigations into the disappearances of missing people in that it is one of the very few cases in which a trace of the missing person has been found after the disappearance. In Killala in Co. Mayo in December 2000 the fleece worn by missing woman Sandra Collins was found five days after she disappeared. It's feared Sandra was murdered and her body concealed. In the days before her fleece was found at the pier in Killala, the entire area had been searched and nothing found. Sandra's family and detectives believe the fleece was planted at the pier by her killer.

It's a simple but frustrating question: was Philip Cairns' schoolbag left in the laneway by someone who was trying to help the investigation, or hinder it? Did the abductor plant the bag in the laneway to take attention away from another search area, or was it left in the laneway by an innocent person who found the bag but didn't want to get involved in the case?

Today the most famous schoolbag in Ireland lies in a plastic evidence bag locked in a safe. When the bag was found, Philip's school journal, a copybook, a maths book and pencil case were inside. Three books were missing: two books required that afternoon for religion class, and a large geography book, *Discovering Geography 1*. These three books have never been located.

When a person close to the Cairns family asked whether the bag and the books still in it could be checked for fingerprints against all the people in the school, a garda told them it would be too big a job, and that all the pupils would have to do so voluntarily. A scientific examination of the bag in November 1986 did not reveal anything of value. However, with recent developments in forensic science, the bag has undergone further testing in recent years, and it's known that it contains what's called 'touch DNA', where the DNA of three people has been detected on the bag. Those three people have not been identified.

For eighteen years until his retirement in 2016, Tom Doyle was the detective sergeant in charge of Philip's case. He told me Philip's schoolbag may one day be the unlocking of the case.

There are many advances that have been made in forensic science in recent years, and there will be even more advances made in the future. Something, which we were unable to detect from a search of Philip's bag in 1986, may be revealed in the future. Philip's schoolbag is kept in a secure location, and it may yet become crucial.

Philip Cairns had a happy life as part of a close-knit family. A number of newspaper articles in subsequent years suggested that in the weeks prior to his abduction he may have been physically attacked, or have been under threat from some unknown person. Those claims resurfaced in recent years on social media. However, the informed belief of those closest to this case is that these claims are simply not true. None of Philip's family believe that anything untoward happened to Philip before the day he was abducted. The family are adamant that he was sleeping normally, eating normally and playing with his friends – all the actions of a boy without a care in the world. His concentration in school was so good that only hours before he disappeared, as his class took turns to read aloud, Philip was able to pick up reading when it wasn't even his turn, after his name was called in error.

Philip spent many happy afternoons fishing with the Dublin City Sea Angling Club and would often travel with his father to the open competitions along the east coast. A few weeks before he disappeared he had taken part in the All-Ireland Juvenile Championships at Garryvoe, Co. Cork. On the day he disappeared he had been looking forward to going away the following weekend fishing with his father. He had also started to learn to swim, and was involved in sports in his new school.

In the days and weeks following the disappearance of Philip Cairns, a sense of fear hung over the country. That fear was compounded by the eerie dumping of Philip's schoolbag close to his home a week after the abduction. Parents around the country refused to let their children walk to school alone and insisted on walking with them or driving them to the school gates, or even keeping them at home. Yet no similar abductions occurred. One detective told me that this fact has led the gardaí to examine a number of possibilities.

The fact that no other boys, or indeed girls, were abducted in the greater Dublin area might suggest the abductor was not necessarily a predator with constant uncontrollable urges to attack. The person would more likely be someone who committed an evil act on impulse, and has managed to control that impulse. That doesn't mean they haven't attacked other children in other ways, but they haven't snatched other children from the roadside. We've also considered the possibility that Philip knew his attacker, and was singled out by the abductor because of this. Another reason that no other abductions occurred might be because the abductor is now dead, or in prison for something else. But we're conscious that there have been a number of reported abduction attempts every year since Philip disappeared.

Philip Cairns' father told me he feared that the person who abducted his son might have tried to strike again.

Even in June 2002, at a spot out on the roadside very close to where Philip would have been walking, a boy about the same age as Philip was approached by a stranger in a car. A car came down from the Rathfarnham area and made a U-turn and stopped close to the boy. The driver said something to the boy like 'Come on, you're late. Get in.' The boy didn't get into the car, and told his parents about the incident that night. The gardaí later said they hadn't made the abduction attempt public because 'nothing happened and nobody had seen anything'. I would wonder if it's the same person who picked up Philip sixteen years before.

In March 2015 the danger posed to children by random abductors was illustrated in a terrifying ordeal in Cullohill, Co. Laois. An eleven-year-old girl was playing with her two younger brothers when a 36-year-old man stopped his jeep and approached the children. The man suddenly grabbed the girl by the waist and pushed her into the jeep through the driver's side. The girl struggled, kicking her legs, but the attacker managed to throw her onto the passenger side and began getting into the vehicle at the driver's door. One of the girl's younger brothers, who was only ten years old, began grabbing at the man, trying to hit him, and pulling at the window of the vehicle. As the boy continued to fight the man, the girl managed to free herself from the other side of the vehicle and get away. The driver fled the scene but was later caught and pleaded guilty to falsely imprisoning the girl. The abductor was Michael Martin, a father of two, originally from Dublin, but with an address in Waterford city. He was jailed for thirteen years.

Was Philip's abductor someone who, like Michael Martin, was a multiple convicted criminal? Martin had ninety-two previous convictions when he tried to abduct the girl; he had suffered trauma in his childhood, having witnessed a friend die tragically; he also had a diagnosed mental disorder. Or is Philip's abductor unlike Michael Martin in every way except a capacity for violence? He could be extremely intelligent, having never come to the attention of gardaí at all, with an ability to conceal his true self. He could be a professional, someone in authority who would not have alarmed Philip as he approached him. There are many possibilities, all still considered by gardaí.

In January 2005 eleven-year-old Robert Holohan vanished from Midleton in east Co. Cork. A massive garda search operation took place as fear gripped the country that an abduction similar to Philip Cairns' had occurred. However, the reality in Robert's case was that he had been killed by a neighbour, Wayne O'Donoghue, who then callously hid the boy's body at Inch Strand, many miles away. Robert's body was found eight days after he disappeared. In a particularly upsetting twist, it would emerge that, along with so many others from the local community, O'Donoghue had taken part in searches for Robert's body, all the while keeping his terrible secret to himself. Detectives investigating Philip Cairns' disappearance have wondered if a similar situation might have existed in his case, whereby someone who assisted in the massive search for Philip was actually the person responsible for taking him from his family.

One detective told me the answer to Philip's case may lie close to where Philip disappeared.

> Philip was a sensible boy, and wasn't foolhardy. He would never have willingly got into a car with someone he didn't know. Therefore he was either dragged into a car in the space of a few seconds or he accepted a lift from a person he knew. If he was dragged in by someone he didn't know, there would have been more of a chance of a struggle, or a scream, or Philip might have dropped his bag. Now, that might have happened and would certainly explain the bag being found dumped close by a week later; but it's almost unbelievable that a child could be basically kidnapped on a busy street and no one to see anything. If I had to guess, I'd say someone he knew stopped and offered him a lift, someone he trusted. If this is true, perhaps it was someone living in the Rathfarnham area, or who worked in the Rathfarnham area.

In November 1986, as the gardaí continued their search for Philip Cairns, a twelve-year-old boy, Ultan Whelan, was chosen to take part in a reconstruction of Philip's last movements for a television appeal.

He was nominated by the principal of Coláiste Éanna after Philip's friend Enda said that Ultan was a good likeness of Philip. As part of the televised appeal, Philip's mother pleaded with the abductor: 'If Philip has been abducted, please let him go. We just want Philip back.'

More than a hundred leads were generated in the hours after the televised reconstruction, as people phoned Rathfarnham Garda Station or called in with information. This brought to over 600 the number of leads gardaí were following up by November 1986. In the first two weeks of the investigation detectives took more than 1,500 written statements, followed up more than 200 reported sightings of Philip Cairns, checked every hostel in Ireland, alerted all ports and airports, carried out house-to-house searches in the Rathfarnham area, and combed woodland and wasteland close to Philip's house. Nothing was found. In the weeks and months after Philip Cairns was abducted, his family were emotionally and physically drained. Alice Cairns spoke to numerous journalists in order to generate publicity, hoping to trigger a break in the case. Philip Snr was taking part in searches day and night. Two weeks after Philip's disappearance another tragedy struck the family when a young relative of Alice's died in Kilkenny following an illness.

The pressure on the whole family was almost intolerable. Philip's four sisters had always looked out for him, and his little brother, Eoin, missed his best friend terribly. Eventually Eoin, Helen and Suzanne were persuaded to return to school, something they all found extremely difficult. Establishing some degree of normality for Philip's brothers and sisters was something that was very important, but almost impossible.

Some weeks after Philip's disappearance, a man contacted the gardaí in Rathfarnham. What he told them would first intrigue then ultimately frustrate them. He said he had been driving along Ballyroan Road from Ballyboden Road between 1.20 and 1.30 p.m. on Thursday, 23 October 1986 – the time Philip is believed to have been abducted. Close to Ballyboden Road he noticed a red car, which he described as being badly parked and obstructing traffic. He said he had seen a boy wearing a grey school jumper and carrying a bag approaching the front passenger door of the parked car. The witness had been angered by the way the car was parked and told the gardaí he had written down the registration number of the car. However, he no longer had the number. He had gone on to the airport, and while he was away his wife had cleaned out his car, and the number was lost. It was only after he learnt of the disappearance of Philip Cairns that he remembered about the badly parked car.

Detectives gritted their teeth, and thanked the man for his help. They knew it wasn't his fault: it wasn't as if he had seen anything that he thought was really suspicious. It was just frustrating that, having had the foresight to write down the registration number of the car, he should then lose it. He was able to describe the driver of the car as possibly about fifty years old, with grey sticking-up hair. The red car might have been a Renault or a Mazda.

In October 1989, three years after Philip's disappearance, gardaí suddenly believed they might be about to unlock the mystery. Detectives received four anonymous phone calls from a man who said he knew 'who had killed Philip Cairns'. The mystery caller, who has never been found, had phoned the confidential number with particular information, which at first convinced gardaí that he was genuine. Over the course of four phone calls he told them that Philip had been driven away from Ballyroan Road that day by a man whose identity was known to the caller. For weeks gardaí spoke to the anonymous caller, each time getting more information from the man, who seemed worried and nervous, but then the calls stopped. When, later that same month, the man had still not been in contact, Superintendent Bill McMunn went on television to reveal that the anonymous calls had been made, and to appeal to the caller to get in contact again.

Bill McMunn told me the calls may have been a cruel hoax.

This man told us he knew who was responsible for abducting Philip, and he called four times. Yet he wouldn't give us the crucial information we wanted. And then the calls stopped. The mystery caller may have met with an accident, or couldn't call us again for some reason; or, as many of us subsequently believed, it might all have been a hoax. It's not right that someone would do that, if that's what happened. We were trying to find a young boy: it's a serious business; but we have to check out all leads, we have to check out everything. I was in the force for forty-three years, and despite all the successes, the unsolved cases do affect you. Gardaí don't like to be beaten.

The abduction of Philip Cairns is only one of a number of crimes to have been committed in the Rathfarnham area in recent decades. During the 1980s the now convicted paedophile Derry O'Rourke lived in the area and appeared to be an upstanding member of the community, happily married and raising his five children. He was a prominent national swimming coach, but beneath it all, over a period of thirty-two years, he was sexually abusing girls he was teaching to swim. From July 1970 until December 1992 he abused at least thirteen girls in changing rooms and other places. In 1997 he was caught and jailed for twelve years.

Another violent man from Rathfarnham, who on the surface appeared to be a committed family man, murdered his wife and a baby girl in 1992. Frank McCann – who, like Derry O'Rourke, was a prominent member of the swimming community – was convicted in 1996 of deliberately starting a fire at his home in Butterfield Avenue, Rathfarnham, in September 1992. His wife, Esther, and an eighteen-month-old baby girl whom the McCanns were rearing, died in the blaze. Local people who witnessed the fire were traumatised by being powerless to do anything to save the victims from the raging fire that engulfed the house. McCann had used a fire accelerant to start the fire, which he lit while standing in the front doorway and throwing in a match as his wife and the baby girl slept upstairs.

Another violent man from Rathfarnham was originally jailed for life for raping one of his nephews in the west of Ireland in 1993. This man, who was single, also admitted sexually assaulting three other boys at his home in Rathfarnham and at hotels around the country on dates between 1989 and 2000. He was also convicted of taking pornographic images of children in the bedroom of his home. This violent man was thirty years old when, in 1989, the first of the known sexual assaults occurred. He did not come to the attention of gardaí until eleven years later, in June 2000, when one of his victims contacted gardaí. The life sentence that was subsequently imposed on the man was later reduced to a ten-year sentence and the convicted rapist now lives in another part of the country.

On 12 November 1994 the gardaí issued a computer-modified photograph showing what Philip Cairns might look like at the age of twenty-one. The process, which used photographs of Philip's parents and siblings at a similar age, tried to interpret Philip's appearance eight years after his disappearance. The technique is similar to the one used as part of a fresh appeal for information in the case of Mary Boyle. Despite the 'aged' photographs of Mary Boyle and Philip Cairns, neither appeal ever led to a definite sighting.

As Mary Boyle has a twin sister, her family had been able to see what Mary might look like as an adult. In contrast, the 'aged' photograph of Philip Cairns was the first opportunity Alice and Philip Snr had to see what their eldest son would have looked like as a man.

The part of Co. Dublin where Philip Cairns disappeared is a densely populated suburban area. Assuming that Philip stayed on the same side of the road as he walked south from his house towards Coláiste Éanna, he would have been walking on the footpath with oncoming traffic to his immediate left. If an oncoming car stopped on the near side of the road and then travelled on in the same direction, it would have brought Philip back past his house and to a junction that links roads to Tallaght, Templeogue, and Rathfarnham. Another possibility is that he was abducted by a person in a car that stopped at one of the side roads to Philip's right as he walked; this car might then have driven either north towards Templeogue or south towards Ballyboden.

Detectives have had to consider many possibilities that can leave even the most focused of minds confused. These possibilities assume that the motorist did not make a U-turn, something that might have stuck in the minds of other motorists. There is also the possibility that whoever abducted Philip did not travel very far but drove towards one of the nearby estates, avoiding the main roads.

In May 2016 the investigation focused on a dying convicted paedophile. Eamonn Cooke had run pirate radio station, Radio Dublin, in the 1970s and '80s, but spent the last years of his life in Arbour Hill Prison having been convicted of sexually assaulting a number of children. A woman who had been a young girl in 1986 was now accusing Cooke of being directly involved in Philip's disappearance. The woman had told detectives in Rathfarnham that she had been in a car with Cooke in October 1986 and that he had collected a boy she believed was Philip. The woman said the car was wine-coloured and did not belong to Cooke. She said she was in the car with him when he had pulled in at a bus stop close to the Blue Haven pub on Ballyroan Road and a young boy had got in. She said the boy knew Cooke and addressed him as 'Mr Cooke'. She said Cooke told the boy to get into the car and he would show him the Radio Dublin studios. The boy said he would be late back to school but Cooke said they would only be a few minutes.

The woman said the boy got into the front passenger seat of the car; he was about thirteen years old and had black hair. She said the boy gave Cooke a cassette tape from his bag. Cooke then drove them to the Radio Dublin studios in Inchicore. The woman said that, through a glass window inside the building, she had then seen Eamonn Cooke push the boy, who then pushed Cooke back. She said Cooke picked up a trophy and hit the boy on the head. The woman said she passed out and did not see the boy again.

The woman said that she could recall being in a car with Eamonn Cooke a few days later and two other girls getting into the vehicle. She said the bag belonging to the boy was in the car, inside a black bag. She said Cooke instructed her to give the bag to the two girls and that they had driven to a laneway where the two other girls had brought the bag. The witness said she did not know the two girls, and never saw them again.

As gardaí read over the woman's statement, they knew that the Blue Haven pub was in the opposite direction to Coláiste Éanna. It would have meant Philip turning left out of his driveway instead of right. No one had reported seeing a boy walking that direction on the day of the abduction. However, now a woman had made a statement outlining very precise detail of childhood memories. Detectives would have to put these allegations to the convicted paedophile the woman was now linking to the case.

Detectives quickly established that Eamonn Cooke had left Arbour Hill Prison and was now in St Francis Hospice in Raheny where he was very ill, at the end stages of cancer. Detective Sergeant Tom Doyle and Detective Garda Nuala Burke went to the hospice and over the course of two days questioned Cooke about the allegations now being made against him.

The questioning was carried out on 21 and 22 May 2016 and the process was difficult. A nurse was with Cooke at all times, and at one point insisted that because of his ill health he should only answer 'Yes' or 'No' to the detective's questions. Cooke was clearly in poor health, and at certain times simply stared at the two gardaí but at other points he did answer questions in a low and at times inaudible voice. Some of his answers were to prove intriguing.

During the first day of questioning Cooke said he had met Philip Cairns, and that Philip had been in his house in Tallaght. He said Philip had been at the radio station in Inchicore once or twice. When asked about any incident at the radio station Cooke replied 'No'. He indicated he could remember Philip's bag being in his car, but when asked if he had put the bag in the laneway he replied 'No', and when asked if he had got someone else to put it in the laneway he replied 'No'. Eventually Cooke said he couldn't help anymore.

The two gardaí returned to the hospice the next day and on this occasion Cooke was told of the full allegation being made against him by the woman. Some of Cooke's responses again tended to put him in the frame, while other answers were at odds with the allegation against him. He again said he knew Philip Cairns, but he said Philip and the girl had not been at the radio station together. Cooke said Philip had travelled by himself to the radio station. He said he supposed he had brought Philip home from the radio station as he brought a lot of kids home. When asked again about the schoolbag being in his car he replied 'No'. The interview ended soon after this.

Cooke had been slightly more lucid on the second occasion, and detectives Doyle and Burke made a final appeal to him to give them any information he had about Philip Cairns, but no more information was forthcoming. Eamonn Cooke died twelve days later, on 4 June. Gardaí had done their best to question him as soon as a statement was made linking him with Philip's disappearance, but his answers in the hospice were confusing. Clearly severely ill and under pain management, he said he knew Philip Cairns but denied attacking him. He said Philip's schoolbag had been in his car, but he denied putting the bag in the laneway or asking anyone else to do it. He said Philip had been in the Radio Dublin studios, but not when the girl (the woman who had now come forward as a witness) would have been there.

Philip's mother Alice does not believe the statements by Eamonn Cooke that her son had been in his house or that he had visited Radio Dublin studios a number of times. In an interview on RTÉ *Prime Time* in June 2016 she thanked the witness who had come forward with the information, and said she believed the woman had done so in good faith, but Alice said her son did not have any link to Radio Dublin and didn't know Cooke. It just didn't sound like Philip at all. Again appealing for the public's help Alice said that whoever had taken Philip was someone her son had 'known slightly, or didn't know at all'.

Despite Cooke's death, detectives continued to investigate the new line of enquiry linking the paedophile with Philip's disappearance. Nineteen boxes of personal belongings, including audio tapes, video tapes and diaries, were taken from Cooke's cell in Arbour Hill and examined by detectives, along with seven boxes recovered from a storage unit at an industrial estate in Ballymount. However, nothing was found to link Philip to Eamonn Cooke. Philip's schoolbag underwent a fresh forensic examination, but Cooke's DNA was not found on it.

An anomaly arose that lessened the possibility that Cooke was a credible suspect in Philip's disappearance. It emerged the house that Cooke indicated he had brought Philip to was not occupied by the paedophile until the year after Philip disappeared. Another house he had lived at in Tallaght in 1986 was also examined but again nothing was found. The old Radio Dublin studios had been demolished, and there were simply no more investigative avenues available. A number of sites were identified where Eamonn Cooke had located transmitters in the Wicklow Mountains for his pirate radio station, but in the absence of any further information there was no prospect of excavations being conducted at any site. A senior garda later recorded that there was no information available to link Eamonn Cooke to Philip Cairns other than the woman who had come forward, and that other lines of enquiry separate to Eamonn Cooke would continue to be pursued.

In mid- to late-2016 a vicious social media campaign was waged by a number of people who attacked the gardaí, claiming the force was trying to pin Philip's abduction on the now deceased paedophile Eamonn Cooke. Those fuelling the campaign failed to realise that detectives had to follow every lead in the case, and that Cooke had made ambiguous statements, which had to be investigated, whereby he had seemed to both incriminate and distance himself from the crime. The campaign claimed Cooke had been a smokescreen to hide the truth and suggested Philip had been the victim of a paedophile ring and that the paedophiles were still being protected because of their social status. Gardaí asked those heading up the campaign for evidence to back up the claims but none was ever provided. Indeed, the campaign failed to mention that those claims had been brought to gardaí by other people years earlier, had been thoroughly investigated and found to have absolutely no merit.

The social media campaign also caused great distress for Philip's family. Some of the commentary had questioned why Philip's family were not more critical of gardaí or were not more vocal online. One of the more outrageous claims made was that Philip had confided in his family that he was being abused. This simply wasn't true. Not only was this claim utter nonsense, it was deeply distressing to Philip's family. Eventually Philip's sister Sandra responded to the hurtful material while speaking at the National Missing Persons Day event in December 2016.

Remembering her brother as a 'happy, contented boy', who, as he began secondary school, was showing a bigger interest in 'music, his clothes and having the right hair style', Sandra said the past thirty years had been heartbreaking for Philip's loved ones.

Sandra acknowledged that so many people had shown a genuine concern for Philip, but admitted that a recent social media campaign had been shocking and deeply distressing.

> Philip has been inaccurately described as a troubled, distressed and vulnerable loner … this callous portrayal of him bears no resemblance to our Philip … some online commentators have said that we, his family, don't own Philip's story. But they fail to realise that for us, it is not a story to be taken up and dropped on a whim. It is our life and our experience that we have to deal with every day.

Sandra thanked the gardaí for their dedicated and continuing work on the case. She added that she feared some of the irresponsible online commentary could stop potential witnesses coming forward.

The National Missing Persons Day event had been established in 2013 and the Cairns family attend every gathering. Reflecting on when Philip disappeared, Sandra told the 2016 event that victim support thirty years ago was very limited and it had been a long time before they had met with other families going through a similar trauma. She praised the Missing Persons Helpline for helping to make those connections.

Whoever left Philip's schoolbag in the laneway close to his home a week after his disappearance holds the key to the case. That person could pinpoint the site of the abduction and so narrow the search, even now. Philip's normal practice was to put his schoolbag over his head and wear it across his chest. When later examined, the bag had not been cut or damaged in any way, so if Philip was wearing it over his head it would have taken a number of seconds for the abductor to take it off and throw it on the roadside, an action that would have been unusual for someone trying to cover their tracks.

Perhaps the more credible possibility is that the bag was removed later at an unknown place. The abductor may then have thrown the bag some distance from the scene of the abduction, where it was found by schoolchildren; or he may have kept the bag and then left it in the laneway himself a week later. If the bag was left by the abductor, detectives believe this was to try to throw them off the scent. It is not thought likely that a person who had committed such a violent and callous act would have risked capture close to the scene of the crime, unless it was to throw some type of smokescreen over the investigation. Many detectives who have mulled over the bag clue so many times feel that the most likely explanation remains that the bag was left in the laneway by an innocent person.

The search for Philip Cairns extended all over the world. While many detectives feel that the answer to Philip's disappearance lies somewhere in south Co. Dublin, every conceivable lead has been followed up. One hypothesis, which received considerable attention, was that Philip was abducted by a religious cult. This possibility was privately examined by the gardaí – indeed premises owned by certain religious groups were searched – but this line of enquiry was ruled out in the early weeks of the investigation. The idea had been fuelled by the fact that two of Philip's religion books were missing from his schoolbag when it was found but ignores the fact that a geography book was also missing, and that all these books had been in Philip's bag only because he had those classes that afternoon. Gardaí also point out that the kind of religious groups capable of such an action were relatively rare in Ireland in 1986. Whoever abducted Philip Cairns is more likely to be someone who was able to blend into the community and not arouse suspicion.

Another idea put forward was that some other unknown person might have abducted Philip and taken him abroad. In the years since Philip's disappearance there have been reported sightings as far away as America and Argentina. All reported sightings are investigated, but none has ever stood up as genuine.

In December 1986, two months after Philip vanished, two boys disappeared in England and were never found. Eleven-year-old Patrick Warren and thirteen-year-old David Spencer were last seen in the town of Solihull, near Birmingham. Patrick and David are among a number of children to vanish throughout Britain in the 1970s and '80s. Philip Cairns is but one of a small number of children to vanish in Ireland. There is nothing to suggest any link between the disappearances.

Alice and Philip Snr were subjected to several false leads and hoaxes after their son disappeared. Some mistakes were genuine and without malice; but a number of people have acted in a callous manner towards a family whose grief has been laid bare for everyone to see. A person close to the family told me some of the added traumas the family has had to suffer down the years.

I'll never forget the night that the schoolbag was found in the laneway. One garda in his excitement actually came into the house and said, 'Philip is around; we've found his bag; we'll have him back home in the next half hour'. Can you imagine hearing that and waiting that night, and waiting, and nothing: Philip doesn't come home, Philip doesn't ever come home; can you imagine? And while that's an example of a false hope that happened through overenthusiasm or stupidity, there have also been really sick people who've targeted the Cairns family. One man once phoned them up pretending to be a garda at a station in north Dublin, saying that he'd found Philip and that he was bringing him home. Again the family waited, and of course nothing happened. That man phoned from what sounded like a busy garda station, so he was in some type of office when he made this hoax call. What type of sick person does something like that? A female garda stayed with the family for weeks after Philip went missing. Some of the phone calls were very upsetting. But you have to answer the phone: the next call could be the one.

Newspaper articles have suggested Philip was the victim of more than one attacker, and that he might have been murdered because he was about to expose a paedophile ring. These distressing articles quote unnamed sources who have never confided this information to gardaí. They have caused immense pain and upset to Philip's family, who are adamant that Philip had nothing troubling him in the weeks before he disappeared. The articles have also angered the gardaí involved in the case.

Just because a journalist writes something doesn't make it true. We've had a number of people come into us with their theory about what happened to Philip. We've had everything suggested to us, from a foreign child-trafficking ring to aliens. It's all wild speculation, and it doesn't help. These journalists need to remember that there is a family left behind here, and there is a memory of a young boy to be honoured and protected. In relation to the 'paedophile ring', there is absolutely no proof. Certain journalists quote unnamed sources, people who have never contacted us with this information. Show me the proof.

Alice and Philip Snr's five remaining children are all now in their forties and fifties. Philip Snr retired from his job as a purchasing manager at the end of 1994. In 2013 he and Alice celebrated their fiftieth wedding anniversary. Sadly, Philip Snr passed away in 2014. The other boys in Philip's class in 1986 are now grown men; most are married and with families of their own. All the while, the search for Philip continues.

In 2009 gardaí began an excavation at a wooded area in Rathfarnham. The search took place near the junction of Whitechurch Road and College Road, close to the M50. A team of geophysicists were on-site to advise officers on how to conduct the search, with specialist equipment being used to look for evidence of soil disturbance. The search followed new information received by detectives but was called off after a few days, with nothing found.

The Cairns family were kept up to date with that search, and indeed all investigative leads down the years. Several gardaí have served as the family liaison officer and become close to the family, including Detective Garda Mary Fallon, Detective Sergeant Tom Doyle, and more recently Garda Maria Dennison.

Tom Doyle worked the case for eighteen years, pledging to do everything possible to find Philip. He got to know the Cairns family well. As the detective sergeant in Rathfarnham from 1998 until 2016, Doyle investigated many other cases that were ultimately solved, including a number of murder cases, but he always went back to Philip's case as one which deserved ongoing garda attention. Now retired, he says detectives in Rathfarnham would dearly love to find Philip.

> It all comes down to one thing: someone knows something that can help us solve this mystery. In all probability there is some person who is tormented every day by their secret and would love to speak out in confidence. It could be a seemingly trivial piece of information that someone has that might fit what we're looking for. Despite the passage of time, the search for Philip will never end.

The current team of investigators are based at Rathfarnham and Tallaght garda stations and include Superintendent Ian Lackey, Detective Inspector John Walsh, Detective Sergeant Tom McManus and Detective Garda David Connolly.

In the mid-1990s the Cairns family came face to face with another family who continue to suffer similar pain. Alice and Philip Snr met Ann and Charlie Boyle, the parents of Mary Boyle, who was six years old when she disappeared in Co. Donegal in March 1977. The families met in the grounds of RTÉ in Donnybrook, Dublin, where they had taken part in a radio discussion about missing people. It was a deeply emotional meeting, and many tears were shed. Later, at Ballyroan Road, the two families talked late into the evening. It was an extraordinary meeting of two families both living a life of uncertainty and both clinging to a chink of hope that their children would someday be found. Although sadly Charlie Boyle and Philip Cairns Snr have since passed away, Ann Boyle and Alice Cairns have attended every National Missing Persons Day event since 2013.

Every anniversary brings media attention. In 2006, on the twentieth anniversary of Philip's disappearance, I interviewed his younger brother Eoin for RTÉ news. Eoin was eleven when his brother disappeared.

We played soccer in our back garden, and with other boys on our road. Philip played hurling for a local team, he loved to go fishing with Dad. We think of Philip and how he should be with us. He is always there in the sense that he is not there. He was my best friend.

CHAPTER 11

MARIOARA ROSTAS: TAKEN IN BROAD DAYLIGHT

On Sunday, 6 January 2008, eighteen-year-old Marioara Rostas was abducted from a Dublin street in broad daylight by a gangland criminal intent on murder. Marioara and her thirteen-year-old brother Dumitru got the train from Donabate into Dublin city that morning to beg at traffic lights at Lombard Street, close to the Births, Deaths and Marriages Office, a short walk from Pearse train station. The killer didn't know Marioara but specifically targeted her, having observed her as she begged. Marioara was of slim build, weighing only eight stone, and was just five feet three inches tall. She was six weeks short of her nineteenth birthday but looked much younger.

Marioara didn't speak English and had been in Ireland less than three weeks. Life was tough for her and her family, but it had been even tougher in their original homeland in western Romania. When her father Dumitru lost his job in a furniture factory back home, the family travelled to Ireland and resorted to begging to get money for food. Marioara was with her family and other members of the Roma community in Ireland and living in a derelict property in north Co. Dublin with no sanitation, electricity or running water. Marioara's parents had first arrived in Ireland in October 2007 and their daughter joined them on 19 December.

A garda investigation would later establish that Marioara's abductor had apparently driven around Dublin at the same time the previous week. Perhaps he had spotted Marioara then. Perhaps on that occasion he was planning to abduct her or someone else but changed his plans because there were too many people around. However, on Sunday, 6 January the killer was ready to strike. Having spent over an hour in the area, he pulled up beside Marioara. Dumitru saw his sister speaking with the driver and approached the vehicle too. He would tell detectives that in the brief discussion between Marioara and the driver it seemed there was a promise of a McDonald's meal. He handed Dumitru €10 and Marioara got into the car.

Dumitru watched his sister being driven away in a Ford Mondeo with a Louth registration. Dumitru couldn't read, but he was able to remember letters and numbers and he would later tell detectives that the registration of the car began with 01-LH. Over the following hours Dumitru waited for his sister to return with the McDonald's meal, but she never did.

From subsequent analysis of a particular 085 mobile phone that pinged off a number of telephone masts, both that day and the following day, it is believed Marioara was driven over the river Liffey to a house on Castle Avenue in Clontarf. Detectives believe the killer had been living in a flat in the house, using a false name.

Whether Marioara was taken directly to Clontarf is not clear. The killer's phone was not active for a five-hour period between 1.15 p.m. and 6.30 p.m. that day. It then pinged close to Clanbrassil Street in Dublin's south inner city. It's possible that he took Marioara directly to

Clontarf, tied her up and left her in the flat, while he then drove to the south inner city, returning to Clontarf later that day. The killer's phone was active in Clontarf from 7.40 p.m. that Sunday night, and would ping off the same mast in Clontarf until the following afternoon.

At some point soon after she got into the killer's car Marioara realised that she was not being taken to McDonald's, but was in fact being taken far away from her brother. At some point she realised the friendly motorist promising her and her brother a meal was in fact a very evil man. She wouldn't have known much of Dublin at all, and she must have felt absolute terror as it dawned on her that she was trapped in the car. The leafy suburb of Clontarf, close to the city centre, became the location where a terrified Roma teenager was forced into a basement flat in a large house on Castle Avenue and locked in a room. It is likely the attacker stayed with Marioara in her makeshift prison in Clontarf that night. Just what exactly happened in that time will never be known.

Garda enquiries established that Marioara was alive for more than twenty-four hours after her abduction, but because the teenager's body was not found until four years later, the post-mortem examination was unable to establish the precise nature of the attacks she suffered before she was killed, specifically if she had been raped or sexually assaulted.

When Marioara didn't return to the area near Pearse train station that Sunday Dumitru eventually left and contacted his parents, explaining what had happened. That night, Marioara's father Dumitru Snr called to the front desk of Pearse Street Garda Station to report his daughter missing. In broken English he tried to explain that his daughter had only been in Ireland since before Christmas, that she did not know Dublin at all, and that if she had said she was returning to her brother, that's what she would have done.

Although in time detectives at Pearse Street Garda Station were to play a key role in finding Marioara's body and establishing much of what had happened in the case, initially gardaí wondered if the answer to Marioara's disappearance lay within the Roma community itself. Perhaps Marioara had been the victim of an arranged marriage, or an attack linked to criminals within the Roma community. It was a natural consideration, given that gardaí in Dublin city had investigated such cases before. Nobody yet knew how wrong that theory was in Marioara's case. It would be many months before the shocking reality of the teenager's murder was laid bare.

At some point in 2007 the killer had driven out on the N81 road towards Blessington and turned off past Manor Kilbride, heading towards the Sally Gap. At Kippure he'd parked and then walked for a mile to a secluded area in a small forest. There he dug three and half feet down into the ground, then two feet wide and five feet long. It was similar to something the IRA would have used to store weapons, but this hide was being built by a young Dublin criminal. The hole would comfortably hold a body. The killer covered the grave with plywood and soil. It was now ready for use.

This killer kept handguns, shotguns and rifles hidden in various places in south Dublin, from Crumlin to Terenure, and across the city in Clontarf. He was close to a gangland assassin from Dublin who had previously hidden out in Carlow and was now across the border in Co. Down. That assassin had already killed a number of men, hiring himself out to a criminal gang involved in a feud in Dublin.

Some gardaí wonder if Marioara's abductor had murdered before. Other detectives think Marioara was his first victim and that his modus operandi, in digging a large hole and cruising Dublin city the week before the abduction, suggests he was working up to killing: he wanted to take a life, maybe he wanted to emulate fellow criminals he looked up to.

Marioara was resourceful. Although vulnerable due to her stature, and at a significant loss in Ireland because she didn't speak English, the teenager had survived a tough upbringing, begging on the streets, living in appalling conditions in Romania and indeed the short time she was in Dublin. We will never know the terror Marioara felt as she was held captive at the house in Clontarf. She must have thought of her younger brother still waiting for her at Pearse train station. The only parts of Dublin that she knew were the area around the train station and the part of Donabate where the family were staying in a derelict house. She had no idea where she was being held. But somehow within her prison in Clontarf she managed to get access to the killer's mobile phone. It was Monday afternoon. Marioara had been held captive for more than twenty-four hours at this stage. Perhaps the killer had fallen asleep in the same room as her. Somehow she got his phone. She rang the first number she could think of – it was the communal mobile phone at the Roma settlement back in Romania. In her haste she keyed in the wrong number the first time, but she got it right the second time. Marioara was contacting her brother Alexandru over 2,600 kilometres away. She keyed in the thirteen digits and pressed the dial button.

The call from Clontarf to Romania was made at 2.42 p.m. Alexandru Rostas was in the home village of Tileagd, which lies close to the Hungarian border. The village is home to a number of Roma families and conditions are very basic.

Alexandru's cousin answered the phone. The phone call lasted five minutes and five seconds. Most of that time was taken up with the cousin running to find Alexandru and give him the phone, telling him it was Marioara on the line from Ireland and she was very upset.

Alexandru took the phone. Marioara said she was somewhere out of Dublin. She said to get their daddy to come and get her. She was crying and sounded very frightened. Again she said to Alexandru to get their daddy to come and get her. Then the phone went dead.

Alexandru immediately contacted his father in Ireland and he also later spoke to Romanian police. In time the number of the Irish mobile phone Mariora used to ring Alexandru would be identified: it was an 085 'ready to go' phone, which was not registered to any specific person. Detectives would eventually build up a picture of the phone's movements at the time of the abduction and murder.

It's likely the killer either woke up in the room in Clontarf or came into the room and found Marioara mid-conversation on the phone. He didn't know what she had said in Romanian, or who exactly she had spoken with. He would have seen the foreign number she'd called, but still, he would have been worried that the suburban prison he had brought her to might somehow be compromised. It's likely he quickly decided to move her from that basement flat to one of a number of locations throughout the city in which he stored items. He knew someone who lived at Brabazon Street, across the river Liffey in the Coombe.

The mobile phone pinged in the south inner city as the killer travelled from Clontarf that Monday evening to move Marioara across Dublin city. It's likely she was in the boot of the Ford Mondeo, either unconscious or gagged and tied up. The house she was brought to on Brabazon Street is in the middle of a populated area close to Meath Street. Yet no one saw anything suspicious.

And no one heard the shots. In a built-up area of Dublin's south inner city, in one of the most heavily policed parts of the country, Marioara was carried or forced to the top floor of a three-storey building and murdered. The teenager was shot four times in the forehead, her killer standing in front of her. One shot was to the left temple, the other three were directly into the forehead. Marioara would have known what was coming.

In the immediate aftermath of Marioara being reported missing in January 2008, gardaí issued a public appeal for information and circulated her photograph to all media. Detectives knew there was a serious concern for the teenager's safety, but it was not until many months later that it became apparent that a Dublin criminal was a suspect in the case. In the early part of 2008 gardaí followed up a number of leads which ultimately led nowhere, and worked to track down all owners of Ford Mondeos with a 01-LH registration.

The first real break in the case came in the summer of 2008 when an anonymous phone call was made to gardaí following an appeal about the missing teenager on the *Crimecall* programme on RTÉ. The caller said detectives should look at a house near a pub on Brabazon Street, though the house had been destroyed by fire the month after Mariaora disappeared. Enquiries by detectives established a link between a Ford Mondeo and the property at Brabazon Street. When the building was forensically examined, Detective Shane Curran found two bullet holes in walls of the house. No trace of Marioara was found at the property, but gardaí feared that she had been murdered in the house.

As well as the fire at Brabazon Street the month following Marioara's murder, a fire was subsequently started at the flat on Castle Avenue in Clontarf where Marioara had been held captive. It would be a number of months before a link was established between the properties. Meanwhile, the criminal continued about his business. He was believed to have committed aggravated burglaries in Rathmines and Terenure in south Dublin, although he was never convicted.

In November and December 2008 gardaí arrested four people in connection with the suspected murder of Marioara Rostas. Three more arrests followed in October 2009. Some of those arrested were questioned as suspects for the actual murder, and others on suspicion of withholding information. All suspects were released without charge. In the absence of Marioara's body, criminal charges would be very difficult. The investigation was being overseen by Superintendent Joe Gannon at Pearse Street, and involved teams of detectives led by the Senior Investigating Officer Michael Cryan at Pearse Street, and Detective Superintendent Gabriel O'Gara and Detective Inspector J.J. Keane at Kevin Street Station.

The detectives knew the answer to Marioara's case lay within a small group of people who were so far refusing to talk. A number of men and women were arrested in Dublin in November 2008 and questioned about Marioara's disappearance, but all were released without charge. Detectives were in the frustrating position of believing they knew the identities of criminals who had information about the case, but in the absence of Marioara's body, it seemed that the case might never be solved. A team of detectives worked consistently on the case throughout 2010 and 2011, but still it seemed there might never be a breakthrough. Then, in November 2011, gardaí learnt of a plot to kill three people: a journalist, a witness in a trial and a garda. This plot, which was hatched from inside Cloverhill Prison, involved the criminal believed to have murdered Marioara. He was on remand in prison charged with a separate offence, but was believed by gardaí to be issuing instructions to people on the outside to kill a number of people on his behalf.

The investigation into this very real plot led gardaí to question another man – and it was this other person who, now under severe pressure, would lead them directly to Marioara's body. This man maintained he had not been involved in the teenager's murder, but had helped another person to bring her body 30 kilometres from Brabazon Street to an isolated forest at Kippure in the Wicklow Mountains. The witness swore that the first time he saw Marioara she was already dead. He said this other person brought him to the top room of the house at Brabazon Street and showed him the body, saying he had shot her dead because she was a witness.

The man who brought detectives to the very forest where Marioara's body was found was never charged with any offence related to the case and was later given immunity for his assistance. He entered the witness protection programme due to his assistance in Marioara's case. He also was never charged in connection with the conspiracy to kill the journalist, garda and trial witness.

Marioara's body was found on Monday, 23 January 2012. It was day thirteen of the search in a small forest at Kippure, Co. Wicklow. During the previous seven days the searchers had felt confident they were in the right area. On 16 January Garda Dermot Walsh had discovered a large empty rectangular hole in the forest. The officer had been operating a mechanical digger when he spotted that the soil was a different colour at a certain point. By slowly scraping the soil at that spot, gardaí had found plywood placed across a hole big enough to hold a body. The discovery of the pit tied in with the information given by the witness who had led them directly to this section of Kippure in the first place.

The search by a dozen gardaí from the south inner-city stations of Pearse Street and Kevin Street, led by Inspector Pat McMenamin, was hard physical work. Rows upon rows of trees had been planted years before and the search involved cutting branches with chainsaws to allow the digger access to parts of the forest. In some sections the trees were too close together so excavation there was done by shovel.

The man who led gardaí to Kippure said he had been present when Marioara's body was buried there. He said that the killer had been looking for a hole he had previously dug in the forest, but, on that night in early January 2008, he had been unable to find it. The witness said it was covered over with plywood but the killer had covered it too well, and that they had to resort to digging another, smaller hole, less than two feet deep. Marioara's body was carried over a mile from the car, which had been parked on the R759 mountain road linking east and west Co. Wicklow. And into this crudely dug hole Marioara's body was dumped, partially covered with tree roots. The witness said the killer danced on Marioara's body to force it down into the ground. The soil was placed back on top.

The killer's phone was turned off for over five hours on the night of 7 January. Before this it pinged near the Long Mile Road where the criminal had gone to a DIY store to get materials to clean up the murder scene at Brabazon Street. He returned to the house and wrapped Marioara's body tightly in plastic bags. He turned off his phone. The phone would remain off from 8.45 p.m. until 1.58 a.m. on the morning of 8 January. Those five hours would have afforded him ample time to drive Marioara's body in the Ford Mondeo from the south inner city to the woodland at Kippure in Co. Wicklow. A second mobile phone, which was in close contact with the killer's phone, was also turned off during the same period. Considering the geography of Kippure, and the fact that the nearest road to where Marioara's body was found is over a mile away, detectives always suspected that more than one person was involved in the burial of Marioara's body.

The Wicklow Mountains have long been used by paramilitaries, criminal gangs and individual killers to hide the bodies of their victims. Within a mile or two of where Marioara's body was discovered lies the spot where Phyllis Murphy's body was found in January 1980. Her killer, John Crerar, did not bury her but covered her naked body with ferns. Further south, for twenty-seven years the body of Danny

McIlhone lay in a secret grave after the IRA shot him dead and buried his body on bogland in July 1981. Searches had begun in 1999 when the IRA said he was buried at Ballynultagh in the Wicklow Mountains, but Danny's body was only located in 2008 after the Independent Commission for the Location of Victims' Remains carried out a fresh search, widening the scope of the search area.

Dublin criminal gangs had also long used the many hiding spots afforded by the mountains. A short distance north of Kippure, the body of Stephen Byrne from Inchicore was found hidden in a ravine in November 2002. He had been shot dead. His murder remains unsolved.

In late January 2012, as gardaí continued to search for Marioara at Kippure, they were aware of a very recent and amazing chance discovery across the mountains at Sliabh na mBan Óg off the old Military Road. A tree had become uprooted following a storm on 10 January 2012, exposing the remains of James Kenny McDonagh who had vanished from Dublin in October 2011. James was last seen driving his car in Bluebell. The car was later found burnt out at Peamount in west Dublin. It is believed James was murdered by a Dublin gang.

For almost 1,500 days Marioara's body lay buried in a foetal position in the forest until a garda from the Technical Bureau, watching the soil as a small digger carefully scraped the surface, suddenly signalled for it to stop. He called his colleagues over.

Marioara's body had been tightly wrapped in eight grey plastic bags and a large sheet of industrial-size plastic wrap. The bags around the body had been securely bound by duct tape. Inside the wrapping, the teenager's body was covered by a bedsheet and a pillow case was over her head. She was dressed in her bra and underwear. Marioara had been shot four times in the head by a .22 calibre weapon. Four bullets were later removed from her head. Similar bullets had been found in the wall of the burnt-out property in Brabazon Street but it was never established if the bullets had come from the same weapon. In fact the gun used to murder Marioara was never identified: the witness who first brought gardaí to the forest at Kippure said he had seen the killer holding a rifle when he showed him Marioara's body in the house at Brabazon Street. The witness described to detectives how, when he saw her body in the house, Marioara's eyes were still open.

The garda investigation unearthed several guns including weapons buried underground at a location on Rathdrum Road in Crumlin. The firearms had been hidden in Wavin pipes. Another Wavin pipe held a gun, knife and balaclava in an underground hide at Bushy Park in south Dublin. Elsewhere in the same park, a .357 Magnum and another shotgun were found buried close to the river Dodder. Two 9 mm firearms were discovered hidden at a nearby ESB substation. But a particularly worrying and sinister discovery by gardaí was that the killer had been storing weapons on the grounds of two private secondary schools in south Dublin. A 9mm handgun was found close to a tennis court at one school, and a three-foot-long Wavin pipe was unearthed close to the football grounds at the other school. The pipe, which was closed at both ends, contained ammunition for a shotgun, a high-calibre handgun and other firearms.

A gun was also found buried in the back garden of the house in Clontarf where Marioara had been held captive, and another was discovered in a stolen car close by. The killer had set fire to the Clontarf flat in July 2008 – the second property he had torched in an attempt to destroy forensic evidence linking him to the crime. One of the guns found during the investigation was later linked to a murder in Cork, which occurred prior to Marioara's murder. Marioara's killer was not involved in the Cork murder, but circumstances simply reflected the reality that weapons are frequently sold and traded.

The man who stood trial for Marioara's murder was found not guilty by a jury: the majority of the evidence against him came from the individual who had led gardaí to Marioara's body and accused the man on trial of committing the abduction and murder. However a jury took less than three hours to return a 'not guilty' verdict. On the day of the not guilty verdict a number of experienced detectives looked visibly shocked as they left court. They were consoled by others who spoke of how good police work had led to Marioara's remains being returned to the Rostas family for burial. The jury didn't hear evidence relating to the mobile phone that pinged off various masts on the day of Marioara's abduction and the following day. This is the phone that Marioara used to ring her brother Alexandru in a desperate attempt to summon help, and which had pinged at times relevant to the crime: at Lombard Street; Castle Avenue, Clontarf; and at Brabazon Street in the south inner city. Certain legal advice held sway that, because of an EU directive relating to the retention of mobile phone data, evidence relating to the phone shouldn't be introduced in the trial. There were eight expert witnesses ready to testify for the prosecution relating to the phone and what evidence could be gleaned from it, but those witnesses were never called to give evidence.

This fact remains a source of great frustration for many of the gardaí who worked on the case, given that this type of mobile phone evidence was subsequently used in a number of other murder cases. Most notably, mobile phone evidence was used in the trial of Graham Dwyer when he was convicted of the murder of Elaine O'Hara. Hundreds of text messages between mobiles in Dwyer's possession and Elaine O'Hara's phone linked the victim and her killer over a period of months prior to the murder.

Although gardaí recovered a significant number of guns during the investigation into Marioara's murder, the Director of Public Prosecutions decided that no charges be brought against anybody. Likewise nobody ever faced charges relating to the conspiracy, uncovered by gardaí, to murder a journalist, a detective and a witness. Detectives had subsequently also discovered a conspiracy to murder a solicitor, which was linked to the same investigation. However, to the great frustration of investigators, ultimately no one, neither Marioara's suspected killer nor anyone else, would be charged in relation to the various conspiracies to murder, and most frustratingly, no one would be convicted of Marioara's murder.

Three gardaí, Detective Inspector Michael Cryan, Sergeant Paul Murphy and Garda Ofelia Hough travelled to the funeral, which took place in Romania on 10 February 2012. As Marioara's body had been so tightly wrapped in large plastic bags in her secret grave in the Wicklow Mountains she had been mummified. Her mother, Marioara Snr, had insisted that she see her daughter's body when it had been taken from the crime scene in Kippure to a funeral home in Dublin. Having her daughter's body back meant so much to the teenager's mother, and indeed to all the family. Now the Rostas family had brought Marioara back to Tileagd close to the Bihor Mountains in Romania.

The funeral service took place by the side of the Rostas house on the edge of Tileagd. In temperatures well below minus 20 degrees Celsius, Marioara's funeral procession travelled through the snow. Dumitru Snr and Marioara Snr and their remaining children were joined by neighbours. Her family laid out some of their daughter's meagre belongings: a red T-shirt – one of just three she owned – a plastic watch and a pair of runners. There, in western Romania, more than 2,600 kilometres from Lombard Street, Castle Avenue, Brabazon Street and Kippure, Marioara Rostas was laid to rest.

Although her murder was never solved, Marioara's body was only located because a person with direct knowledge assisted gardaí and pointed out the specific section of forest where he had helped bury the body. That man – who became a State witness – did not face any charges relating to his assistance in hiding Marioara's body. This fact has been highlighted by other families desperate for their loved ones' bodies to be returned to them; they would forego any prosecution if it meant getting them back.

Dumitru Rostas Jnr was just thirteen when he saw his big sister get into a car in Dublin city and disappear. His recollection, that the car had a 01-LH reg and was a Ford Mondeo, would greatly assist in focusing an investigation that would eventually identify a suspect who had no criminal convictions but was quickly ascending the gangland ladder. Although the Rostas family returned to Romania in the aftermath of Marioara's murder, in 2014 they revisited the scene where Marioara's body lay hidden for four years. Two gardaí, Jonathan Petrie and Paul Murphy, brought Mariora's father, Dumitru Snr, and her brother, Dumitru Jnr, to lay flowers and say prayers. The Rostas family occasionally return to Ireland and in December 2018 they called in to say hello to officers at Pearse Street Garda Station. The family greatly appreciate the work done by gardaí in finding Marioara's body.

In 2014 the Rostas family were interviewed on RTÉ's *Prime Time* programme. Dumitru Jnr said the loss of his sister was always with him.

> As her brother I am sad all the time, she is no longer here. There is a pain, a dreadful pain deep down in my soul for the rest of my life. We were there begging and in two seconds she was no longer there.

Nobody has yet been brought to justice for Marioara's abduction and murder. It is a sad and stark message: it is possible to entice a teenager into a car in the centre of Dublin, abduct her, hold her captive at two locations in suburban Dublin, shoot her dead and bury her body in the Wicklow Mountains – and get away with it.

CHAPTER 12

IRELAND'S MISSING

There are almost 900 people listed as long-term missing in Ireland, a stark and shocking figure. Behind every statistic is a family left bereft, reliant on gardaí to investigate their loved one's case. In more than two decades of researching missing persons cases, I know the dedication of dozens upon dozens of individual gardaí cannot be questioned: men and women who often continue to work in their spare time to investigate cases where leads have gone cold. However, I believe the area of missing persons continues to be one that is under-resourced in An Garda Síochána, and I know that is a view shared by many gardaí and families of the missing.

Somewhere on this island lie the bodies of missing people. Some have been murdered, others have suffered a fatal accident or have died as a result of a personal tragedy. It is imperative that gardaí be given more resources and expertise to search for missing people. Even a brief examination of some previous cases show that a number of searches have not been as thorough as they should have been. It is to be hoped that, from these tragic cases, lessons have been learned.

For 950 days the body of Michael Murphy lay close to Killiney Dart station in south Co. Dublin. His case is one example of poor garda work in a missing persons case. Michael was last seen alive in June 2002, a short distance from where his body would eventually be found by chance. He had been reported missing soon after his disappearance, and some searches did take place – albeit inadequate – as it was not until February 2005 that workmen building a new lift at the southbound platform of Killiney station discovered Michael's skeletal remains. Building the new lift involved knocking down a seven-foot high wall, which separated the train station from adjoining cliffs. A short time after demolition work began, a worker found Michael's body in undergrowth. It is shocking that for over two and a half years Michael's body lay close to where he was last seen alive.

The body of 78-year-old Maura Reynolds lay undiscovered for more than two years after she disappeared from a nursing home in Bray. Maura had Alzheimer's and had also been diagnosed with cancer. She disappeared after walking out of Tara Nursing Home in Bray on Christmas night 2005. Extensive searches took place along the coastline, and the open ground at Bray Head was also searched with the assistance of sniffer dogs, who failed to detect that Maura's body was actually lying in dense undergrowth halfway up Bray Head.

It was only when a man ventured down a steep incline to cut down trees, which were blocking a satellite television signal, that Maura Reynolds' body was found on 19 February 2008. An inquest jury later found that Maura most likely died due to exposure and hypothermia. Every inch of Bray Head had obviously not been searched by gardaí. Relying on sniffer dogs to search areas that were almost inaccessible to humans had been ineffective in this instance. The chance discovery of her body almost twenty-six months after she went missing meant Maura could eventually be laid to rest in her native Donegal.

For almost three weeks Paul McQuaid's body lay in a lane a few hundred yards from Grafton Street in central Dublin. While thousands of people walked along one of the city's busiest streets during May 2001, close by a young man who had wandered down a lane off Wicklow Street, and fallen off a railing, lay dead. Though Paul's body was found on private property owned by a bank, it seems almost incredible that an isolated lane so close to where the man disappeared was not searched. Paul McQuaid had last been seen outside Judge Roy Bean's bar on Nassau Street.

One of the most distressing aspects of this case is the fact that it was later discovered that there was CCTV of a figure – later confirmed as Paul McQuaid – walking towards the lane. Detectives had conducted an intensive search, including the river Liffey and numerous areas between Judge Roy Bean's and Paul's home in Clontarf in north Dublin. But one of the gardaí who worked on the case accepts that they failed to fully search the immediate area around Nassau Street.

Basically, we should have tried to put ourselves in Paul's shoes. He had come out of the pub in Nassau Street, and he had had a few drinks. What we failed to do was try and think like Paul. We were thinking that, logically, he might have tried to make his way home to Clontarf, but for some reason he headed up Grafton Street instead of down towards Trinity College. So we were wrong from the start. The exact place where his body was found was actually private property, a back entrance in the basement of a bank, and it was a security guard from the bank who found Paul's body. Even if we had looked in from the alleyway it would have been almost, if not totally, impossible to see Paul; but that is still not good enough. We are truly sorry for his family. We could have found him sooner.

Another case in which gardaí did not quickly find a body within or near their immediate search area was the murder of the 28-year-old German journalist Bettina Poeschel in Donore, Co. Meath, in September 2001. For twenty-three days Bettina's body lay in dense undergrowth about 15 yards off the main Drogheda road close to Donore. A massive investigation had been launched soon after her disappearance on 25 September, yet search parties failed to find the murdered woman until a garda made the shocking discovery while searching the almost inaccessible terrain on 17 October.

Bettina's body was found very close to where she was most probably travelling. Gardaí knew she had taken the train from Dublin to Drogheda, and she had told a friend she was planning to visit the passage tomb at Newgrange, about three miles from Donore. Yet for twenty-three days her body lay hidden in undergrowth in Donore, exposed to the elements. The failure to find Bettina's body sooner was to lead in turn to a delay of several months before her remains were released to her family by the coroner for repatriation to Germany. The family later thanked the gardaí for their hard work in eventually finding Bettina and for catching her killer – Michael Murphy had previously killed another woman in Co. Louth and had served a sentence for manslaughter for that crime before he murdered Bettina. Murphy is now serving a life sentence for Bettina's murder.

In 2012 members of the Blackwater Sub-Aqua Search and Rescue team were performing routine exercises in the local river in Fermoy, Co. Cork, when one diver spotted the wreckage of a car beneath the silt. Further investigation revealed a body inside the vehicle. Purely by chance, the body of William Fennessy was recovered inside his Daihatsu Charade. The car had entered the river in 1990 and had over time become covered in silt so that it remained hidden for twenty-two years. All that time William Fennessy's body lay within the vehicle a few hundred metres upstream from the town bridge. The 54-year-old had disappeared in Fermoy in March 1990. Despite the garda investigation at that time, the local river had not been adequately searched. The chance discovery of William's body was a huge source of relief for his family who had waited so long for news. But the circumstances of the recovery of his body begged the question: how many more bodies still lie in rivers and lakes throughout the country?

Fermoy is also the scene of the bizarre disappearance of married couple Conor and Sheila Dwyer, who were in their sixties when they were last seen in April 1991. When gardaí searched their home they found all their personal belongings, including clothes, money and passports, still in the house. The only thing missing was the couple's car, a Toyota Cressida, registration number 5797 ZT. Despite extensive international police assistance, no trace of the car, or of the missing couple, has been found.

County Cork has been the location for several missing persons investigations. Michelle McCormick vanished from Owenahincha Caravan Park in suspicious circumstances in 1993 while Frank McCarthy disappeared from Cork city in the same year. In a particularly concerning case, Cathal O'Brien, a 23-year-old college graduate from Co. Wexford and 42-year-old Kevin Ball both disappeared from a house in Wellington Terrace, Cork, in April 1994. In December of the same year 32-year-old Patrick O'Driscoll, who lived in the same house, also vanished. Gardaí began an intensive investigation, and within months Fred Flannery, who had also been living in Wellington Terrace, was charged with Patrick's murder. When his trial began at the Central Criminal Court in June 1996 a teenage witness told the jury he had seen body parts in a cupboard in the house, and he had been shown a coal bag in which, he was told, Patrick O'Driscoll's body was hidden.

But the trial was halted amid extraordinary scenes after Mr Justice Robert Barr found that certain evidence had been suppressed. Mr Justice Barr directed that Fred Flannery be acquitted of the murder charge, and he walked free from court. A month later Patrick O'Driscoll's dismembered body was found buried in a sports bag in a shallow grave in the grounds of Lotabeg House in Cork. Fred Flannery died in May 2003, but detectives believe other people still alive have information about the murder of Patrick O'Driscoll and the disappearances of Cathal O'Brien and Kevin Ball.

Cathal was a graduate of Waterford RTC and was a socially concerned young man who worked with the Simon Community in Cork. During his work he met and befriended Kevin Ball. The failure of gardaí to find the remains of both men has been a source of great distress to their families. Cathal's father Séamus travelled from his home in Co. Wexford and spent many days digging in fields around Cork city looking for his son. More recently detectives in Cork have been carrying out a cold-case review of these unsolved disappearances.

In one of the most baffling cases gardaí have investigated in recent years, Tina Satchwell disappeared in Youghal, Co. Cork, on 20 March 2017. Tina lived with Richard, her husband of twenty-five years, at Grattan Street in Youghal. The couple had met in Leicester, where Tina was living for a while. They married and moved to Co. Cork, settling first in Fermoy, Tina's home town, and later in Youghal.

The couple spent most of their time together and were a familiar sight at car boot sales in Co. Cork in places such as Rathcormac, Blarney and Castletownroche. The day before Tina vanished, they had visited a car boot sale in Carrigtwohill.

The next day Richard drove to Aldi in Dungarvan at around 10 a.m. Before he left the house he made Tina a cup of tea and some breakfast. When Richard arrived home at 2 p.m., Tina was gone. Her house keys were on the floor and her mobile phone was also in the house. He later established that two suitcases, as well as €26,000 in cash, were missing from the house.

There was no CCTV footage of Tina leaving Youghal that day. The garda investigation highlighted the ongoing lack of adequate CCTV cameras in many Irish towns. Richard made a number of public appeals for Tina to return home. He said he didn't believe anyone had attacked Tina, saying instead that he believed she had left because 'she obviously felt she needed a break, to get her thoughts together, her head straight'.

A team of detectives headquartered at Midleton Garda Station followed numerous leads, and in January 2018 gardaí carried out a major search of woodland at Carrigtwohill. This followed reports that a woman matching Tina's description and a man had been seen entering the wood, but only the man had been observed coming out later on. However, no trace of Tina was found during that search, or indeed during any of the other searches conducted in Youghal and other parts of Co. Cork.

In Co. Galway, a cold-case review continues into the disappearance of mother of seven Barbara Walsh, who vanished from her home in Carna in the Connemara Gaeltacht in 1985. The original investigation was inadequate. The locals spoke Irish, yet witness statements were taken in English. This meant that important nuances may have been lost in translation. Two gardaí who had earlier attended a house party at Barbara's cottage were among the first officers to investigate her disappearance. Specialist detectives were not drafted in to conduct the questioning. A major search of land close to Barbara's home in 2015 failed to uncover anything. Some of her family believe there are other locations in Carna that should be searched, and they have asked gardaí to do so.

Another long-term missing woman is Alice Clifford, who was fifty-seven when she disappeared from St Loman's Hospital in Dublin in 1979. In 2017 one of Alice's daughters, Patricia, told the National Missing Persons Day event that there had been four decades of inaction by gardaí, and she said her family had become disheartened that major mistakes were still being made in relation to her mother's case.

She highlighted the fact that major building work for a new housing development had recently taken place on the grounds of St Loman's Hospital. Given the fact that gardaí had previously excavated a section of land there while searching for Alice in 2013, her family said they would have thought that the builders of the new homes would have been informed that there was a possibility a body might be found during the building work. However, the family said they were shocked to discover the builders had never been told about Alice's case. Patricia called on the government to increase communications between various agencies relating to missing people.

Throughout the country there are historic cases of missing people that should be reinvestigated. Dutch woman Aleida 'Leidy' Kaspersma vanished near Kenmare, Co. Kerry, in 1978. Leidy was living with her English boyfriend Nick Wheatley close to Barrerneen Mountain near Kenmare when she disappeared. Nick later told gardaí he had recently told Leidy he wanted to break up with her, and he said the last time he saw her was when she abruptly got out of their car on the short journey home from Kenmare at 4.30 p.m. on Monday, 2 July 1978. Leidy has not been seen since; her family in Holland have urged gardaí to carry out a cold-case review of her disappearance.

Further west in Co. Kerry, on the Iveragh Peninsula, father of four Brooke Pickard was abducted and killed and his body concealed. Brooke was attacked by an armed gang at a beach car park in Castle Cove, Co. Kerry in April 1991. He had moved from England with his wife Penny to start a new life. It's believed Brooke was lured to the isolated spot near Sneem by someone he knew who pretended they had run out of petrol. When Brooke arrived at the car park he was attacked, bundled into his own van and driven away. Brooke's van was later found abandoned at an isolated forest east of Waterville. Several men from Belfast are suspected of involvement in attacking Brooke and gardaí also believe people living in Co. Kerry and Co. Cork have information about what happened to him. A major excavation of land in 2016 failed to find any trace of Brooke. A man in his sixties was arrested in Kilkenny that same year, but no charges were brought. Penny and the rest of his family still appeal to those who know where his body lies to pass on that information.

Several cases involve criminals hiding the bodies of people they have murdered. William Maughan and his girlfriend Anna Varslavane are missing, believed murdered, since 14 April 2015. Detectives believe the couple were attacked in Gormanston, Co. Meath, by members of a criminal gang. Despite an extensive investigation the couple have not been found. The case has been the subject of a review by detectives from the Garda Cold Case Unit, and officers have vowed to continue the search for the couple. William and Anna were planning to move back to Tallaght on the day they were attacked. William's parents Joe and Nell have repeatedly urged anyone with information to come forward.

Another double disappearance is that of two men, David Lyndsay and Alan Napper, both from north Co. Dublin, who were last seen in Clane, Co. Kildare, in July 2008. It's believed the men were murdered in a house in Warrenpoint, Co. Down. Another missing man, believed murdered, is Patrick Lawlor from Darndale who vanished in December

2004. Patrick was only twenty-three when he disappeared and his family have long campaigned for answers in his case. It is thought Patrick was murdered by a north-Dublin-based criminal gang.

The discovery of the body of another Patrick Lawlor followed intensive detective work by gardaí in Ballyfermot. Seventeen-year-old Patrick was murdered in January 1999, and for three years his body lay in a shallow grave close to the Ninth Lock of the Grand Canal at Clondalkin, Dublin, showing how easily killers can bury bodies in suburban areas. Another similar case was that of 22-year-old Neil Hanlon, whose body lay concealed in a shallow grave on open land in a populated area in Crumlin, Dublin for five months. Neil was last seen in September 2001 close to his home, less than a quarter of a mile from where his body was found.

In 2010 an inquest was held into the death of a man whose body was never recovered. Jock Corbally from Finglas was beaten to death in a field near Baldonnel in February 1996. The jury reached its finding after hearing evidence gleaned by detectives during a fourteen-year investigation. Detectives had established Jock Corbally had been beaten to death with a pickaxe handle, a lead pipe and a baseball bat, but despite extensive searches they never found his body.

The body of a British Army officer, Captain Robert Nairac, who was shot dead by the IRA in Ravensdale, Co. Louth in May 1977, has also never been found. Geoff Knupfer from the Independent Commission for the Location of Victims' Remains believes Robert Nairac's body can still be retrieved, but the IRA has refused to divulge information about the location of his remains. The IRA has given general locations of the bodies of two other men but still their bodies have not been located: Columba McVeigh, who was abducted in Dublin and killed in 1975, is buried somewhere at Bragan Bog in Co. Monaghan; and Joe Lynskey, who disappeared from Belfast in 1972, is buried in Co. Meath.

The IRA did give information leading to the recovery of bodies in counties Monaghan, Wicklow, Meath, Antrim and Louth, but Jean McConville's was only found by chance. Even after excavations failed to find her body in 1999, the IRA insisted it had buried the mother of ten at Templeton Beach in Co. Louth, but in fact her body was found by accident in 2003 at nearby Shellinghill Beach.

A case that remains very much in the minds of the public is that of 22-year-old Trevor Deely from Naas, Co. Kildare, who disappeared while walking home from a Christmas party in Dublin, where he lived, in the early hours of 8 December 2000. Trevor's family and friends conducted a massive poster and publicity campaign in the aftermath of his disappearance. When last seen at 4.15 a.m., Trevor was walking down Haddington Road, close to Baggot Street Bridge. Earlier that night he had been socialising with colleagues from the Asset Management Department of the Bank of Ireland. He had started his night at Copper Face Jacks in Harcourt Street, later going to the Hilton Hotel in Charlemont Place at 9 p.m. At 2.15 a.m. he left the Hilton and went to Buck Whaleys nightclub on Leeson Street. He left there at 3.30 a.m. and went back to his office to check his email and pick up a blue ACC golf umbrella.

In 2017 detectives released CCTV imagery showing an unidentified man standing at the gate as Trevor entered his workplace in the early hours. The man appears to converse with Trevor who continues on inside the premises. The CCTV footage had been converted from video to digital form and the grainy imagery enhanced. The footage clearly shows a man hanging around the building before Trevor arrives and standing close to him as Trevor opens the gate. This man has never been identified. It was stormy when Trevor left the office at 4 a.m.; he is seen on footage opening up the umbrella, walking away and is last recorded on CCTV walking down Haddington Road alone at 4.15 a.m.

In 2017 as part of a cold-case review of Trevor's disappearance, a section of land at Chapelizod was excavated, but no trace of Trevor was found. In the days and weeks after Trevor disappeared, a massive search took place, which included searching the waters of the Grand Canal. Nothing was found. Despite a massive and ongoing publicity campaign, including a reward of €100,000, the case remains unsolved.

There are many cases where families believe the original investigations were not of an acceptable standard. Priscilla Clarke is missing, believed drowned, since 3 May 1988. It's thought she was swept away trying to save the life of Lynda Kavanagh, with whom she had been horse riding in Enniskerry that day. Lynda's body was later recovered from the swollen waters of the river Dargle, but Priscilla's has never been found.

Priscilla's sister Claire was horrified to learn years later that the body of a woman had been washed up on a beach in Co. Wexford in 1995. Her family were never informed and the body was buried without identification. Claire successfully lobbied the Minister for Justice at the time, Brian Lenihan TD, to grant an exhumation and a DNA sample from the body was taken. It was not a match for Priscilla, but Claire's work in highlighting the case of the unidentified woman helped encourage people to agitate for something to be done to identify the more than twenty bodies buried across Ireland.

In a shocking development, Claire established that the skull of the unidentified woman buried in Co. Wexford had been lost by the State. The rest of the woman's body had been buried in 1996, but her skull had been brought to Dublin for the important purpose of studying the woman's dental work to try and identify her. However, it had been mislaid. In recent years extensive searches were carried out at the state pathologist's office, at a university and at a private residence, but the skull was not located. The woman still lies unidentified in Crosstown Cemetery, Co. Wexford.

In the same graveyard lies the unidentified body of one of the passengers from the Tuskar Rock Air Disaster of 1968. The Aer Lingus flight from Cork to London perished off the Co. Wexford coast, claiming the lives of all sixty-one people on board. Most of the bodies were never recovered from the waters off Co. Wexford, but among those bodies that were retrieved one was too badly damaged to be identified. In an era before DNA testing, the body was buried unidentified. However, retired detective Gerry Kealy is currently working on trying to identify the body. Some years ago a DNA sample was taken, and Gerry is tracking down family members of those whose bodies were never recovered.

Gerry Kealy is typical of many gardaí who worked on missing persons cases. While the issue of missing persons was long neglected by the garda force as a whole, many individual officers, like Gerry, often worked on their days off chasing up leads in the hope of a breakthrough. Another retired garda, Tosh Lavery, has also worked tirelessly to raise awareness of missing persons cases. As a member of the Garda Water Unit, Tosh recovered many bodies of people who had been reported missing. His experiences have guided his ongoing strenuous work as an advocate for missing people.

Sergeant Richie Lynch and Garda Ciara McNulty from the Garda Missing Persons Bureau have spent a significant amount of time in recent years taking DNA samples from families of missing people. Many of the cases are decades old and predate a time when family liaison officers existed. Regretfully, there are dozens upon dozens of families whose loved ones went missing in the 1970s or '80s, or even the '90s, whose cases have been long forgotten as investigating gardaí retired from the force. The Garda Missing Persons Bureau is seeking to change that.

The Bureau has been running a special investigation, called Operation Runabay, which is comparing cases of missing Irish people with the more than 600 unidentified bodies in Britain. More than 100 of those cases are people whose bodies were found on the western British seaboard. Most are likely people who entered the sea in Britain, but the garda work has already borne fruit. Richie Lynch has established contact with Don Kenyon, a police officer from the North Wales Police, and a number of historic cases in Wales have been identified as missing Irish people. In 2017, through DNA comparisons, the body of Pauline Finlay was repatriated to Ireland from the Welsh cemetery where she had been buried in 1994. A similar DNA match in 2018 established that a body washed up in Wales in 1986 was Brendan Dowley, last seen in Kilkenny getting on a bus to Dublin for onward travel by ferry.

Another case recently solved was that of Joseph Reilly, last seen in Dublin in 2007, whose body was washed up on a beach near Dundalk and then lay unidentified in a Co. Louth graveyard for ten years. DNA from Joseph's siblings provided a match and finally solved the case. Touchingly, local people in Lordship in Co. Louth had tended to the grave and erected a plaque, which stated that one day the man's family would find him.

2018 brought amazing news for three families of long-term missing people, when a new forensic process allowed for DNA samples to be extracted from three unidentified bodies. Those profiles provided matches with members of the three families who had given their DNA to the database managed by Forensic Science Ireland. Eighteen years after Gussie Shanahan disappeared in Limerick his family was told a body recovered from the river Shannon in 2001 was that of the twenty-year-old. Gussie was laid to rest alongside his mother. Meanwhile, Teresa Gallagher was told that a body recovered in Dublin in 2002 was that of her son James, who vanished in 1999. The family of Margaret Glennon, who disappeared in 1995 in north Co. Dublin, were told that a body found near Swords was that of their loved one. Solving these cases has given great hope that more bodies recovered in Ireland can now be identified. However, many of these cases will need to be exhumed in order to extract a DNA sample. Currently there are unidentified bodies in counties Leitrim, Cork, Wexford, Wicklow, Galway and Dublin.

In 2013 the Department of Justice hosted the first National Missing Persons Day event at Farmleigh. At last there was formal recognition by the State of the number of people missing in Ireland. By the time the sixth such annual event was held in December 2018 the venue had to be changed to the larger venue of King's Inns in Dublin city due to the volume of people who wished to attend and remember their missing loved ones. The event honours all those missing in Ireland, and also Irish citizens missing abroad. John McMeel is missing in the United States since 1997; J.P. Grealis is missing in Holland since 2008; Christopher Gilroy is missing in Spain since 2009; and journalist

Jonathan Spollen is missing in India since 2012. A prominent case is Amy Fitzpatrick, a fifteen-year-old Dublin girl who vanished in Spain on New Year's Day 2008. Amy's father Christopher has recently urged the Irish government to ask Spanish police to carry out a cold-case review of Amy's case.

Families of missing people have provided huge support for one another. Fr Aquinas Duffy, whose cousin Gussie Shanahan was missing for eighteen years, set up www.missing.ie, which provides a constant source of information. A special section of www.garda.ie also features the cases of missing people.

Modern technology now plays a significant role in assisting gardaí to investigate certain missing persons cases. The Child Rescue Ireland (CRI) alert system has been used to good effect in recent years, with media outlets being asked to issue descriptions of people or vehicles when there is an immediate concern for the welfare of missing children. Gardaí have also been working in conjunction with Facebook to organise for all Irish account holders to be alerted to such garda appeals. Electronic motorway signs have also been utilised to display details of vehicles that officers wish to urgently locate.

There is a growing awareness within An Garda Síochána that a number of historic missing persons cases were not originally investigated to a standard that would be expected today. Gardaí have had many laudable successes in other areas of policing, for example in tackling dissident republicans and organised crime. The Criminal Assets Bureau has garnered international praise for hitting criminals in their pockets and taking back ill-gotten gains; but further resources are required when it comes to missing people so that detectives might re-examine what went wrong with so many older investigations.

While gardaí have failed to come up with the answers that the public and, more importantly, the families of missing people want, they remain dogged in their determination to find the answers, to find missing people and in many instances, to find killers. Missing persons cases are time-consuming and resource-intensive. More manpower is crucial to solving more cases.

One of the oldest missing persons cases is Jimmy O'Neill, who was sixteen years old when he disappeared from Waterford in 1947. His younger brother Frank is now in his seventies and in recent years gave his DNA to be kept on file at the database established in recent years by Forensic Science Ireland. The database now has samples from more than 150 families of missing people.

Close to 9,500 people are reported missing in Ireland every year. That's more than five times the annual figure when I wrote the first edition of this book in 2003. The vast majority of those reported missing will eventually be found, but many will not. Despite improvements in policing and greater expertise in some sections of An Garda Síochána, the overall number of missing persons is increasing year by year. This is despite an ever improving response time by gardaí, who use broadcast and social media to publicise many missing persons cases quicker than ever before. But there is a historic legacy of inaction, missed opportunities and sometimes piecemeal or inadequate investigations that must be rectified. Almost 900 people are now listed as long-term missing in Ireland. How can 900 people disappear on an island the size of Ireland and never be found? Amid calls for more action to be taken by the State and the gardaí, the devastating effects of the loss of a loved one are evident in the homes and the hearts of the families of Ireland's missing.

ACKNOWLEDGEMENTS

This book would not have been possible without the kind assistance of many families of missing people. To each and every person who spoke with me, I give my profound thanks for your time and trust. The first family I met, many years ago, was that of Jo Jo Dullard. Jo Jo's sister Mary immediately put me in touch with many other families missing a loved one, and I am very grateful for that. Sadly, Mary passed away in 2018.

Many gardaí gave invaluable assistance during my research. Ultimately they were discussing investigations that have so far failed to reach a conclusion. Their frustrations at failing to solve cases, and in some cases to catch murderers, were clearly evident during our conversations, briefings and interviews.

Thank you to Superintendent Liam Geraghty and Superintendent John Ferris of the Garda Press Office, and thank you to Inspector Conor O'Murchú. A special thanks to Sergeant Damian Hogan for invaluable initial assistance a number of years ago. Thank you also to former Head of the Garda Press Office, Superintendent John Farrelly.

Thank you to Sergeant Richie Lynch and Garda Ciara McNulty of the Garda Missing Persons Bureau. Thanks also to Paul Flood, formerly of the Bureau, and the late Sergeant Mick Kennedy.

I thank the following retired and serving gardaí, all of whom gave of their time without hesitation: Tony Hickey, Martin Donnellan, John O'Brien, Tony Brislane, John Roche, Liam Murphy, Barry Walsh, John McFadden, Ian Lackey, Tony Sourke, Bill McMunn, Michael

Duffy, Gerry Murray, Chris Delaney, John Dunleavy, Declan Goode, Tom Doyle, Pat Campbell, Joe Molloy, Gary Kavanagh, Mick Dalton, Seán Leydon, Tosh Lavery, Gerry Kealy, Syl Hipwell, Jim Sheridan, Brendan McArdle, Eamonn Maloney, Pat Marry, Aubrey Steedman, Mary Fallon, Val Smith, Noel Lynagh, John Harrington, William Doyle, Noel Mooney, Alan Bailey, Declan Liddane and Jason Miley.

There are other gardaí who are not named. *Go raibh míle maith agaibh go léir.*

Thank you also to the many other people who gave of their time during the writing of this book, including many friends of missing people. Thank you to journalist Fintan Lambe for all his work on unidentified bodies in Co. Wexford, which helped uncover the true national picture.

Thank you to Fergal Tobin, former Publishing Director at Gill & Macmillan (now Gill Books), for setting me on this road. More recently thank you to Commissioning Editor Sarah Liddy, Managing Editor Catherine Gough, Director Nicki Howard, and all the team at Gill Books including Deborah Marsh, Mairéad O'Keeffe, Teresa Daly, Ellen Monnelly, Avril Cannon, Seán Hayes, Paul Neilan and Sarah McCoy. Thank you to solicitor Kieran Kelly at Fanning and Kelly.

Thank you to my friends in journalism, both in crime reporting and beyond, for their ongoing support. Thank you especially to my colleagues in RTÉ, in particular the team at *Prime Time*, and thank you also to my former colleagues in Today FM. Thank you to my first boss Barry Flynn for giving me my break in journalism in Midlands Radio 3, and further back, thank you to the staff of St Mark's Primary and Secondary Schools in Tallaght.

On a personal level I thank my parents, Patricia O'Neill and Barry Cummins, and my brother Mark for their support.

I especially thank my wonderful children Ruby and Conor, and also my amazing wife Grace for her constant enthusiasm, guidance and suggestions, and without whom I could not have completed this book.

You may reach me at barry.cummins@rte.ie

Please also visit:
www.missing.ie
www.missingpersons.ie
www.garda.ie

Contact the Missing Persons Helpline on 1890 442 552
Contact the Missing Persons Association on 087 960 9885
The Garda Confidential Line is 1800 666 111